CAN EVANGELICALS LEARN FROM WORLD RELIGIONS?

Jesus, Revelation & Religious Traditions

GERALD R. MCDERMOTT

InterVarsity Press
Downers Grove, Illinois

InterVarsity Press
P.O. Box 1400, Downers Grove, IL 60515
World Wide Web: www.ivpress.com
E-mail: mail@ivpress.com

InterVarsity Press® is the book-publishing division of InterVarsity Christian Fellowship/USA®, a student movement active on campus at hundreds of universities, colleges and schools of nursing in the United States of America, and a member movement of the International Fellowship of Evangelical Students. For information about local and regional activities, write Public Relations Dept., InterVarsity Christian Fellowship/USA, 6400 Schroeder Rd., P.O. Box 7895, Madison, WI 53707-7895.

Cover photograph: SuperStock

ISBN 0-8308-2274-7

Printed in the United States of America ∞

Library of Congress Cataloging-in-Publication Data

McDermott, Gerald R. (Gerald Robert)
  Can evangelicals learn from world religions?: Jesus, Revelation & religious traditions/
Gerald R. McDermott.
    p. cm.
  Includes bibliographical references.
  ISBN 0-8308-2274-7 (pbk.)
  1. Christianity and other religions. 2. Theology of religions (Christian theology) I.
Title.
  BR127.M365 2000
  261.2—dc21
                                         00-040756

| 19 | 18 | 17 | 16 | 15 | 14 | 13 | 12 | 11 | 10 | 9 | 8 | 7 | 6 | 5 | 4 | 3 |
| 15 | 14 | 13 | 12 | 11 | 10 | 09 | 08 | 07 | 06 | 05 | 04 | 03 | 02 |

To my friend Avi Zakai,
who inspired this book

Contents

Acknowledgments

Like all authors I have many to thank for helping me write this book. Roanoke College gave me summer research grants that allowed me to finish several chapters. Bill and Connie Fintel loaned me their lake home for a week, where I organized the first three chapters. Robert Benne continually encouraged me professionally; he and Ned Wisnefske set a tone in our religion and philosophy department that makes teaching and writing there a delight. George Hunsinger helped teach me what it means to do Christian theology.

Several scholars gave me important critical feedback; I have not responded in ways that will fully please them all, and the residual errors are mine, not theirs: Alan Pieratt, Valerie Hoffman, Paul Griffiths, Hans Zorn, Brent Sandy and Bruce Reichenbach. Thanks are due also to Winfried Corduan and an anonymous IVP reader. Their criticisms and suggestions were very helpful.

Finally, I owe the most to Jean and my three boys, who make it so much fun to come home each day.

Introduction

When Lin Yutang was growing up as the son of a Christian pastor in early twentieth-century China, Chinese Christians regarded the Confucian classics as dangerous pagan nonsense. So Lin's father never schooled his son in the rich cultural heritage of their ancient civilization. In his spiritual autobiography, *From Pagan to Christian*,[1] Lin explains that when he went to college and realized that fundamentalist fear had prevented him from appreciating the best of his native culture, he was enraged. "I had been cheated of my national heritage. That was what a good Puritan Christian education could do to a Chinese boy. [So] I determined to plunge into the great stream of our national consciousness."[2]

With the delight of an orphan finding his long-lost parents, Lin devoured Chinese philosophy and folklore and abandoned the Christian faith in which he had been reared. He went on to become one of China's leading *literati* of the twentieth century. He wrote many books extolling the glories of Far Eastern thought and culture, and, by implication, denouncing the cultural insensitivity of Christianity.

In the twilight of his life, Yutang returned to the Christian faith of his childhood. His new faith was deeper and wiser than that of his youth, both chastened and enlightened by his earlier encounters

---

[1]Lin Yutang, *From Pagan to Christian* (London: Beinemann, 1960).
[2]Ibid., p. 35.

with the Buddhist, Confucian and Daoist traditions.

American evangelicalism today is more worldly wise than the fundamentalism of Lin's boyhood. It is more open to human culture and plays a much larger role in the production of culture. Yet in its attitude toward other religions American evangelicalism is remarkably similar to that Chinese fundamentalism. Like its distant Asian cousin it has often regarded non-Christian religion as taboo—consisting of either foolish nonsense or demonic delusions. Sometimes it has granted these religions a certain benign respect that acknowledges limited points of convergence with Christian doctrine. But rarely, if ever, has it regarded non-Christian religion as something from which it can learn. As a result, Christian understanding of its own revelation is less than it could be. More important, Christian witness to non-Christians has created a rock of stumbling for Christians and non-Christians alike. How many non-Christians have decided to stop listening because Christians have shown no appreciation for what might be true in their religions?

Arguably, the church's greatest challenge in the next century will be the problem of the scandal of particularity.[3] More than ever before, Christians will need to explain why they follow Jesus and not the Buddha or Confucius or Krishna or Muhammad. But if, while relating their faith to the faiths, Christians treat non-Christian religions as netherworlds of unmixed darkness, the church's message will be a scandal not of particularity but of arrogant obscurantism.

Kosuke Koyama tells of a missionary couple arriving in Bangkok who told their host that all Thai religion (chiefly Theravada Buddhism) was the worship of demons (30 million people and 700 years of tradition brushed aside in one instant, Koyama notes) and that the (then) 800 million citizens of the People's Republic of China

---

[3]"Scandal of particularity" refers to the conviction that God has revealed Himself in particular places and times, especially through the Jews and Jesus, and not to every human being in history in equal measure.

were—according to the missionaries—all atheists and therefore unsaved, making the country an enemy of the gospel.[4] Thankfully most missionaries I know do not display such cultural insensitivity. However, this kind of evangelistic approach, which ignorantly assumes that non-Christians have no knowledge of God and that their traditions are worthless and pernicious, may do more harm than good to the name of Christ. It tells non-Christians that Christians are not interested in learning about them and have no respect for their cultures. Often it communicates the message that Christians are interested in people not as human individuals but only as representatives of systems of thought. In the language of Martin Buber, we regard the other person not as a Thou demanding respect but as an It to be accepted only conditionally.[5]

Recent evangelical introductions to the problem of other religions have built commendably on foundations laid by J. N. D. Anderson and Stephen Neill.[6] Anderson and Neill opened up the "heathen" worlds to the evangelical West, showing that many non-Christians also seek salvation and have personal relationships with their gods. In the last decade Clark Pinnock and John Sanders have argued for an inclusivist understanding of salvation, and Harold Netland has shed new light on the question of truth in the religions.[7] Yet no evangelicals have focused—as nonevangelicals Keith Ward, Diana Eck and Paul Knitter have done—on the revelatory value of truth in

---

[4]Kosuke Koyama, *Waterbuffalo Theology* (Maryknoll, N.Y.: Orbis, 1974), p. 213.
[5]Martin Buber, *I and Thou*, 2d ed. (New York: Charles Scribner's Sons, 1938).
[6]J. N. D. Anderson, *Christianity and Comparative Religion* (Downers Grove, Ill.: InterVarsity Press, 1970; rev. ed., *Christianity and the World Religions* [Downers Grove, Ill.: InterVarsity Press, 1984]); J. N. D. Anderson, ed., *The World's Religions* (Grand Rapids, Mich.: Eerdmans, 1976); Stephen Neill, *Christian Faith and Other Faiths* (Downers Grove, Ill.: InterVarsity Press, 1984).
[7]John Sanders, *No Other Name: An Investigation into the Destiny of the Unevangelized* (Grand Rapids, Mich.: Eerdmans, 1992); Clark Pinnock, *A Wideness in God's Mercy: The Finality of Jesus Christ in a World of Religions* (Grand Rapids, Mich.: Zondervan, 1992); Harold A. Netland, *Dissonant Voices: Religious Pluralism and the Question of Truth* (Grand Rapids, Mich.: Eerdmans, 1991).

non-Christian religions.[8] Anderson and Neill showed that there are limited convergences between Christian and non-Christian traditions, and Pinnock has argued that there might be truths Christians can learn from religious others. But as far as I know, no evangelicals have yet examined the religions in any sort of substantive way for what Christians can learn without sacrificing, as Knitter and John Hick do, the finality of Christ.[9]

This book is the beginning of an evangelical theology of the religions that addresses not the question of salvation but the problem of truth and revelation, and takes seriously the normative claims of other traditions. It explores the biblical propositions that Jesus is the light that enlightens every person (Jn 1:9) and that God has not left Himself without a witness among non-Christian traditions (Acts 14:17). It argues that if Saint Augustine learned from Neo-Platonism to better understand the gospel, if Thomas Aquinas learned from Aristotle to better understand the Scriptures, and if John Calvin learned from Renaissance humanism, perhaps evangelicals may be able to learn from the Buddha—and other great religious thinkers and traditions—things that can help them more clearly understand God's revelation in Christ. It is an introductory word in a conversation that I hope will go much further among evangelicals.

The first five chapters are theoretical, making the case that evangelicals can learn from world religions. The first two chapters are prolegomena. In chapter one I define what I mean by evangelical and then briefly review how evangelical scholars have treated the

---

[8]Keith Ward, *Religion and Revelation* (Oxford: Clarendon, 1994); Diana Eck, *Encountering God: A Spiritual Journey from Bozeman to Banaras* (Boston: Beacon, 1993); Paul Knitter, *No Other Name?* (Maryknoll, N.Y.: Orbis, 1985). See also Francis X. Clooney, *Hindu Wisdom for All God's Children* (Maryknoll, N.Y.: Orbis, 1998), and Kenneth Cracknell, *Justice, Courtesy and Love: Theologians and Missionaries Encounter World Religions, 1846-1914* (London: Epworth, 1998).

[9]John Hick, *God Has Many Names* (Philadelphia: Westminster Press, 1982), and *An Interpretation of Religion* (New Haven, Conn.: Yale University Press, 1989); Knitter, *No Other Name?*

religions until the late 1990s. In chapter two I define revelation and try to sort out how evangelicals should interpret revelation. Then in chapter three I argue that the Bible suggests that God has sometimes given revelation of Himself to those outside Israel and the church, and that the church has sometimes learned from those "outsiders." In chapter four I make a theological argument for the notion of revelation in the religions, using (among other things) Jonathan Edwards's understandings of covenant and typology. I claim that there is revelation of a sort in at least some of the religions—neither general nor special revelation but "revealed types." In chapter five I show that three important Christian theologians used thinking from outside the church to help them understand the revelation of Christ.

The next four chapters are case studies, as it were, in which I apply my theoretical conclusions to some real-world traditions. Chapters six through nine treat four major non-Christian religious traditions (Buddhism, Daoism, Confucianism and Islam) and suggest what evangelicals can learn from them. This list of four is meant to be suggestive, not exhaustive. I have not treated Hinduism or Sikhism or animism or the host of other religions in the world. And of course there are many, many more things that could be said about and learned from the four traditions I do consider. These four are intended to be a representative sampling and hopefully a stimulus for other evangelical scholars to take up where I leave off. The last chapter considers objections made to this project and responds to each one of them.

Some readers may object, upon reading chapters six through nine, that I am not really learning anything at all from these traditions because most of the concepts I discuss are so similar to Christian concepts. But if we reexamine what takes place in most learning, I think it will become clear that the same kind of learning is suggested in this book. And as readers follow the argument in these chapters, they will see that most similar ideas in other religions are nevertheless still different in both content and context.

Let me explain what I mean by "most" learning. It seems to me that most learning is a matter not of seeing entirely new things but of seeing old things in new ways. Religiously and theologically, learning means new understanding of familiar concepts more often than it means assimilating wholly new articles of faith. So for example, we grow in our understanding of Christ by perceiving more deeply or vividly His holiness or love, or by relating His holiness to His love in ways we had not considered before. This learning by seeing the old in new ways is far more common than learning by being introduced to completely new concepts, such as when one is first introduced to the concept of the Trinity. That is, most learning about the Trinity is not in its introduction as a new concept but in trying to understand the meaning of the Trinity and how that meaning changes our view of God. In other words, most often Christians learn by seeing a familiar concept from new vantage points.

Most learning in the history of Christian thought has been the same. It has involved elucidating and unraveling the implications of the original blinding revelation of God in Christ. Sure, there have been moments of receiving wholly new concepts that interpret that revelation, such as the atonement, but far more of the learning has involved slow and patient understanding of what the basic concepts mean. That understanding has unfolded along many different lines, but I would suggest three typical ways in which new understanding or insight comes: placing a new emphasis on a part of the revelation of Christ so that revelation as a whole takes on new light; seeing an old concept, which has previously helped us understand Christ from a new perspective; and developing ideas further by way of new application, relationship or implication.

The first way of seeing old ideas in new light has been to shift emphasis. According to Harvard historian Edmund Morgan:

> Change in Christian thought, even so radical a change as the Reformation,
> has usually been a matter of emphasis, of giving certain ideas a greater

weight than was previously accorded them or of carrying one idea to its logical conclusion at the expense of another. In this way one age slides into the next, and an intellectual revolution may be achieved by the expression of ideas that everyone had always professed to accept.[10]

Thus Luther changed the theological agenda of Christendom not by introducing a wholly new concept of justification but by placing new emphasis on selected strands within the Augustinian tradition.[11] Justification by grace through faith was not foreign to the Christian tradition before Luther, but when Luther placed paramount emphasis on the idea and situated it at the center of Christian faith, all the rest of what had been revealed looked new and different. Both Luther and Calvin are known for what has been unjustly called the "invention" of preaching merely because they placed new emphasis on a neglected tradition in Christian churches. Similarly, I will argue that Islam's emphasis on submission to God can help evangelicals correct a misplaced emphasis on self-determination. And the Confucian tradition's determination to do what is right regardless of circumstances can help evangelicals regain a proper emphasis on Christian discipleship. In both cases real learning is possible.

John Henry Newman said that great ideas have many aspects.[12] By this he meant that history's truly great ideas have many dimensions; the ideas are so rich in meaning that no one view or aspect can even begin to exhaust the content of the idea. This is the second way in which we can learn—by seeing a familiar idea from a new aspect or vantage point.

Certainly Christ is history's greatest idea.[13] It would not be too

---

[10]Edmund Morgan, ed., *Puritan Political Ideas: 1558-1794* (Indianapolis: Bobbs-Merrill, 1965), p. xiii.

[11]See Harry S. McSorley, *Luther Right or Wrong? An Ecumenical-Theological Study of Luther's Major Work, "The Bondage of the Will"* (New York: Newman Press, 1969).

[12]On ideas and aspects, see John Henry Newman, *An Essay on the Development of Christian Doctrine*, 6th ed. (Notre Dame, Ind.: University of Notre Dame Press, 1989), chap. 1, section 1.

[13]I refer to the conception, not the personhood, of Christ, Who is infinitely more than an idea.

much to say that the idea of Christ is *infinitely* rich in meaning since in Christ "all things hold together" and in Him are hid "all the treasures of wisdom and knowledge" (Col 1:17; 2:3). This must mean, at least, that all of reality is somehow comprehended in and by Christ. Hence there is an infinite number of aspects or vantage points from which to see the idea of Christ, each of which will show something new and unique about what it means for God to be in Christ. This also means that as a church we may have only begun the journey of understanding Christ—that there may be far more to Christ that the church will learn as it reflects on Scripture and tradition—and perhaps other religions—with the help of the Holy Spirit.

As often as not, new aspects or perspectives on the meaning of Christ come from looking at Christ through the lens of another tradition—to the degree that that is possible. For example, in chapter five I will examine how Thomas Aquinas gained new insights into the meaning of Christ by looking through Aristotelian tradition. In chapter six I propose that looking through the window of Buddhist analysis of desire as a compulsive clinging of the ego helps us understand more clearly what Paul meant by the fallen self and what Luther meant by the self *curvatus in se* (curved in upon itself).

A third way we learn is through developing a concept by teasing out its implications or relating it to other concepts. Revelation, Newman wrote, is not a revealed system but a concatenation of detached and incomplete truths belonging to a vast system never fully revealed in history.[14] In eternity all Christian doctrines will fit together, but now, in time, many of the connections remain mysterious. The history of theology is a history of slowly drawing more and more connections; one of the earliest, for instance, was the development of Trinitarian doctrine in the first few centuries after the com-

---

[14]Francis McGrath, *John Henry Newman: Universal Revelation* (Tunbridge Wells: Burns and Oates, 1997), p. 123.

pletion of the New Testament. After several centuries of struggle, the church finally connected God's oneness with the three Persons revealed in Scripture in a way that made both theological and doxological sense. This was a drawing out into explicit doctrine what was implicit in the testimony of Scripture.

This drawing out started even within the history of revelation in the Bible. When Hosea and the other prophets proclaimed that God wanted not sacrifice but mercy, they were making explicit what was implicit in the Pentateuch. Paul, Peter and John seem to have derived a lion's share of their insights, under the inspiration of the Spirit, by reflecting on what Jesus had taught in germ form in His miracles, parables, replies and censures.[15] In the second half of this book I explore how we can learn from other religions by following similar patterns. Muslim boldness in the public square, for example, can help evangelicals see how faith and action can relate in ways not previously seen. Just as Aquinas used Aristotle to develop the concept of analogy that is only implicit in Scripture, by studying Daoist *wu-wei* evangelicals can learn about the implications of biblical injunctions to wait on God. Other traditions, then, can help us make explicit what is only implicit in our present understanding of Christ. This is a kind of learning that sees not entirely new doctrines (although that is theoretically possible) but old doctrines and concepts in new ways.

One caveat on learning from similar ideas in other religions: we can never see the ideas as other religions see them. Each idea is colored and shaped by the framework in which it fits, and the whole framework grows out of a different set of loves and hatreds (or "affections," as Jonathan Edwards called them).[16] Since each idea is properly seen only within the context of the framework in which it

---

[15]Paul knew something of Jesus' teachings from oral tradition. See N. T. Wright, *The New Testament and the People of God* (Minneapolis: Fortress, 1992), esp. pp. 407-8.

[16]Jonathan Edwards, *Religious Affections*, ed. John E. Smith, vol. 2 of *The Works of Jonathan Edwards* (New Haven, Conn.: Yale University Press, 1959).

fits, and we can never properly see that framework unless we share the affections of those religionists who love that framework, we will never see the idea or piece as they see it. So I can never understand *wu-wei* as Daoists understand it. It is clearly seen only by those who see the Dao as final reality—a conviction and vision that I do not and cannot share. Nevertheless, I can learn enough from the concept—however imperfectly I understand it—to help me see new things about God's revelation in Christ.

Furthermore, when evangelicals use ideas from other traditions to better interpret God in Christ, they will inevitably change the shape of those ideas by fitting them into their Christian framework. That is the nature of all human understanding; because it looks through its own perspective, what it sees is colored and partly shaped by that perspective. Therefore, when evangelicals learn from ideas in other traditions, the learning that emerges will have a distinctly (evangelical) Christian contour and flavor. So when I learn from Daoist *wu-wei*, my interpretation of it is shaped by my Christian framework, and the way that I use it to change a bit of my Christian framework is still distinctly Christian. But this does not change the fact that I have nevertheless learned something new from my encounter with Daoist *wu-wei*. My understanding of *wu-wei* is limited by my Christian affections and perspective, and my use of it will be distinctly Christian, but I can still say that I now see my union with Christ differently because of my encounter with Daoist *wu-wei*. I have *learned*.

So I agree with Augustine's conviction that one cannot fully understand a religion unless one believes it: *crede ut intelligas* (believe so that you may understand). As I have suggested, this cuts both ways. On the one hand, it means that I do not have "inside" knowledge of Buddhism or Islam or any of the other non-Christian faiths I discuss, and so I miss something, perhaps much, of their internal dynamics. On the other hand, commitment to my Christian faith gives me a small measure of the mind of Christ on these other faiths, and so I am at the same time perhaps privy to insight into them that their own devotees do not share. (I say "perhaps" because while I am sure that Christian revelation offers insight into other religions, I am less sure to what extent I have appropriated that insight.) So while my own commitments prevent me from seeing a large part of the inner dynamics of another faith, I may also be able to understand something of that faith that its own devotees do not.

I approach this topic with, I hope, requisite humility. That is, I need to acknowledge that I have not read the non-Christian sacred texts in their original languages, and we all know that much is lost in translation. Nor have I traveled extensively to see these religions in their "thick" descriptions, as Geertz has put it.[17] But I have studied and taught these texts and traditions for some years, have traveled to the Middle East to study Islam, and have discussed these issues with friends who are devotees of the religions I discuss in this book.

There are several dangers involved in studying the faiths of others. Christian students may be tempted to water down or compromise their own Christian truth in an attempt to make themselves more acceptable to those who do not share their convictions. They may flirt with commitment to another faith and wind up committed neither to Jesus nor to the new tradition, in the mistaken impression that they must suspend their own commitments in order to understand the commitments of others. They do not realize that, for one thing, there is no such thing as a person without any commitment. When we drop commitment to one tradition, we inevitably assume commitment to another (which may be our own self-concocted tradition). The Enlightenment assumption that we can be neutral observers in regarding religions is one of the great myths of modernity. Those who endeavor to seek understanding without commitment also fail to understand that commitment is necessary for the

---

[17]Clifford Geertz, *The Interpretation of Cultures* (New York: Basic Books, 1973).

deepest understandings. While commitment to Jesus precludes commitment to the finality of other faiths, it does not rule out acceptance of the truths that other faiths may contain. It also opens one up to insight into the reality that other faiths attempt to assess.

Another danger is that the very young in faith will explore other traditions in depth while their knowledge of their own faith is shallow. The result may be spiritual confusion in which nothing is clear and everything seems relatively true. This is something like an immigrant coming to America and trying to learn English and two other languages at the same time. It would be far better to concentrate on English and achieve some competence in that language before trying to learn additional languages. For this reason I would encourage new believers to get grounded in Christ and His revelation in Scripture before they start exploring all the intricacies of other exotic religions. But for those who are moderately grounded in Christ and beginning to wonder how Christ relates to other religions, this may be a good place to begin.[18]

Finally, a word about my words for God. In an appendix at the end of the book, I explain both why I use masculine pronouns for God and why I capitalize them. Readers who have trouble with that practice may want to turn to the appendix before they begin reading chapter one.

---

[18]I would also recommend to beginners in this subject Winfried Corduan, *Neighboring Faiths: A Christian Introduction to World Religions* (Downers Grove, Ill.: InterVarsity Press, 1998); Kenneth Cragg, *The Christ and the Faiths* (Philadelphia: Westminster Press, 1986); and Neill, *Christian Faith and Other Faiths.*

1

EVANGELICALS
& THE
|WORLD RELIGIONS|

O NE OF THE BOONS OF POSTMODERNISM IS THAT NOW EVANGELI-
cals are on a level playing field. No longer can nonevangelical scholars claim that while their work is conducted with cool objectivity,
evangelical scholarship is fundamentally different because it operates with "hot" presuppositions.[1] If the postmoderns have taught us
anything, it is that all scholarship is "hot"—which means "interested" in the Marxist sense. Every scholar—for that matter, every
human being—looks at the world through lenses shaped by that
person's history and situation. The scholar who claims to be free
from all prejudice and tradition is naive or dishonest. There is no
scholar whose presuppositions do not influence the way he or she
sees, and indeed what he or she sees.[2] If there is a universal norm of

---

[1]I do not mean that all nonevangelicals *see* evangelicals as on a level playing field but that
the scholarly community has increasingly adopted a framework that requires them to see
the field that way.
[2]One thinks of Thomas Kuhn's now classic *The Structure of Scientific Revolutions*, 2d ed.

reasonableness, there is no human access to it.[3]

Hence the claim of those still operating by Enlightenment presuppositions, that their knowledge is objective because they determine to separate faith from their research, while that of others—particularly evangelicals—is utterly subjective because they permit faith to influence their work, now seems silly. It calls to mind the observation made by philosopher of science Paul Feyerabend that "there is hardly any difference between the members of a primitive tribe who defend their laws because they are the laws of the gods . . . and a rationalist who appeals to objective standards, except that the former know what they are doing while the latter does not."[4] In more philosophical language, frameworks of rationality are not universal but are socially and historically located.

Therefore, it does not necessarily detract from the objectivity[5] of this book to say that I will look at the question of revelation in the

---

(Chicago: University of Chicago Press, 1970), which argued that scientists, like ordinary people, tend to see only what they are trained to see. Because they depend on inferences that are difficult to make, they are prone to see only what the dominant paradigm has suggested they ought to see.

[3]I find illuminating David C. Clark's distinction between a modest foundationalism that posits an ultimate perspective or conceptual scheme that human forms of reasoning at best approximate in varying degrees and a classical foundationalism that claims an ultimate perspective or conceptual scheme that all humans can realize if they think in a neutral or purely objective manner. The latter appears to be mythical, the former more realistic. Even George Lindbeck, who has been interpreted as something of a relativist (I think, inaccurately), seems to hold to something like this modest foundationalism: "The issue is not whether there are universal forms of reasonableness, but whether these can be formulated in some neutral, framework-independent language." David C. Clark, "Relativism, Fideism and the Promise of Postliberalism," in The Nature of Confession: Evangelicals and Postliberals in Conversation, ed. Timothy R. Phillips and Dennis L. Okholm (Downers Grove, Ill.: InterVarsity Press, 1996), pp. 107-20; George A. Lindbeck, The Nature of Doctrine: Religion and Theology in a Postliberal Age (Philadelphia: Westminster Press, 1984), p. 130.

[4]Paul K. Feyerabend, Science in a Free Society (London: Verso, 1983), p. 82, cited in Alister McGrath, A Passion for Truth: The Intellectual Coherence of Evangelicalism (Downers Grove, Ill.: InterVarsity Press, 1996), p. 90.

[5]Obviously I do not claim pure objectivity, which no one possesses. But one can be more or less objective, while stating one's presuppositions, by handling evidence with greater or lesser degrees of fairness to the data.

religions from an evangelical perspective. It does mean that my interpretation and conclusions will probably differ from someone who uses a nonevangelical or non-Christian perspective. But it does not mean that my reasoning will necessarily be less fair or more perspectival.

The above statement, of course, begs a further question. What do I mean by *evangelical?* Like *love* and *religion,* it is notoriously difficult to define. There seem to be as many definitions as there are people who use the word. To cite just a few, Dan Rather (who is not an evangelical but like many in the media typically conflates *evangelical* and *fundamentalist*) would understand it differently from the way it is understood by Jerry Falwell or Jimmy Carter, both of whom claim to be evangelicals but use the word in markedly different ways.

Part of the problem is that there are so many different kinds of evangelicals. For example, there are very conservative evangelicals who jealously guard a literalist version of biblical inerrancy and tend to be polemical and separatist (from liberals and other evangelicals); they are difficult to distinguish from those I will define later in this chapter as fundamentalists. There are other inerrantists, however, like many who work in the Evangelical Theological Society, who are engaged in creative scholarship and dialogue with communities well outside their own. Then there are those whom Gabriel Fackre calls "old evangelicals," for whom religious experience takes priority over all else; they emphasize the experience of regeneration and mass evangelism. There are also the "neoevangelicals," for whom the gospel's social implications and apologetic persuasiveness are most important. Other groups include the "justice and peace" evangelicals, who oppose the Religious Right (made up largely of politically conservative evangelicals) and espouse a "radical political agenda associated with Anabaptist roots in the sixteenth century," and "charismatic evangelicals," who champion the work of the Holy Spirit in tongues, healing and exuberant worship. "Ecumenical evangelicals" are commonly found in the mainline denominations; they make common cause with nonevangelicals in those churches on social concerns and the historic creeds and liturgies.[6] And there are still other kinds—many of which are eclectic combinations of disparate elements from the above six groups. After surveying the large panorama of groups calling themselves evangelical, it becomes apparent that evangelicalism resembles not so much an assortment of groups as a long continuum, with a wide range of differing positions varying from one another on a host of issues.

So how can one make sense of the word? It is clear that I cannot speak for all evangelicals. Nor would I want to. But I can and will speak for a position that I think is both historically and theologically grounded in broad streams of evangelicalism. It also draws from classical Christian sources both before and outside the relatively recent historical phenomenon known as evangelicalism, but many of its most distinctive emphases derive from thinkers and movements that have been characterized as evangelical.

I will proceed both historically and theologically. That is, I will provide something of a historical definition by examining the highlights of three centuries of evangelical history. Then I will stipulate a theological definition by suggesting what I take to be the best of the evangelical tradition. Others will no doubt differ with me over what is the best, and theirs may be as well grounded or better grounded than mine. I will argue simply that the way I define the word is grounded in evangelical principles. That is, this is not the only definition of evangelicalism that can be grounded both in evangelical history and theology, but it is the one that I will presuppose when using the word *evangelical* in this book.

Articulating my definition of the word will also enable my readers to determine whether I am truly an evangelical. Some may wonder

---

[6]Much of this analysis comes from Gabriel Fackre, *Ecumenical Faith in Evangelical Perspective* (Grand Rapids, Mich.: Eerdmans, 1993), pp. 22-23.

after finishing the book, for some of my proposals travel beyond what most evangelicals have said in the past about the world religions. Staking out my understanding of the word will also help readers determine if the proposals suggested in the remainder of the book are consistent with the definition stipulated in this chapter.

Historical Highlights

The word *evangelical* is derived from the Greek noun *euangelion*, which means "glad tidings," "good news" or "gospel," the last of which goes back to an Old English word for "God talk."[7] Three times the New Testament says that someone who proclaims the gospel of Christ dying for our sins is an *euangelistēs* (evangelist).[8] There are signs of what could be called an evangelical spirit[9] throughout church history, from the early church and its fathers through Augustine, Ambrose, Bernard of Clairvaux, Thomas Aquinas and Blaise Pascal to the Reformation precursors John Wycliffe, Jan Hus and Girolamo Savonarola. But the word was first used of Catholic writers who early in the sixteenth century tried to revert to more biblical beliefs and practices than were current in the late medieval church. Then at the Reformation the name was given to Lutherans who focused on the doctrine of justification by grace

---

[7]Some of the best discussions in the United States regarding the meaning of evangelicalism are found in George M. Marsden, "The Evangelical Denomination," in *Evangelicalism and Modern America*, ed. George M. Marsden (Grand Rapids, Mich.: Eerdmans, 1984); Marsden, *Understanding Evangelicalism and Fundamentalism* (Grand Rapids, Mich.: Eerdmans, 1991); Douglas A. Sweeney, "The Essential Evangelicalism Dialectic: The Historiography of the Early Neo-Evangelical Movement and the Observer-Participant Dilemma," *Church History* 60 (March 1991): 70-84; Donald W. Dayton and Robert K. Johnston, eds., *The Variety of American Evangelicalism* (Knoxville: University of Tennessee Press; Downers Grove, Ill.: InterVarsity Press, 1991); Mark A. Noll, *The Scandal of the Evangelical Mind* (Grand Rapids, Mich.: Eerdmans; Leicester: Inter-Varsity Press, 1994); Mark A. Noll, David W. Bebbington and George Rawlyk, eds., *Evangelicalism: Comparative Studies of Popular Protestantism in North America, the British Isles, and Beyond, 1700-1990* (New York: Oxford University Press, 1994).

[8]Acts 21:8; Ephesians 4:11; 2 Timothy 4:5.

[9]I mean by this—as I will explain in what follows—an emphasis on the authority of Scripture, preaching, the cross of Christ and conversion.

through faith and who sought to renew the church based on what they found in Scripture.[10]

The more recent roots of today's movement lie in the trans-Atlantic revivals of the 1730s and 1740s, led by Jonathan Edwards, John Wesley and George Whitefield, who highlighted the authority of Scripture, the work of Christ in salvation and the New Birth. This movement was shaped by the Puritan legacy of preaching and conversion, but it stressed more emphatically the sense of assurance of salvation. It was also molded in part by Pietism, which emphasized warmth of feeling, sometimes at the expense of doctrine, and by Enlightenment modes of thinking, which appealed to the authority of John Locke and used his method of testing opinions by experience.

These Enlightenment influences were strengthened during the high tide of common-sense philosophy in the nineteenth century, a philosophy that promised the unerring value of intuition. While Edwards had insisted that fallen reason can never know the majesty of God, Charles Hodge suggested that to know the words of Scripture was to know the realities to which the words pointed.[11] In this century Carl Henry has put more emphasis on the intellectual principles one can derive from Scripture than on the biblical narratives, a pattern that Hans Frei has identified as characteristic of the Enlightenment mentality.[12]

Today's evangelicalism emerged as a self-conscious reaction against

---

[10]Alister McGrath, *Evangelicalism and the Future of Christianity* (Downers Grove, Ill.: Inter-Varsity Press, 1995), pp. 20-22. Today in Europe it is the word used for Lutherans and Reformed, who are derived theologically from the sixteenth-century Reformation.

[11]For Jonathan Edwards on reason, see, for example, "A Divine and Supernatural Light," in *A Jonathan Edwards Reader,* ed. John E. Smith, Harry S. Stout and Kenneth P. Minkema (New Haven, Conn.: Yale University Press, 1995), pp. 105-23; Charles Hodge, introduction to *Systematic Theology* (Grand Rapids, Mich.: Eerdmans, 1986), 1:1-17.

[12]George Hunsinger, "What Can Evangelicals and Postliberals Learn from Each Other? The Carl Henry-Hans Frei Exchange Reconsidered," in *The Nature of Confession,* ed. Timothy R. Phillips and Dennis L. Okholm (Downers Grove, Ill.: InterVarsity Press, 1996), pp. 134-50.

fundamentalism, which began shortly after 1910 as a series of pamphlets making reasoned arguments against Protestant liberalism but then degenerated into a reactionary "oppositionalism" that lost its link with the historic creeds of the church and tended to ignore the social demands of the gospel. As one scholar has described it, it was "too otherworldly," "anti-intellectual," legalistic, moralistic and anti-ecumenical.[13]

The deliberate use of the term *evangelical* in this century dates to the formation in 1942 of the National Association of Evangelicals, which was a careful attempt to distinguish evangelicalism from fundamentalism. In contrast to the fundamentalist separation from modern culture, the "new evangelicals" (led by E. J. Carnell, Harold Ockenga, Carl Henry and Billy Graham) were committed to engaging with culture in an attempt to transform it through the gospel.[14]

In the half century since, evangelicals have become prominent players on the American landscape.[15] They have gained political clout and numerical strength. Recent studies suggest that "evangelicals now constitute the largest and most active component of religious life in America." A 1992 survey identified 25.7 percent of the population as "white evangelicals" and another 7.8 percent as "black Protestants," most of whom could be classified as evangelicals.[16]

---

[13]Martin E. Marty, "What is Fundamentalism? Theological Perspectives," in *Fundamentalism as an Ecumenical Challenge*, ed. Hans Küng and Jürgen Moltmann (London: SCM Press, 1992), p. 3; see also R. V. Pierard, "Evangelicalism," in *Evangelical Dictionary of Theology*, ed. Walter A. Elwell (Grand Rapids, Mich.: Baker, 1984), pp. 381-82.

[14]For a fascinating account of a leading outpost of the "neo-evangelical" movement, see George M. Marsden, *Reforming Fundamentalism: Fuller Seminary and the New Evangelicalism* (Grand Rapids, Mich.: Eerdmans, 1987).

[15]At the same time it must be noted that, as Noll has put it, evangelicalism "has always been made up of shifting movements, temporary alliances, and the lengthened shadows of individuals" (Noll, *Scandal of the Evangelical Mind*, p. 8).

[16]"Akron Survey of Religion and Politics in America," conducted by John Green, James Guth, Lyman Kellstedt and Corwin Smidt, cited in Noll, *Scandal of the Evangelical Mind*, p. 9 n. 8. In an important recent book Christian Smith and Michael Emerson argue that evangelicals are prominent not because they retreat from modernity but precisely because they engage it (*American Evangelicals: Embattled and Thriving* [Chicago: University of Chicago Press, 1998]).

Evangelical theology has matured at the same time that many evangelicals have concentrated on peripheral matters (such as the rapture and other questionable eschatological details) and equated the logical conclusions of dogma with dogma itself (particular formulations of biblical inerrancy, double predestination, the second blessing and the millennium).

Theological Definition

Although Karl Barth is not an evangelical in the American or British sense of the word, his definition of the word aptly summarizes what I consider to be the best work in evangelical theology today: "*Evangelical* means informed by the gospel of Jesus Christ, as heard afresh in the 16th-century Reformation by a direct return to Holy Scripture."[17] Many scholars have attempted to delineate in more detail what evangelical theology is about, but Alister McGrath's six "fundamental convictions" seem to capture the most important distinctives.[18]

1. *The majesty of Jesus Christ, both as incarnate God and Lord and as Savior of sinful humanity.* Evangelical theology is radically Christ-centered, which has three implications. First, we know God only through Christ. As the apostle John wrote, "Grace and truth came through Jesus Christ. No one has ever seen God. It is God the only Son, who is close to the Father's heart, who has made him known" (Jn 1:17-18 NRSV). There is knowledge of God the Creator (Calvin's helpful phrase) in the creation, but all that knowledge is distorted until one's perspective is clarified by knowledge of God the Redeemer (Christ).

Second, we are saved by Christ's life, death and resurrection. Apart from the cross, there is no salvation, which means that all theology must start with the cross. Hence at the center of the Christian

---

[17]Quoted in Donald G. Bloesch, *God, Authority, and Salvation*, vol. 1 of *Essentials of Evangelical Theology* (San Francisco: Harper & Row, 1978), p. 7.
[18]McGrath, *Evangelicalism and the Future of Christianity*, pp. 53-87.

faith is the work of God in Christ, Who chose us before the foundation of the world (Eph 1:4) before we could even begin to think about choosing Him. For this reason I think the "reformist" wing of evangelical theology goes astray when it declares that the "enduring essence of Christianity is a work of God in the life of the human person, variously called conversion, regeneration, or being born again."[19] This is dangerously humanocentric, particularly when reformists further assert that "doctrines are never as central as the experience of meeting God."[20] This last statement may reflect an important admonition that we are not saved by our theology, but it can also suggest that our religious experience is more decisive than what God has done in Christ. In addition, it can lead to a perilous subjectivism, the sort that led Schleiermacher to derive faith from experience rather than from the biblical revelation of Christ. It demonstrates that evangelical theology needs to learn both from the Reformation's emphasis on the primacy of Scripture and justification by grace through faith, and from the Trinitarian and christological consensus of the early church.[21]

Third, belief that the cross is central means that we need the cross because of our fallenness. Evangelicals believe that no dimension of our lives is free from sin. Sin is not just inherent weakness or ignorance but also positive rebellion against God's law; it is moral and spiritual blindness and bondage to powers beyond our control. Its

---

[19]Roger E. Olson, "The Future of Evangelical Theology," *Christianity Today*, February 9, 1998, p. 44. While I disagree with this aspect of the reformist approach, I affirm its conviction that God's Spirit continues to give the church illumination of the revelation in Christ, which sometimes leads to new understanding of that revelation. As the English separatist minister John Robinson stated it, "The Lord has more truth and light yet to break forth out of his Holy Word." See Keith L. Sprunger, "John Robinson," in *Dictionary of Christianity in America*, ed. Daniel Reid et al. (Downers Grove, Ill.: InterVarsity Press, 1990), p. 1022.

[20]Olson, "Future of Evangelical Theology," p. 44.

[21]It may be objected that the second half of this book takes a deep dive into subjectivity since it focuses on the experience of other religions. Yet I continue to hold in those chapters that our final norm for interpreting those experiences and doctrines is the doctrine of Christ as delivered in Scripture and the creeds.

manifestations are pride, lust for power, sensuousness, selfishness, fear and disdain for spiritual things. The propensity to sin is present from birth; its power cannot be broken by human effort, and the ultimate result is separation from God.

2. *The lordship of the Holy Spirit, Who is necessary for the application of the presence and work of Christ.* Like many other Christians, evangelicals have tended to neglect the third member of the Trinity, despite the emphasis given to the Spirit by Calvin and Edwards, and the Puritans' insistence on the role of the Holy Spirit in regeneration. Recently, however, evangelical theologians have begun to give more systematic attention to the third Person of the Trinity.[22]

3. *The supreme authority of Scripture.* By this, evangelicals mean that they regard the biblical canon as the most determinative source of knowledge of God and as a guide to Christian living. The Bible is not the limit of reading or the only source of this knowledge, but it is the evangelical's center of gravity. Rather than restricting us to a narrow range of knowledge or experience, acknowledging the authority of Scripture is liberating because it frees us from the slavish demand that we follow every cultural trend and provides a framework with which we can evaluate those trends. It claims that God has chosen to reveal Himself through Scripture; therefore, to submit to biblical authority is to receive God as God has chosen to be known, not as we would like God to be.

The best of evangelical theology believes that the language of Scripture is culturally conditioned but that through it God has nevertheless conveyed the eternal, unconditioned Word. It also teaches that Scripture is to be interpreted with the help of reason and the best tools of scholarship; attention is to be paid to the

---

[22]See, for example, Clark Pinnock, *Flame of Love: A Theology of the Holy Spirit* (Downers Grove, Ill.: InterVarsity Press, 1996); Thomas Oden, *Life in the Spirit,* vol. 3 of *Systematic Theology* (San Francisco: HarperSanFrancisco, 1992), esp. chaps. 1, 2 and 5; see also the work by the New Testament scholar Gordon Fee, *God's Empowering Presence: The Holy Spirit in the Letters of Paul* (Peabody, Mass.: Hendrickson, 1994).

genre of a biblical passage, so that, for example, poetry is to be read as poetry and not as a set of scientific propositions. And finally, we should read the Bible *for* ourselves, not *by* ourselves. Luther and Calvin never meant private interpretation of Scripture to be elevated over the consensus of the Christian community, which includes the historic creeds and great theologies of the last two thousand years.

This is not bibliolatry, for Christianity is the religion not of a book but of a person. Luther said that Scripture is but the manger and swaddling clothes in which Christ is laid and that all the Bible points to Christ. This means that any interpretation of Scripture that does not relate understanding of God to the God revealed in Christ falls short. It also means that any talk of God that does not focus finally on Christ is finally unchristian.[23]

Since the heart of Scripture is Christ and God's preparation of a people for the Christ, theology should pay preeminent attention to the narratives about Jesus and God's people. Unfortunately, some evangelical theologians after Jonathan Edwards (such as B. B. Warfield, Charles Hodge and Carl Henry) have marginalized the narrative character of Scripture and tended to reduce Scripture to a set of principles or concepts.[24] Recently, however, evangelical theologians have begun to reorient their theology around narrative, a reorientation that naturally follows from the recognition that the God of Scripture is a God of history, the narrative of Whose history is found in Holy Scripture.[25]

---

[23]This does not mean that the Messiah is always the explicit or even implicit reference of an Old Testament passage, but it does mean that the meaning of all the Old Testament can be explicated fully only by eventual reference to Christ.

[24]Even the recent emphasis on worldview can be seen as a part of the Enlightenment legacy that subtly distorts the biblical revelation. See Gregory A. Clark, "The Nature of Conversion: How the Rhetoric of Worldview Philosophy Can Betray Evangelicals," in *The Nature of Confession,* ed. Timothy R. Phillips and Dennis L. Okholm (Downers Grove, Ill.: InterVarsity Press, 1996), pp. 201-18.

[25]Gabriel Fackre, Donald Bloesch, Stanley Grenz and others. Narrative theology grew out of the work of Karl Barth, Hans Frei, H. Richard Niebuhr and George Lindbeck.

4. The need for personal conversion. Because of the Puritan and Pietist legacies from which Edwards, Whitefield and Wesley learned, evangelicals have placed more emphasis on conversion than have most other Christians. This does not require an emotional experience or even that one remember an initial commitment to Christ. Some Christians can never remember a time when they did *not* trust Christ. It does require personal repentance and trust in the person and work of Christ—not simply intellectual acceptance of Christian doctrine.[26]

5. The priority of evangelism for both individuals and the church as a whole. The fundamental motivation for evangelism, as McGrath has pointed out, is generosity—the desire to share the great news of salvation with others.[27] Evangelicalism is not our message but Christ's proclamation to His world that He is its creator, redeemer and lord.

6. The importance of Christian community for spiritual nourishment, fellowship and growth. Evangelicals have often tended to be individualistic, ignoring the community when it was convenient. But the evangelical tradition, particularly in its Reformation and eighteenth-century roots, has usually insisted on the indispensability of the Christian community for spiritual maturity. This is critical for hermeneutics, as I pointed out above in the discussion of Scripture. The Holy Spirit has been active in the church from the beginning, continually and progressively unfolding the truth of the Word. To read Scripture properly, therefore, means listening to what the Spirit has told the church throughout the ages. As J. I. Packer puts it, "To treat the principle of biblical authority as a prohibition against reading and learning from the book of church history is not an evangeli-

---

[26]Some may object that this is what Roger Olson meant by his statement that experience is more central than doctrine. But the danger of Olson's statement—when isolated from the larger body of his thought—is that experience can then be seen to take interpretive priority over doctrine. This submits our understanding of the work of Christ to the fallen ego, not to the objective revelation of God in Jesus.

[27]McGrath, *Evangelicalism and the Future of Christianity*, p. 76.

cal, but an anabaptist mistake."[28] Tradition is a history of discipleship, which means that we will grow spiritually only as we listen to others in the community of believers, which extends back through the ages. As evangelicals we are free to enjoy the Lutheran doctrine of the priesthood of every believer, reading and interpreting the Bible for ourselves. But woe unto us if we ignore the riches of wisdom available to us in tradition, which will protect us from the errors and superficiality that result from reading the Bible *by* ourselves.

Every one of the above six distinctives is shared by most other Christians. What makes this list evangelical, however, is the degree of emphasis that evangelicals place on the six marks and the forms that they take. For example, all Christians say evangelism is important at one level or another, but not all define the evangelistic message in the Christocentric terms that evangelicals use. Some regard social service as evangelism, and others do not consider conversion to faith in Christ to be necessary. Nor do all regard evangelism with the same urgency. When Billy Graham conducted his first crusade in New York City, some Protestant mainline leaders ridiculed his efforts—not only because he did not emphasize structural social reform but also because they regarded personal evangelism as theologically wrong-headed.[29] Now some of those same churches speak of personal evangelism as essential to the growth of the church in the world, but they send out proportionately fewer missionaries and do less to train their members for the task of evangelism than their evangelical counterparts typically do.

Evangelicals differ in the relative importance they place on these six distinctives, the precise interpretations they make of each, and

---

[28]J. I. Packer, *Fundamentalism and the Word of God* (London: Inter-Varsity Press, 1958), p. 48, cited in McGrath, *Evangelicalism and the Future of Christianity*, p. 84 n. 77.

[29]*Christianity and Crisis* 16 (March 5, 1956): 18. Reinhold Niebuhr was particularly critical of what he perceived to be Graham's use of "Madison Avenue" marketing techniques and regarded Graham's style of evangelism as "pietistic individualism" (Richard Fox, *Reinhold Niebuhr: A Biography* [San Francisco: Harper & Row, 1985], pp. 265-66).

additional distinctives they wish to highlight. Generally, however, evangelical theology is willing to tolerate diversity where central issues are not involved. As Richard Baxter put it, "In essentials, unity; in non-essentials, freedom; and in all things, charity." So, for example, there are many different evangelical understandings of biblical authority, the role of women, ecclesiology, sacraments, liturgy, worship style and gifts of the Spirit.

Finally, it will help provide further clarity by distinguishing evangelical theology from its most prominent Protestant alternatives today—fundamentalism, orthodoxy, liberalism and postliberalism. I do not mean by this list to suggest that Catholics cannot be evangelicals. There are many Catholics who would affirm the above six distinctives, but the distinctives refer primarily to Protestants because official Catholic doctrine denies the supreme authority of Scripture, choosing instead to posit a dual authority of Scripture and Catholic tradition. So while there are many points of agreement between evangelicals and most Catholics,[30] Catholic theology will differ with evangelical thought at a number of junctures.

Evangelicalism Versus Fundamentalism

Evangelicalism is most often confused with fundamentalism, so I will first identify points at which these two approaches diverge. I should say at the outset that, as for all generalizations, there will be plenty of exceptions to the "rules" that follow and that these are no more than tendencies or directions in which members of these two constituencies move. They should be regarded as ideal types that are valuable not so much in their historical value (there may be no one individual who perfectly fits either type) as in their heuristic import.

---

[30]See, for instance, the two recent statements by leading evangelicals and Catholics, which show that the sixteenth-century divide between Catholics and Protestants on justification and other issues has narrowed considerably: "Evangelicals and Catholics Together: The Christian Mission in the Third Millennium," *First Things*, May 1994, pp. 15-22; "The Gift of Salvation," *First Things*, January 1998, pp. 20-23.

The sum total for each type roughly approximates a distinctive pattern of thinking.[31]

1. *Interpretation of Scripture.* Fundamentalists tend to read Scripture more literally, while evangelicals tend to look more carefully at genre and literary and historical context.[32] Another way of saying this is that fundamentalists tend to assume that the meaning of Scripture is obvious from a single reading, while evangelicals want to talk about layers of meaning. For example, more fundamentalists will understand the first three chapters of Genesis to contain, among other things, scientific statements about beginnings, while evangelicals will focus more on the theological character of those stories— that the author/editor was more interested in showing that the earth has a Creator, for example, than precisely how the earth was created.

2. *Culture.* Fundamentalists question the value of human culture that is not created by Christians or related to the Bible, whereas evangelicals see God's "common grace" working in and through all human culture. For them, Mozart may not have been an orthodox Christian and possibly more flawed than most, but his music is a priceless gift of God. Culture is tainted by sin, as are all other human productions, but it nevertheless can reflect God's glory.

3. *Social action.* There was a time when fundamentalists considered efforts to help the poor to be a sign of liberal theology because proponents of the social gospel during the modernist controversy of the 1920s were theological liberals.[33] Until recently many funda-

---

[31]Donald Dayton discusses the historical dimensions of these patterns in his *Discovering an Evangelical Heritage* (Peabody, Mass.: Hendrickson, 1988).

[32]Confusion often abounds, however, when people talk about literalism and fundamentalists. It is not true that fundamentalists interpret every word of the Bible in literal fashion; for example, I do not know any fundamentalists who think God is literally a rock (Ps 18:2) or Jesus a door (Jn 10:7). And even the most liberal Christians take the Bible literally when it asserts that God is one (Deut 6:4).

[33]George M. Marsden, *Fundamentalism and American Culture: The Shaping of Twentieth-Century Evangelicalism: 1870-1925* (New York: Oxford University Press, 1980), pp. 85-93. See also Joel Carpenter, *Revive Us Again: The Reawakenings of American Fundamentalism* (New York: Oxford University Press, 1997), esp. pp. 118, 193.

mentalists limited their view of Christian social action to struggles for religious freedom and against abortion. Evangelicals have been more vocal in their declarations that the gospel also calls us to fight racism, sexism and poverty.[34]

4. *Separatism.* For many decades in this century, fundamentalists preached that Christians should separate themselves from liberal Christians (which sometimes meant evangelicals) and even from conservatives who associated with liberals. This is why some fundamentalists refuse to support Billy Graham: Graham asks for help from mainline Protestant and Catholic churches and sends his converts back to these churches for further nurture. Evangelical theology puts more emphasis on engagement with culture with the aim of transforming it and on working with other Christians toward common religious and social goals.

5. *Dialogue with liberals.* Fundamentalists have tended in the past to believe that liberal Christians (those who denied Jesus' resurrection, the sinful nature of humanity, the efficacy of the atonement or fundamentalist views of biblical inerrancy) were Christian in name only, that there was nothing to learn from them and that there was no use trying to talk to them once they refused to accept the fundamentalist version of the gospel. The evangelical approach is to talk with those of more liberal persuasions in an effort to persuade and perhaps even learn.[35]

6. *The nature of Christianity.* Although most fundamentalists preach salvation by grace, they also tend to focus so much on rules and restrictions (dos and don'ts) that their church members could get the impression that the heart of Christianity is a set of laws gov-

---

[34]I should also say, however, that many fundamentalist churches (and parachurch organizations such as the Salvation Army) have provided spiritual and material uplift for the poor for well over a century.

[35]For examples of this kind of dialogue, see David L. Edwards and John Stott, *Evangelical Essentials: A Liberal-Evangelical Dialogue* (Downers Grove, Ill.: InterVarsity Press, 1988); Clark H. Pinnock and Delwin Brown, *Theological Crossfire: An Evangelical/Liberal Dialogue* (Eugene, Ore.: Wipf & Stock, 1998).

erning outward behavior. There is an equal danger in evangelical churches, but evangelical theology focuses more on the person and work of Christ as the heart of the Christian faith.

7. *Fissiparousness*. Many evangelical groups have fractured and then broken again over what seems to later generations to have been minor issues. But the tendency seems worse among fundamentalism, for which differences of doctrine, often on rather minor issues, are considered important enough to warrant starting a new congregation or even denomination. Because evangelical theology makes more of the distinction between essentials and nonessentials, evangelicals are more willing to remain, for example, in mainline Protestant churches.

Protestant Orthodoxy, Liberalism and Postliberalism

Evangelicalism differs from classical Protestant orthodoxy not so much in its doctrines, which are very similar, but in its method. Evangelicalism tends to emphasize the primacy of Scripture more radically than do the Protestant traditions out of which it grew. That is, it subscribes to the doctrines of the great creeds of the church not because the creeds teach the doctrines but because the doctrines have biblical support. It listens to the great fathers and mothers of the church (and not only since the Reformation) and learns with the utmost respect from the historic confessions, but it also wants to receive them with critical care. It wants to be open to further light breaking out from the Word that might compel a reshaping or reformulation of historic understandings. The best of evangelical theology will never reject the basic doctrines of the Trinity, Christology and salvation, which come from the historic creeds, but will be open to new light from the Spirit about how to apply them. What the church believed about slavery and women for many centuries are two examples of further light from the Spirit that led to new understandings of the biblical revelation. Furthermore, while the two are not mutually exclusive, evangelicalism values personal faith in Jesus Christ over loyalty to creeds and dogmas. It is wary of arid orthodoxy that lacks the warmth of personal faith.

Evangelicals reject liberalism's faith in human experience as a final norm for truth and morality. Against the homogenizing tendency of liberal theology, which would postulate an underlying religiosity common to all faiths, evangelical theology emphasizes the particularity of Christian revelation and the uniqueness of Christian spirituality. While liberals place a premium on personal autonomy and appeal to internal norms (conscience and religious experience), evangelicals stress human responsibility to God, Who has given us external norms in Jesus Christ and Scripture.

Evangelicals have learned much from the more recent "research program" called postliberalism, which has been inspired by Karl Barth, Hans Frei and George Lindbeck.[36] According to William Placher, a prominent postliberal, this method of theology highlights the primacy of narrative as an interpretive category for Scripture, asserts the hermeneutical primacy of the world created by the biblical narratives over the world of human experience and claims the primacy of language over experience.[37] Evangelicals cheer postliberals' emphasis on the distinctiveness of Christianity, Scripture as the supreme source of ideas and values, the centrality of Jesus Christ, and Christian community.

But for evangelicals the problem with postliberalism is that it tends to reduce truth to a matter of internal consistency. It has a very difficult time answering the question, Why be a Christian and not a Buddhist? Rather than describing the two visions and talking about how one is more truthful than the other, postliberals refuse to acknowledge points of contact between Christians and non-Christians. But evangelicals insist that there is biblical precedent for identifying points of contact in experience, reason and culture.

---

[36]"Research program" is the description given by both appreciative evangelicals and postliberals themselves. See Phillips and Okholm, eds., *Nature of Confession*, pp. 13, 246.
[37]William C. Placher, "Paul Ricoeur and Postliberal Theology: A Conflict of Interpretations," *Modern Theology* 4 (1987): 35-52.

Paul wrote that knowledge of God the Creator can be gained outside of Christ (Rom 1:18-20). Luke testified that God has not left Himself without witness (Acts 14). While evangelicals agree with postliberals that only the work of the Holy Spirit can bring someone to faith, evangelicals believe that reason and experience, drawing on points of contact between those within and those outside the circle of faith, can be used by the Spirit to help deliver the gift of faith.

Postliberals are also unclear on the nature of revelation. They deny that the Bible is an objective revelation from God and say instead that the Bible can contain the Word when the Holy Spirit so moves. Perhaps as a result, they do not clearly determine whether the gospel stories are fictional or real.[38] Evangelicals put more emphasis on the objective nature of the biblical revelation. With postliberals they emphasize the necessity of the Spirit's illumination to give true understanding of the Person featured in the biblical story, but they assert that the Spirit inspired the writing of the texts in such a way that the Bible is the Word of God even if no one ever receives it as such. The Gospels are not merely stories that help us perform a Christian life by portraying a Christ Who may or may not have been Jesus of Nazareth; rather, they show us the true Jesus Who also was the Christ.

Evangelicals on the World Religions

When evangelicals have considered the world religions, for the most part they have focused on the questions of truth (do all the religions teach the same essential truths? is truth propositional or ineffable?) and salvation (can non-Christians be saved?), not revelation (is there divine revelation in the religions?). Evangelicals' concern for revelation has extended only to the point at which it affects the question of salvation. They have asked only if non-Christians can be saved

---

[38]See McGrath, *Passion for Truth,* pp. 157-61, for more on this.

through general revelation or if the truth in other religions—if there be any—can save them. No evangelical scholar of whom I am aware has launched a serious study of the question of whether truth has been given by God to the religions.

Recent evangelical discussion of the religions, which has centered almost exclusively on the question of salvation, has used the restrictivist-pluralist-inclusivist typology as a framework of understanding. This is a way of categorizing the three principal answers to the question of whether non-Christians can be saved. Restrictivists say that all the unevangelized are doomed to hell, for one must make explicit confession of Jesus during this life in order to be saved. Salvation is available only to those who have become confessing Christians. Augustine, John Calvin, R. C. Sproul and Ronald Nash have been prominent exponents of this view.[39]

Pluralists say there are many ways to salvation, many roads to heaven and union with God. Jesus is only one. One can be a Buddhist or Muslim and get to God apart from Jesus. Jesus is therefore the savior of some but not all. Others are saved by other saviors. John Hick, Paul Knitter, Wilfred Cantwell Smith and Aloysius Pieris are well-known proponents of this approach.[40]

Inclusivists say that Jesus is ontologically but not epistemologi-

---

[39]Augustine, *Letter to Deogratius*, in Nicene and Post-Nicene Fathers, ser. 1, ed. Philip Schaff (1886; reprint, Grand Rapids, Mich.: Eerdmans, 1974), 1:416-18; John Calvin, *Institutes of the Christian Religion*, ed. John T. McNeill, trans. Ford Lewis Battles (Philadelphia: Westminster Press, 1960), 2.6.1; R. C. Sproul, *Reason to Believe* (Grand Rapids, Mich.: Zondervan, 1982), pp. 47-59; Ronald Nash, *Is Jesus the Only Savior?* (Grand Rapids, Mich.: Zondervan, 1994). For other discussions of this question, see Millard J. Erickson, *How Shall They Be Saved? The Destiny of Those Who Do Not Hear of Jesus* (Grand Rapids, Mich.: Baker, 1996); John Sanders, ed., *What About Those Who Have Never Heard? Three Views on the Destiny of the Unevangelized* (Downers Grove, Ill.: InterVarsity Press, 1995).

[40]John Hick, *The Myth of God Incarnate* (Philadelphia: Westminster Press, 1977), and *An Interpretation of Religion* (New Haven, Conn.: Yale University Press, 1989); Paul Knitter, *No Other Name?* (Maryknoll, N.Y.: Orbis, 1985); Wilfred Cantwell Smith, *Faith and Belief* (Princeton, N.J.: Princeton University Press, 1979), and *Towards a World Theology* (Maryknoll, N.Y.: Orbis, 1981); Aloysius Pieris, *An Asian Theology of Liberation* (Maryknoll, N.Y.: Orbis, 1988).

cally necessary for salvation. That is, no one is saved apart from Jesus' work and person, but one does not have to know Jesus during this life to be saved by Him. Salvation is therefore available to those who profess other religions but only by means of the hidden Christ. If a Chinese peasant who has never heard of Jesus nevertheless knows from nature and conscience that there is a moral God whose law he finds in his heart, and realizes that this law condemns him, and throws himself upon this God's mercy, he is really casting himself upon Christ, Who is the mercy of God. Jesus saves him not because he is a good man but because he is among the elect whom He has chosen to save through His life, death and resurrection. Jesus has given this man faith and repentance as gifts. Not all inclusivists state their schemes in precisely this manner, but the following have embraced some version of what has just been outlined: Clement of Alexandria, Justin Martyr, Irenaeus, John Wesley, C. S. Lewis, Clark Pinnock, John Sanders, J. N. D. Anderson and Millard Erickson.[41]

In this book I will not argue for one of these over the others since my focus is not on salvation but on the question of revelation in the religions. Suffice it to say that all evangelical thinkers of whom I am aware reject pluralism because of such clear textual testimonies as John 14:6 and Acts 4:12 that Jesus is the only savior and way to God. Evangelicals are divided between restrictivism and inclusivism,

---

[41]Clement of Alexandria *Stromata* 1.5, 15; 5.5, 13; 6.6-8, 17; 7.2; Justin Martyr *First Apology* 46; Irenaeus *Against Heresies* 4.6.5-7; 4.20.6-7; 2.6.1; John Wesley, "The General Spread of the Gospel," in *The Works of John Wesley*, 3rd ed. (Peabody, Mass.: Hendrickson, 1986), 6:286; John Wesley, "On Faith," in *Works*, 7:197; C. S. Lewis, *Mere Christianity* (New York: Macmillan, 1967), pp. 65, 176, and *God in the Dock*, ed. Walter Hooper (Grand Rapids, Mich.: Eerdmans, 1970), p. 102; John Sanders, *No Other Name: An Investigation into the Destiny of the Unevangelized* (Grand Rapids, Mich.: Eerdmans, 1992); Clark Pinnock, *A Wideness in God's Mercy: The Finality of Jesus Christ in a World of Religions* (Grand Rapids, Mich.: Zondervan, 1992); J. N. D. Anderson, *Christianity and Comparative Religion* (Downers Grove, Mich.: InterVarsity Press, 1977); Millard Erickson, "Hope for Those Who Haven't Heard? Yes, But . . . ," *Evangelical Missions Quarterly* 11 (August 1975): 124.

but since the Reformation, inclusivism has steadily gained favor and is beginning to challenge restrictivism for supremacy among published evangelical thinkers.[42]

It needs to be noted, however, that this typology has recently collapsed among nonevangelicals, and the question of salvation has now taken a radical turn. Evangelicals will no doubt begin to explore this new development. Joseph DiNoia was the first prominent scholar to signal this new turn, and S. Mark Heim has now given it its fullest explication.[43] They have argued that inclusivism is incoherent because the religions have different ends. Inclusivism seems to suggest that other religions seek a goal similar to that of Christians—union with an infinite, personal God.[44] How then is one to make sense of Theravada Buddhists, who do not believe in such a God and have no such goal?

Not only is inclusivism problematic in view of the plurality of goals in the religions, but closer inspection seems to indicate (DiNoia and Heim suggest) that all the religions are exclusive (restrictivist, in a sense) in their claims. That is, if we take the religions in their thickest historical and empirical descriptions, we find that they all teach that their religious goals can be met by following their religion alone (in the restrictivist sense, consciously appropriating their methods during this life). Hence each religion is a "one and only"—the only way to its kind of salvation. So inclusivism does not work because it assumes there is only one salvation to be pursued by all the religions when in reality there are many.

Neither does pluralism cohere, because it is crypto-inclusivist. It

---

[42]Sanders, *No Other Name*, p. 216 n. 1.

[43]Joseph DiNoia, "The Universality of Salvation and the Diversity of Religious Aims," *World Mission* (Winter 1981-1982): 4-15; S. Mark Heim, *Salvations: Truth and Difference in Religion* (Maryknoll, N.Y.: Orbis, 1995).

[44]Of course, most inclusivist scholars are not so naive as to think that systems such as advaita vedanta are theistic. The point that DiNoia and Heim make is that the ends of the religions are so radically diverse that it is impossible to think of them as leading by different routes to the same destination.

claims to believe in many goals but actually believes in only one—for
Hick, it is reality-centeredness; for Knitter, orthopraxis that pursues
liberation from social oppression; for Wilfred Cantwell Smith, universal common rationality and a universal quality of faith. Each of these
goals is very different from what real practitioners of the religions say
they are about. While real believers say very different things about the
divine and how to reach it, pluralists insist they are all talking about
the same thing. In effect, then, pluralists deny any pluralism of real
consequence. Like inclusivists, they say there is only one end for all.

DiNoia and Heim argue not only that the religions teach different
goals or salvations but that there may actually *be* different salvations.
These different ends are not for the same person at the same time but
for different people, or for the same person at different times. Moreover, they say that this reality of different ends may be "providentially"
provided by God. In other words, Theravadin Buddhists may indeed
experience nirvana, and Muslims may indeed find Paradise. So there
are three types of religious fulfillment: lostness, incomplete religious
fulfillment through a non-Christian religion, and communion with
the triune God—the last of which only Christian faith provides.

DiNoia and Heim make philosophical and theological arguments
for this notion, appealing to the Neo-Platonic Great Chain of Being
and its concept of plenitude and to the Christian doctrine of the
Trinity that functions as a "template for diversity." They refer to
Dante's circles of Paradise, in which each soul receives its dearest
desire. Evangelicals will note the stunning absence of any attempt to
make a biblical argument for this scenario.

Evangelicals may also start to rethink their use of the old typology, and some will want to see if there is biblical evidence for a plurality of salvations. Note, however, that this discussion still revolves
around the question of salvation. Despite signs of biblical support
for the notion of revelation in the religions,[45] and a large number of

---

[45]See chapter three.

orthodox Catholic scholars working on this question for some decades, evangelicals have hardly begun to ask the question. John G. Stackhouse Jr. and Clark Pinnock have started to pose the question, and Pinnock has done some preliminary exploration, but nothing more has been attempted.[46] It is time to go further.

---

[46]John G. Stackhouse Jr., "Evangelicals Reconsider World Religions: Betraying or Affirming the Tradition?" *Christian Century,* September 8-15, 1993, pp. 858-65; Pinnock, *Wideness in God's Mercy,* esp. chaps. 3 and 4.

2

WHAT IS
|REVELATION?|

SINCE THIS IS A STUDY OF THE POSSIBILITY OF REVELATION IN OTHER religions, it is first necessary to define what is meant by *revelation*. The term has been a commonplace in theology only since the Enlightenment, when the English Deists launched a frontal attack on the notion that God had made Himself known through media beyond nature and reason. Deists argued that a God who revealed Himself only to Jews and Christians was an arbitrary monster in whom right-thinking persons could not believe, for a just God would have made Himself known to all human beings, not just those who fell within the scope of the Judeo-Christian tradition. Hence since the Enlightenment it has been customary to refer to two sources of knowledge about God: (1) nature and reason, which are available to all, and (2) revelation, which is available to those with access to the Bible.[1]

---

[1] When the distinction is made between revelation on the one hand, and nature and reason on the other, "special revelation" is meant—what can be learned of salvation from the Bible. Nature and reason taken together were later called "general" revelation. I will elaborate on this distinction later in this chapter.

For good secondary accounts of deism, see Gerald R. Cragg, *The Church and the Age*

Definition

Etymologically, the word *revelation*, which comes from the Latin *revelo*, goes back to the Hebrew *gala* and the Greek *apokalyptō*, both of which mean the unveiling of something that was hidden so that it might then be seen and known for what it is. The sense of this is conveyed by the author of Ephesians: "In former generations this mystery was not made known to humankind, as it has now been revealed to his holy apostles and prophets by the Spirit" (Eph 3:5, author's translation).

For the authors of Scripture, then, revelation is the unveiling of a previously hidden mystery. More important, however, it is God Who uncovers the mystery. God has taken the initiative to disclose His plans, character and very being to His human creatures. God has shown Himself and His ways to selected human beings, who in turn have passed down to us what they have seen, heard and experienced:

> We declare to you what was from the beginning, what we have heard, what we have seen with our eyes, what we have looked at and touched with our hands, concerning the word of life—this life was revealed, and we have seen it and testify to it, and declare to you the eternal life that was with the Father and was revealed to us—we declare to you what we have seen and heard so that you also may have fellowship with us; and truly our fellowship is with the Father and with his Son Jesus Christ. (1 Jn 1:1-3)

As this passage makes clear, revelation for the biblical authors was not the product of human seeking or imagination but a divine gift to creatures who otherwise have only distorted ideas about the

of Reason 1648-1789 (New York: Penguin, 1960), and *Reason and Authority in the Eighteenth Century* (Cambridge: Cambridge University Press, 1964); Robert E. Sullivan, *John Toland and the Deist Controversy: A Study in Adaptations* (Cambridge, Mass.: Harvard University Press); Peter Byrne, *Natural Religion and the Nature of Religion: The Legacy of Deism* (London: Routledge, 1989); Peter Harrison, *"Religion" and the Religions in the English Enlightenment* (Cambridge: Cambridge University Press, 1990); J. A. I. Champion, *The Pillars of Priostcraft Shaken: The Church of England and Its Enemies 1660-1730* (Cambridge: Cambridge University Press, 1992). The best contemporary account is John Leland, *A View of the Principal Deistical Writers* (1755-1757; reprint, New York: Garland, 1978).

divine: we were "dead" in our sins and "darkened" in our understanding of God when God took the initiative to open our eyes and ears to see God's reality and redemptive designs (Eph 2:1; 4:18; cf. Mt 11:25-27; 16:17; 2 Cor 4:6). Apart from revelation, our speculations about the divine are only "foolishness" and in fact contradict true knowledge of God (Rom 1:21-26; 1 Cor 2:14). Even if sin were not a barrier to knowing the divine, there is still a vast ontological gulf between us and the transcendent realm. God is so far from humanity in His mode of being that human beings can not see Him (Jn 1:18; 1 Tim 6:16; cf. Ex 33:20) or find Him by searching (Job 11:7; 23:3-9) or guess His thoughts (Is 55:8-9). As Søren Kierkegaard famously expressed it, there is an "infinite qualitative distinction between God and man."[2] It is for these reasons that Pascal said that God alone can speak well of God.

The word *revelation* refers not only to the process of God disclosing His purposes and being but also to the knowledge of God that results from that disclosure. This knowledge then reveals the meaning of all the rest of reality. As Thomas Oden has put it, receiving and understanding God's revelation is an experience through which we see all the rest of experience.[3] Lesslie Newbigin has compared it to Kepler's discovery of his third law. In Kepler's words, "At last I have brought it to light and recognized its truth beyond all my hopes. . . . The pure Sun itself of the most marvellous contemplation has shone forth." Newbigin adds that while Kepler proclaimed, "I have brought it to light," the biblical prophets testified, "God spoke to me."[4] If the provenance of revelation was different, the result was similar: it is an event that makes all other events intelligible.

This is the way revelation worked for the Israelites and early

---

[2]Søren Kierkegaard, *Training in Christianity*, in *A Kierkegaard Anthology*, ed. Robert Bretall (New York: Modern Library, 1946), p. 391.
[3]Thomas C. Oden, *The Living God*, vol. 1 of *Systematic Theology* (San Francisco: Harper & Row, 1987), p. 333.
[4]Lesslie Newbigin, *The Gospel in a Pluralist Society* (Grand Rapids, Mich.: Eerdmans, 1989), p. 59.

Christians. Human experience took on cosmic meaning when seen through the prism of revelatory events captured by Scripture. The author of Exodus told his readers, "When in the future your child asks you, 'What does this mean?' you shall answer, 'By strength of hand the LORD brought us out of Egypt, from the house of slavery'" (Ex 13:14). When the first Christians were persecuted for their faith or saw miraculous healings, it was the death and resurrection of Christ that explained these events (Acts 1—5). In other words, the content of revelation was a God Whose character and nature were revealed primarily in narratives about His work of redemption, which began in the counsels of the godhead in eternity and will continue until the eschatological establishment of a kingdom headed by the Son. It is this story, which began with Adam and Abraham and the Jews and continued through the incarnation, that demonstrates to all the cosmos God's holiness, faithfulness and sovereignty. It shows that, in the Trinity, God is a society of love and that Jesus was God's last revelation to humanity. For He was the image of God, in Whom all the divine fullness dwelled (2 Cor 4:4; Col 1:15; Heb 1:3).[5]

If revelation conveys knowledge, it is not merely information that provides new insight. The divine disclosure demands whole-hearted trust in what is revealed; it inspires a faith that, if properly received, entails obedience (Rom 1:5; 16:26). Those who receive this revelation are called not to mere mental assent but to an openness that is self-involving and transforming.

Media and Modes

Through what media or modes does revelation come? According to the biblical witness, they are many and varied. God spoke through lots (1 Sam 10; Acts 1:24-26), visions (1 Kings 22:17-23), audible

---

[5]For a theological understanding of this narrative, see Jonathan Edwards, *A History of the Work of Redemption,* ed. John F. Wilson (New Haven, Conn.: Yale University Press, 1989), pp. 111-530.

voice (1 Sam 3:1-14), dreams (Gen 28:10-17), interpretation of dreams (Gen 40—41), angels (Judg 13:15-20), inspiration of prophecy (Jer 1), wisdom (Proverbs), historical events (such as the exodus), metaphors (Ps 18:2), parables (Mt 13:1-50), and stories {the gospel accounts of Jesus' life, passion and resurrection).

Sometimes the biblical text says simply that God revealed Himself—to Jacob (Gen 35:7, 9) and Samuel (1 Sam 3:21), for example. God appeared in human form to Abraham (Gen 18:1—19:1), and Jacob wrestled with God (Gen 32:24-30). Moses saw His back (Ex 33:21-23) but, according to the text, sometimes spoke with God "face to face" (Num 12:8; Deut 34:10).

In the New Testament we are told that Jesus controls the knowledge of God by choosing those to whom He reveals the Father (Mt 11:27). He spoke in parables both to reveal the nature of the kingdom to His disciples and to keep its mysteries hidden from those not ready or able to hear (Mt 13:11-15). But it was His very Person that was the fullest revelation of God (Jn 1:1). Now the Word had become a human being (Jn 1:17), so to know Jesus was to know God (Jn 14:9). God had revealed Himself in "many and various ways" during the Old Testament era, but the history of revelation culminated in Jesus Himself (Heb 1:1-2). The Holy Spirit was sent to continue the revelatory function of the Son through the inspired writings of the apostolic generation (Jn 14:25-26; 16:12-15; 1 Jn 2:20, 27).

Revelation in Nature?

In twentieth-century theology Karl Barth initiated a debate over whether God also reveals Himself through nature in what is sometimes called "natural revelation."[6] There is biblical evidence that, while unregenerate humans cannot properly interpret this revela-

---

[6]Of course this was not a new subject in the history of theology, but Barth has made it particularly compelling in this century.

tion, nature nevertheless provides knowledge about God. The psalmist declares that "the heavens are telling the glory of God; and the firmament proclaims his handiwork" (Ps 19:1). Luke reports Paul's words at Lystra that God gave a witness to Himself in His provision of nature's seasons, rain and food (Acts 14:17); then at Athens Paul again proclaimed that God created the earth's seasons and geography so that human beings would "search for God and perhaps grope for him and find him" (Acts 17:26-27). In his letter to the Romans, Paul wrote that "what can be known about God is plain" to those who suppress the truth "because God has shown it to them. Ever since the creation of the world his eternal power and divine nature, invisible though they are, have been understood and seen through the things he has made" (Rom 1:19-20).

It was on the basis of these and similar passages that John Calvin and Jonathan Edwards argued that God has given objective revelation of Himself in nature. Calvin said that God the Creator (not God the Redeemer, Who is known only through Christ) can be known by reflection on the created order, which is a mirror or theater for the display of God's presence, nature and attributes.[7] Calvin also believed that the historical process itself gave witness of God. He pointed to such biblical passages as those in the prophets, where Isaiah and Habakkuk, for example, discerned God working through Assyria and the Chaldeans (Is 10:5-6; Hab 1:5-6). Edwards used natural revelation as a foundation for cosmological (based on the notion that all things require a Cause for their existence) and teleological (inferring a Designer responsible for the design of the cosmos) arguments for the existence of God.[8]

Both Calvin and Edwards were responding to Paul's second chap-

---

[7] John Calvin, *Institutes of the Christian Religion,* ed. John T. McNeill (Philadelphia: Westminster Press, 1960), 1.5.

[8] Jonathan Edwards, *Freedom of the Will,* ed. Paul Ramsey (New Haven, Conn.: Yale University Press, 1957), pp. 181-82; Miscellanies entry 267 [subsequent Miscellanies entries will be designated as "Misc. ##"], Edwards Papers, Beinecke Rare Book and Manuscript Li-

ter in Romans, in which he said that the human conscience contains divinely implanted testimony to God's moral law: "What the law requires is written on their hearts, to which their own conscience also bears witness" (Rom 2:15). For Calvin this was part of his grounding for what he called a *sensus divinitatis* found in every human being—a sense of the divine that points the human being to God.[9] Edwards also wrote of an innate, prereflective awareness of God, a natural inclination that prejudices the soul to believe in God: "That secret intimation and sort of inward testimony that men have upon occasion of the being of God."[10] For this eighteenth-century theologian, nature was full of evidence for God: "[God is] manifest in ourselves, in our own bodies and souls, and in everything about us wherever we turn our eye, whether to heaven, or to the earth, the air, or the seas."[11]

Edwards agreed with Calvin that nature points only to God the Creator, not God the Redeemer, and that knowledge of only the former is insufficient for salvation. The American theologian asserted that knowledge of God the Creator reveals to humanity something of what is required to please God but not how to find God when He has been displeased. So nature shows that there is a God Who makes moral demands, but it does not show how sinners can be restored to that God after they have failed to meet those demands. Nature reveals God, he wrote, but no one has ever come to God through nature alone. Even if some had come to God through nature, they still would not know whether God wanted to save them or damn them.[12] Edwards also claimed that while nature

---

brary, Yale University. See also Gerald McDermott, *Jonathan Edwards Confronts the Gods: Christian Theology, Enlightenment Religion, and Non-Christian Faiths* (New York: Oxford University Press, 2000), chap. 3.

[9]Calvin *Institutes* 1.3.1.

[10]Edwards, Misc. 268.

[11]Jonathan Edwards, "Man's Natural Blindness in Religion," in *The Works of Jonathan Edwards*, ed. Edward Hickman (Edinburgh: Banner of Truth, 1974), 2:252.

[12]Edwards, Misc. 1304. See also McDermott, *Jonathan Edwards Confronts the Gods*, chap. 3.

can tell us something about the truth of God, it cannot reveal to us the reality of God. I shall explain this shortly in my discussion of the interpretation of revelation. So for neither Calvin nor Edwards is revelation in nature a basis upon which to build a revealed theology—which must come by special revelation about Christ in a manner qualitatively different from what has been revealed through nature. Nor does natural revelation mean that humanity has an innate capacity for finding God apart from grace. Only the action of the Holy Spirit can reveal the true God to a person; apart from this work, that person is dead in his or her sins.

Another way of putting this has been to differentiate between *general* and *special* revelation. The former is given to all human beings through nature and conscience (Rom 1:18-20; 2:14-15), while the latter has come through Israel and Jesus Christ and therefore has been made known only to those who have had access to those traditions. The former reveals God's existence, power and moral demands, while only the latter shows how we can find relief for our inevitable failure to meet those demands. There is value in this distinction and in the language used to describe it. The distinction shows us that while many do not have full knowledge of the way of salvation, all have access to some knowledge of God. It also suggests that we may be able to discover some of God's truth in the wider world outside the sphere of special revelation. The language of revelation used for both sides of the distinction affirms that knowledge of God given to non-Christians has been *revealed* by God. It may not be enough for salvation, but it is nevertheless true knowledge about God given by God Himself.

While this distinction opens up the question of revelation in the religions, it also causes difficulties. Some revelation in the religions falls under neither side of the distinction as the two sides are usually defined, for some truth claims in the religions that seem to mirror or deepen what we know from Scripture are peculiar to only one or a few religions. Since they are not accessible to all, they cannot be

called instances of general revelation as the term is conventionally used. Nor do they fall under special revelation, which is usually taken to mean truths about how to gain salvation from sin and death. The Daoist concept of *wu-wei*, for example, describes a way of surrendering to the divine that is known to few and yet says nothing about how we can gain forgiveness for our refusals to surrender.[13] Hence it is neither general nor special revelation. In chapter four I shall argue that there is another category that can account for this phenomenon.

Karl Barth protested that the biblical passages typically used to support knowledge of God in nature have been misinterpreted by generations of readers, particularly since the Enlightenment. In fact, he alleged, the Old Testament passages show no knowledge of God apart from knowledge of the God of Israel (those outside of Israel use nature only for idolatrous purposes), and Paul indicates that this knowledge of God gained through nature leads only to condemnation.[14] In Barth's famous battle with Emil Brunner over natural revelation he accused Brunner of the error of *analogia entis,* by which (according to Barth) we seek knowledge of God on the basis of the perfection of human attributes. For Barth the biblical way was the *analogia relationis,* by which we know ourselves only by relationship to God through Jesus Christ. Hence testimonies of God in nature are not revelation because they are invariably misunderstood; they falsify rather than illumine. The only knowledge we have of God is in the face of Christ (2 Cor 4:6).[15]

---

[13]Daoist *wu-wei* is a kind of surrender to the essence and spirit of the cosmos. Philosophical Daoists would not necessarily call this surrender divine, and they do not believe in a god from whom one would seek forgiveness, but I describe *wu-wei* in this way to help Christians understand this concept in their own terms (I will go further in chapter seven) and to show that this tells us nothing about salvation.

[14]Karl Barth, *Church Dogmatics,* II/1 (Edinburgh: T & T Clark, 1957), pp. 130-33.

[15]Karl Barth, *Nein! Antwort an Emil Brunner,* Theologische Existenz heute 14 (Munich: Kaiser, 1934); English translation in Karl Barth and Emil Brunner, *Natural Theology: Comprising "Nature and Grace"* (London: G. Bles, The Centenary Press, 1946).

In my judgment Barth was right to insist that saving knowledge of God requires not just objective knowledge of God but also subjective understanding of that knowledge. However, in his attempt to defend Christian revelation against the German Christian religion based on blood and soil (with which he associated Brunner's natural theology), he overreacted. He argued, for example, that the voices of the cosmos in Psalm 19 are dumb because the text says "their voice is not heard" (Ps 19:3). But the psalmist probably meant that there is no *audible* voice, for he goes on to say that that voice "goes out through *all* the earth, and their words to the *end* of the world" (Ps 19:4; emphasis added). This seems to speak of God's revelation going to those who have not heard of the Lord of Israel—not just to Israelites, as Barth had suggested. Paul makes it clear that the revelation of God's law is made to *every* human heart (Rom 2:14). Barth accurately noted that many biblical writers suggest that these voices are not heard properly, if at all. Nevertheless, this and other texts indicate that there is genuine disclosure of God given through the cosmos and the human person—even if that disclosure is not seen or understood by many. Condemnation is indeed the result of some of this revelation (Rom 1:20), but Scripture also hints that the Spirit uses this revelation, no doubt in conjunction with others, to lead some to God (Acts 17:27; Rom 2:15). As G. C. Berkouwer put it, Barth's interpretation seems to be special pleading: "[Barth's exegesis] is more the result of an a priori view of revelation than an unprejudiced reading of the text itself."[16]

The Nature of the Truth of Revelation

Debate has raged not only over the question of whether genuine revelation is given by God through nature. Scholars and other interpreters have also contested the nature of the truth conveyed by

---

[16]G. C. Berkouwer, *General Revelation* (Grand Rapids, Mich.: Eerdmans, 1983), p. 154, cited in Gabriel Fackre, *The Doctrine of Revelation: A Narrative Interpretation* (Grand Rapids, Mich.: Eerdmans, 1997), p. 50.

revelation. This argument—or more accurately, series of arguments—has concerned three questions. First, is revelation an event or a proposition expressed in words? Second, is God's truth capable of being conceptualized, or is it ineffable? Third, what is the relationship between revelation and Scripture?

The first question is whether God's revelation is more properly described as an event in history that is described by human words or as God's speech conveyed to human subjects in verbal and propositional form. Those who favor the first view argue that truth in Scripture refers primarily to the Christ-event: God's self-revelation to humanity as the Christ in the person of Jesus. Hence for the biblical writers truth is something that *happens*. Truth is not a series of statements but comprises events in history such as the exodus and a person in history named Jesus of Nazareth. Borrowing Calvin's language of accommodation, these interpreters say that God has accommodated Himself to our capacity by revealing Himself in our history through these historical events. Revelation, then, is first and foremost a historical event. As Barth put it, revelation demands historical predicates.

This view can be corroborated by Scripture quite easily. Scripture represents God as manifesting His presence to human beings in a variety of ways and instances—many of which can be described as events. He revealed His presence to Abraham, Isaac and Jacob, Moses, Paul and many others (Gen 35:7; Ex 6:3; Num 12:6-8; Gal 1:15-16). There were the theophanies at the burning bush, Mount Sinai and the river Chebar (Ex 3:2—4:18; 19:11-20; Ezek 1). The angel of the Lord seems to have been a manifestation of Yahweh Himself (Gen 16:10; Ex 3:2—4:18; Judg 13:9-23). John said, "The Word became flesh and lived among us" (Jn 1:14). There is no doubt that Scripture portrays Jesus as God's paramount revelation. All these manifestations of God's presence were more events than messages.

It is equally clear that for the biblical writers revealed truth was not only something that happened but also something that was *told*. In Scripture God also revealed Himself by *speaking* His *purposes* to

His people. This divine speech was historical insofar as it was communicated to human beings who lived in history and received these communications at a given place and time. The reception of the message and the consequent reiteration of the message in human words can thus be considered something of a historical event, but the revelation itself is better characterized as a message from God than as an event in history.

Consider, for example, God's frequent statements of His purposes—that is, His communication of His character, plans and demands. He spoke to Noah, Abraham and Moses not only of His plans and purposes for them but also of His ultimate purposes for His people and the rest of humanity (Gen 6:13-21; 12:1-18; 15:13-21; 17:15-21; 18:17-33; Ex 3:7-22).[17] Then He declared to Israel the laws and promises of His covenant in Exodus 20—23; Deuteronomy 6:13-25; 28; Psalms 78:5-8; 147:19. He told Amos that He would do nothing without revealing His purposes to His prophets (Amos 3:7). Christ told His disciples all He heard from His Father and promised He would send the Spirit to complete His instruction to them (Jn 15:15; 16:12-15). Paul said that God revealed to him the mystery of His eternal purpose in Christ (Eph 1:9-14; 3:3-11), and John testified that Jesus revealed to him what would come to pass shortly (Rev 1:1).

The biblical evidence, then, shows that the distinction between revelation as event and revelation as word is a false dichotomy. Both are prominent in Scripture. In fact, neither is complete without the other. Word interprets event, and events fulfill promises made with words. The exodus was interpreted by words that sought to use Israel's liberation as a reminder of God's grace and motivation to keep the terms of the covenant. The prophets' words promising a messiah and new covenant were fulfilled by Jesus and His kingdom.

---

[17]For this and the next paragraph I am indebted to J. I. Packer, "Revelation," in *The New Bible Dictionary*, ed. J. D. Douglas (Grand Rapids, Mich.: Eerdmans, 1962).

A second question has concerned the intelligibility of revealed truth: is it capable of being communicated with words, or is it ineffable? Early in this century Rudolf Otto published what has now become a classic, *Das Heilige,* in which he (rightly) argued that as much attention ought to be paid to the nonrational (as opposed to irrational) dimension of religion as to the rational. But he also claimed that the otherness of the divine, which he called the "numinous," "completely eludes apprehension in terms of concepts."[18] It can be experienced only as an intuition; no coherent description of it can be formulated in language.

In a later version of what could be called the ineffability thesis, the Swiss theologian Emil Brunner proposed that revelation should not be construed in terms of communication of information about God but rather should be understood as a dynamic, dialectical encounter between God and humans. Hence the truth of revelation is not propositional but existential and can be expressed only in terms of a personal encounter of the human "I" with God's "Thou" in Jesus Christ.[19]

More recently, the Harvard historian of religion Wilfred Cantwell Smith has distinguished between the external "cumulative tradition" of religious communities and the inner faith of the religious believer. Only the latter, he claims, constitutes significant religious truth. Therefore, we should think of religious truth not in terms of propositional statements about God, self or world but rather as indicators of personal integrity, sincerity, faithfulness, authenticity of life and one's success in appropriating certain beliefs in one's life and conduct.[20] The conclusion of all three of these thinkers is that there exists a higher level of religious truth to which the principle of non

---

[18]Rudolf Otto, *The Idea of the Holy,* trans. J. Harvey (New York: Oxford University Press, 1950), pp. 5-6.
[19]Emil Brunner, *Truth as Encounter,* 2nd ed. (Philadelphia: Westminster Press, 1964).
[20]Wilfred Cantwell Smith, *The Meaning and End of Religion* (New York: Harper & Row, 1962).

contradiction does not apply. At this level, nothing about God can be known in rational terms.

The first problem with this position is that the biblical data indicate, as I have already noted, that God often spoke His purposes, plans and demands to His people. He communicated in rational terms, or at least messages that were then expressed in rational terms, to human beings. So while it is clear from Scripture that much of revelation is nonrational (Jesus was a person not a proposition), it is clear that some of it can be expressed in propositional terms.

Harold Netland has also pointed out philosophical problems with the position that revelation can never be expressed in propositional terms. The proposition that no truths about God can be known, for example, is self-refuting. The statement itself is a truth that is presumably capable of being known. Negative knowledge about God presupposes positive knowledge. For instance, if God is incorporeal, then He is not tall, short or even a physical being at all.[21]

Furthermore, the attempt to resolve the question of how different religions relate to one another by appeal to a higher (ineffable) form of religious truth that is not limited by the principle of noncontradiction is epistemologically untenable, for any attempt to state the distinction between lower and higher will have to appeal to the principle of noncontradiction. Either there is a higher level or there is not. One cannot say there is and there is not at the same time. Hence the higher level is not beyond all distinctions and logical principles.

Some religious truth is indeed ineffable. Paul said that the love of Christ "surpasses knowledge" (Eph 3:19), and much (probably most) of the divine cannot be known by human beings. But the very concept of revelation suggests that God has made some dimensions

---

[21]Harold Netland, *Dissonant Voices: Religious Pluralism and the Question of Truth* (Grand Rapids, Mich.: Eerdmans, 1991), chap. 4.

of His being and ways known to us. Hence we can know something of God *ad nos*. As Thomas Aquinas argued, our knowledge about God is neither univocal nor equivocal but analogical. Our knowledge about God, gained from revelation, is neither identical to its referent nor meaningless but contains both similarities to its referent and differences. We see through a glass darkly, which means we see something.[22]

Another way of putting this is to say that Scripture and theology provide us with models of God. A model is never the same thing as what it represents. But by understanding it, the mind can grasp something of the reality to which it points. For example, the stories of Jesus in the Gospels do not give us the full reality of Jesus, but nevertheless they provide us with something of His person, character and teaching.[23]

Therefore, by grasping the words and images of revelation in Scripture, we can grasp something of the reality of God Himself. This applies not only to the words and symbols of Scripture but also to the historical events described therein. No historical account is an exact reconstruction; it is always an interpretive picture. Yet because the historical accounts in Scripture were superintended by the Holy Spirit's inspiration, they can show us something of both the character and the purposes of God. When the objective content of Scripture is illuminated by the Holy Spirit (which I will discuss below), the reader can encounter the divine.

Therefore, as Gavin D'Costa has argued, we *can* know something about God, and it can be expressed in rational terms. The economic Trinity is the immanent Trinity. The Trinity as made known to us through redemption is not a different Reality from the triune deity-in-Itself. The knowledge of God we have been given through revelation is not simply a human construction (although our understand-

---

[22]Thomas Aquinas *Summa Theologiae* 1.13.1-6, 12.

[23]Colin Brown, "Revelation," in *The New International Dictionary of New Testament Theology*, ed. Colin Brown (Grand Rapids, Mich.: Zondervan, 1978), 3:336-37.

ing and formulation of revelation will always be conditioned by our finite and fallen perspectives). Our knowledge of God is not so broken that we can know nothing of Who God is and what He is like.

The third question, which asks whether the Bible is revelation or merely the witness to revelation, is related to the first question concerning revelation as event or word. Those who have said, following Barth, that revelation is always event, have also said, following Barth, that the Bible is not revelation in itself but the witness to revelation. This view of the Bible is based on Barth's motif of actualism, which thinks in terms of events and relationships rather than things or substances. God's being, Barth taught, is always a being in act. Just as our relationship to God is never possessed once and for all but is continually established anew by the ongoing activity of grace, so revelation is always an event or happening and never a thing.[24] Therefore the Bible, which is a thing, can never be identified with the Word of God, which is continually established anew according to the divine good pleasure. The Spirit often uses it to communicate a dynamic and living word to a person who reads it or hears it, but apart from that dynamic illumination of the Spirit, the Bible is not the Word or revelation of God.

Barth's understanding of the relation of revelation to Scripture seems too occasionalist to do justice to the Scripture's own witness to itself. New Testament authors regard Old Testament passages as authoritative utterances of God (Mt 19:4-5; Acts 4:25-6; Heb 1:5-14; 3:7-11). The question "Have you not read . . . ?" is virtually the equivalent of "Do you not know that God has said . . . ?" (Mt 12:3; 21:16; 22:31; Mk 2:25; 12:10, 26; Lk 6:3). And the phrase "it is written" carries the full weight of divine authority (Mt 11:10; 21:13; 26:24, 31; Mk 9:12-3; 11:17; 14:21, 27; Lk 7:27; 19:46). Occasionally *God* and *Scripture* are used interchangeably (Rom 9:17; cf. Ex 9:16; Gal 3:8; cf.

---

[24]See George Hunsinger, *How to Read Karl Barth: The Shape of His Theology* (New York: Oxford University Press, 1991), pp. 30-32, 76-102; Barth, *Church Dogmatics*, II/1, pp. 257-321.

Gen 12:3; Mt 19:4-5; cf. Gen 2:24).

So while Scripture claims that its *written* deposit was inspired by the Spirit (2 Tim 3:16; 2 Pet 1:20-21; 3:2, 15-16; cf. 1 Tim 5:18), Barth connects inspiration only with the psyche of the believer. Geoffrey W. Bromiley, chief translator of Barth's *Church Dogmatics*, concludes that Barth stressed the present ministry of the Holy Spirit at the expense of the once-for-all work of the Spirit in the authorship of Scripture.[25] Edwards, in contrast, provides a more (biblically) balanced way to incorporate both the objective character of revelation in the Bible and the need for subjective illumination to the believer.

Dimensions of Revelation

So far I have used opposing terms to describe revelation (event or proposition, rational or ineffable, objective or subjective) and have suggested that each pair is a false dichotomoy. Revelation comprehends both events and propositions about those events, it is both ineffable at points and capable of rational description at others, and it involves both an objective content of knowledge about God as well as a process or activity of the Spirit. Yet even this does not go far enough. To stop here would give a narrow and unnecessarily limited view of revelation. It is far better to say that revelation involves not one or two but many dimensions.

Catholic theologian Avery Dulles has helpfully outlined five models of revelation, which do a better job of surveying the vast range of ways in which God has revealed Himself to His creation.[26] The models are not mutually exclusive but complementary, like theories of light as both particle and wave. All theological models are deficient representations of limited aspects of the mysteries of faith, and they are not of equal value. But the combination of the

---

[25]Geoffrey W. Bromiley, *Historical Theology: An Introduction* (Grand Rapids, Mich.: Eerdmans, 1978), pp. 420-21.

[26]Avery Dulles, *Models of Revelation* (Garden City, N.Y.: Doubleday, 1983).

five presents a fuller and more subtly delineated description of revelation as found in Scripture than do the three polarities discussed above.

1. *Revelation as doctrine.* This way of looking at Scripture sees it as containing clear, propositional statements that are the data from which church doctrines can be derived. It sees the events of Scripture as interpreted only by the words of Scripture. This view does not endorse a dictation theory of inspiration but emphasizes the propositional content of revelation. It asserts that faith is not blind but a reasonable act of trust that rests on both external and internal validations of the Bible.

2. *Revelation as history.* This view claims to return to Semitic historical concreteness in a flight from Greek metaphysics, which is thought to dominate the first view. Revelation, it is claimed, is not a collection of doctrines but a story. Proponents of this view are correct in emphasizing the importance of narrative in Scripture, but not at the expense of the nonnarrative sections, such as Proverbs and James. Dulles suggests mediating these first two views by saying that the historical event in Scripture is the material element in revelation while the word that interprets it is the formal element. Revelation is complex, which means that the next three models are needed as well.

3. *Revelation as inner experience.* This considers revelation as an interior experience of grace or communion with God, in which spiritual perception is immediate to the individual. Some proponents of this view would say it is not necessarily dependent on Christ, while others hold that in this sense revelation is merely the heightening of the normal and universal experiences of the moral and mystical life. I contend that in order for it to be Christian revelation it must be mediated by Christ and that there is a fundamental discontinuity between natural experience and supernatural revelation. So while some versions of this view conflict with an evangelical understanding of revelation, it nevertheless reminds the evangelical that revelation contains

not only an objective pole (the first and second models) but also a subjective pole, in which the objective content of revelation is personally appropriated by the believer through the work of the Spirit.

4. *Revelation as dialectical presence.* This is the notion that God is not an object to be known by inference from nature or history, by direct perception or by propositional teaching. God is utterly transcendent; He encounters the human subject only when it pleases Him by a word in which faith recognizes Him to be present. Therefore the word of God both reveals and conceals God. Just as Jesus was not recognized as God by most of His contemporaries, so too the Word of God is not seen for what it is unless God in His pleasure decides to reveal it as such. While this view unnecessarily restricts the objective content of revelation, it is a potent warning that illumination of the Word is a necessary part of revelation and that evangelicals run the danger of domesticating the divine when they forget this.

5. *Revelation as new awareness.* Proponents of this last view worry that the four preceding views can be too individualistic and otherworldly. They maintain that revelation is an expansion of consciousness or shift in perspective that engages people to join in works of social liberation. It is a presentation of paradigmatic events that stimulate the imagination to restructure one's experience. Truth is practical and salvational, and has no fixed content. Evangelicals insist that revelation has content indeed, but they can agree that the illumination of the Spirit works on the written revelation of Scripture to bring about a new consciousness. This new awareness will be concerned not only with individual salvation but also with the material and social well-being of others.

Why have I introduced Dulles's five models of revelation? It could be argued that they are contradictory—some refer to revelation as a body of knowledge while others see revelation as a process of knowing. The first stoutly affirms revelation as propositional, but the last argues for awareness that includes but transcends propositions. My point is that revelation is multidimensional. It must be if it is the self-manifestation of the triune God, Who is the infinite fountain of all being and beauty. God necessarily subsumes all of reality, so it stands to reason that His revelation of Himself would include every dimension of reality.

Therefore, while each of these models is incomplete when taken in isolation from the others, each contributes to an understanding of the polydimensional phenomena gathered under the word *revelation*. Like everything else about God, revelation is always distorted when considered from only one perspective. Since it is *God's* revelation, we must expect that it will be at least as complex and multidimensional as the most profound temporal realities we experience. And then some! So even the ideas we glean from these five models do not begin to exhaust the meaning of God's revelation. They do, however, begin to open us to the plethora of meanings for the word, and they suggest that when we ask about revelation in other religions, we must be open to a variety of ways in which that might happen.

The Interpretation of Revelation

If revelation and the nature of its truth have been difficult to define, interpreting revelation is not a simple matter either. Let me first comment briefly on sources and method. I have already suggested that Scripture is the principal testimony to the triune God's true identity but that tradition and reason are and ought to be integral components of the process of interpreting Scripture. Gabriel Fackre has given us a handy way to relate these sources to one another. Scripture, he has written recently, ought to play a magisterial role, church tradition and conversation a ministerial role, and general human experience (which can never be separated from the use of reason) a catalytic and contextual role. Another way of putting this, according to Fackre, is to say that Christ is the center of faith, the gospel is the substance, and tradition is a guide to interpreting both.

In this process the eye of faith, as he puts it, looks under the illumination of the Holy Spirit through the world.[27]

There are many things to be said about method, but I will limit my discussion of this to two points. First, one needs to approach this weighty matter of divine revelation with humility. As Dionysius put it centuries ago, our language is fragmentary and fragile. We strive with all our might in broken language to talk about what is finally quite indescribable.[28] Though we can talk about truth in rational terms, we must recognize the broken and incomplete character of everything we say about the divine, for we are using finite language to capture an infinite reality. Therefore, Kierkegaard said, there is an element of comedy in all talk about God, which we who have received a measure of grace should be quick to confess.[29] It is rather ridiculous, when we recognize our insignificance, to presume to declare monumental truths about God, for He is "not only infinitely greater and more excellent than all other being, but he is the head of the universal system of existence; the foundation and fountain of all being and all beauty; from whom all is perfectly derived, and on whom all is most absolutely and perfectly dependent; of whom, and through whom, and to whom is all being and all perfection; and whose being and beauty is as it were the sum and comprehension of all existence and excellence: much more than the sun is the fountain and summary comprehension of all the light and brightness of the day."[30] Of course, one of the great miracles of grace is that this fountain of existence has condescended to share its knowledge of itself with us. But even after we have gratefully

---

[27]Fackre, Doctrine of Revelation, p. 13.

[28]Pseudo-Dionysius, Divine Names, trans. C. E. Rolt (London: SPCK, 1975), 1.1ff., cited in Oden, Living God, p. 321.

[29]Søren Kierkegaard, Concluding Unscientific Postscript, trans. David F. Swenson and Walter Lowrie (Princeton: Princeton University Press, 1941), pp. 250-51, cited in Oden, Living God, p. 321.

[30]Jonathan Edwards, The Nature of True Virtue, ed. Paul Ramsey (New Haven, Conn.: Yale University Press, 1989), p. 551.

acknowledged that stupendous fact, we must further observe with humility that our interpretation of that revelation is necessarily flawed because of our sin and finitude.

Second, we must observe the Reformation principle that Scripture is self-interpreting. Or, to put it another way, Scripture is a unified whole given to the church by the Spirit of God—not by scholars using the historico-critical method whose deliberations we nervously await while deciding what to believe. My point is not that scholarship has nothing to tell us about the Bible but that we must receive its judgments critically while recognizing that the presuppositions governing much of what has passed for objective biblical criticism has been shown to be as prejudiced as the most unabashed fundamentalist commentaries.[31] Therefore, we would do well to heed the advice of the English Reformers who warned biblical interpreters not to "expound one place of Scripture [so] that it is repugnant to another."[32] God's written revelation is a seamless whole, parts of which we dare not tear out without the risk of rendering the whole incoherent.

But there is far more to interpretation than simply having, knowing and relating one part of Scripture to another. There is also what I have been calling the illumination of the Holy Spirit. This is a divine operation in the mind and heart of a recipient of grace that confirms to that recipient the reality of a supernatural truth or person. This is what enabled Peter to recognize that Jesus was the Christ: "Blessed are you, Simon son of Jonah! For flesh and blood has not revealed this to you, but my Father in heaven" (Mt 16:17). It is what showed Paul the truth and reality of the gospel: "I did not receive [the gospel] from a human source, nor was I taught it, but I received it

---

[31]A good introduction to the methodological problems surrounding biblical scholarship is found in N. T. Wright, *The New Testament and the People of God* (Minneapolis: Fortress, 1992), esp. chaps. 1-5.

[32]Article 20, "The Thirty-Nine Articles," in *Documents of the English Reformation*, ed. Gerald Bray (Minneapolis: Fortress, 1994), p. 297.

through a revelation of Jesus Christ" (Gal 1:12). It is also what he prayed for the Ephesians to receive: "I pray the God of our Lord Jesus Christ, the Father of glory, may give you a spirit of wisdom and revelation as you come to know him, so that, with the eyes of your heart enlightened, you may know what is the hope to which he has called you [and] what are the riches of his glorious inheritance among the saints" (Eph 1:17-18). The absence of illumination explains why so many could not understand the gospel: "Those who are unspiritual do not receive the gifts of God's Spirit, for they are foolishness to them, and they are unable to understand them because they are spiritually discerned. . . . In their case the god of this world has blinded the minds of the unbelievers, to keep them from seeing the light of the gospel of the glory of Christ, who is the image of God" (1 Cor 2:14; 2 Cor 4:4). But its presence is the cause of faith for believers: "For it is the God who said, 'Let light shine out of darkness,' who has shone in our hearts to give the light of the knowledge of the glory of God in the face of Jesus Christ" (2 Cor 4:6).

This is what John Calvin referred to as the "sealing of the Spirit," which is necessary for one to discern the truth of the Scriptures.[33] Both Calvin and Jonathan Edwards argued that an unregenerate person cannot receive the Bible as the Word of God by the force of arguments from reason. They agreed that the best argument for Scripture's divine origin is the Bible itself and that one can appreciate the force of its "self-validation" only by the work of the Holy Spirit. According to Edwards,

> Natural men may indeed have a common belief of many things in the Word, as they have of probable histories. But the faith of the godly, whereby they believe the Word of God to be true, is from the intrinsic signatures of divinity which they see in it. They see that excellency and that image of God in the Word that constrains the mind to assent to it and embrace it as true and

---

[33]Calvin *Institutes* 1.7.4-5.

divine. There are signatures of divine majesty to be seen in the Word, and signatures of divine wisdom and of divine holiness, and the evident marks of divine grace that make it evident that the Word of God did proceed from a divine majesty and wisdom, and holiness and grace.[34]

If the illumination of the Spirit is necessary to show that the Bible is the Word of 'God, it is also necessary to properly interpret it. The biggest part of interpretation is opening the eyes of the believer to the Reality behind and to which Scripture points. Thus, reading the words alone is not enough, even if one believes the Bible is divine revelation. Edwards said that words have no natural power to open up the divine reality. They have the capacity to convey to the mind the notions that are the subject matter of the Word, but only the Spirit can convey what Edwards called the "sense of the heart" that alone can shine light on divine realities.[35]

Even intellectual apprehension of and assent to the truths of Christ's redemption are insufficient. What is needed is a vision of the *beauty* of God in Christ, which for Edwards involved a personal knowledge and appreciation for the love that God showed in the incarnation and passion of His Son. This is a recognition—which comes only by the illumination of the Holy Spirit—that "God is God, and distinguished from all other beings, and exalted above 'em, chiefly by his divine beauty, which is infinitely diverse from all other beauty."[36]

It is this vision of the divine beauty that makes divine realities seem not only true but real. For Edwards this spelled the difference between "familiar" and "personal" knowledge of another. We can be familiar with William Jefferson Clinton by virtue of the many newspaper and magazine articles we have read about him and the televi-

---

[34]Jonathan Edwards, "Profitable Hearers of the Word," in *Sermons and Discourses 1723-1729*, ed. Kenneth P. Minkema, vol. 14 of *The Works of Jonathan Edwards* (New Haven, Conn.: Yale University Press, 1997), pp. 251-52.

[35]Jonathan Edwards, "A Divine and Supernatural Light," in *Selected Writings of Jonathan Edwards*, ed. Harold P. Simonson (Prospect Heights, Ill.: Waveland, 1970), pp. 65-88.

[36]Jonathan Edwards, *Religious Affections*, ed. John E. Smith, vol. 2 of *The Works of Jonathan Edwards* (New Haven, Conn.: Yale University Press, 1959), p. 298.

sion news programs we have watched. On the basis of this input we can say that we are familiar with Clinton and believe that certain things said about him are true. But if we actually meet him and spend several hours with the man, then we might say, in Edwards's sense of the word, that what we thought was true we now know to be real. We have personal knowledge. This is approximately the distinction that Edwards made between believing that certain divine things are true and being convinced of their reality. Edwards himself used the analogy of knowing that honey is sweet. Until we have actually tasted honey, we can believe the sweetness of honey to be true because of universal reports we have heard about it. But when we taste it for ourselves for the first time, we know not only that honey's sweetness is true but also that it is *real*.

Edwards insisted that without this seeing of the divine beauty, which comes only by the illumination of the Holy Spirit, revelation has not been truly revealed to us: "Unless this is seen, nothing is seen. . . . This is the beauty of the godhead, and the divinity of Divinity . . . without which God himself (if that were possible to be) would be an infinite evil: without which, we ourselves had better not have been; and without which there had better have been no being. He therefore in effect has nothing, that knows not this."[37]

If Edwards is right (and I think he is), we must reject not only the sufficiency of natural revelation but also the sufficiency of written revelation. That is, neither represents the fullness of revelation that is necessary for the knowledge that the triune God is not only true but real. Written revelation in Scripture is necessary for rational knowledge while spiritual revelation of the beauty of God in Christ is necessary to give full meaning to that rational knowledge. This is why, as Edwards remarked, the devil can know about Christ and still behave like the devil. Therefore, he concluded, a person can know the attributes of God, the Trinity and salvation by Christ and

---

[37] Ibid., p. 274.

nevertheless lack saving grace. Without the illumination of the Spirit, knowledge about Christ gained through revelation is no guarantee of salvation.[38]

For this reason I think Edwards did a better job of balancing the subjective and objective poles in revelation than did Barth. Barth rightly stressed the subjective pole, in reaction against, among other things, dry and sterile orthodoxies that seem to presume that mental assent to Christian doctrine is sufficient. The Swiss theologian properly emphasized God's dynamic activity of the Spirit, by which the human subject sees and acts by repeated acts of grace, rather than looking solely to a realm and book that were completed two millennia ago. But Barth marginalized the inspiration of Scripture and failed to give proper attention to the work of the Spirit in superintending the writing and selection of the biblical canon. In contrast, Edwards highlighted both the work of the Spirit in producing an authoritative Scripture and the work of the Spirit in the church to open the eyes of readers and hearers to the realities to which Scripture points so that they may participate in those realities.

Because both poles of revelation are required, interpretation is open to distortion—particularly by those who have objective revelation but not the subjective illumination of the Spirit. Theologically, this is the proposition that God is free to hide or disclose Himself, even in the act of revelation. Revelation overrides neither human nor divine freedom.

This notion of God's freedom to conceal even within revelation is based on biblical indications that God hides Himself even to those given revelation and keeps some things secret while revealing others (Is 45:15; Deut 29:29). Jesus revealed His humanity and some of His divine powers to thousands during His earthly sojourn, but His true identity was kept hidden from most of them (Mt 11:25-27). Even the disciples' "eyes were kept from recognizing him" on the

---

[38]See McDermott, *Jonathan Edwards Confronts the Gods,* chap. 3.

road to Emmaus (Lk 24:16). This divine freedom also follows from the biblical emphasis on God's sovereignty, which means His ultimate lordship over all of history, including His sharing of His self-knowledge with His human creatures (Eph 1:11; 2 Cor 6:18). One implication of this, which will be discussed further in chapter four, is that revelation can remain within a religion as a partly or even totally concealed revelation. Christians might see that revelation in a way that transforms the religion out of all recognition to an adherent but that nonetheless is faithful to the intent of the author of the revelation, God's Spirit. An example of this is the early church's interpretations of prophetic passages in Torah that it felt pointed to Jesus as the Christ; most Jewish readers of these same passages either believed that the prophecies pointed to someone other than Jesus if they considered the passage to be messianic (often they did not), or they understood the words to refer to the people of Israel as a whole.[39]

Finally, then, the most important criterion in interpreting revelation is christological. As Clark Pinnock has pointed out, what the Spirit says can never oppose the revelation we have of Christ because we are told that the Spirit's role is to glorify Christ and what Christ shows us of God (Jn 14:26; 16:13-14; 1 Jn 4:2-3).[40]

D'Costa adds that since the immanent Trinity is the economic Trinity, we cannot discover anything new about God *in se* that is unrelated or contradictory to the second person of the economic Trinity—the only Trinity we know. Therefore, we can know that we will never find a fourth or fifth person in God. Allah and Brahman, for example, must be understood within the context of the triune God. They may give us hints of hidden riches within the Trinity that we had not previously seen, but such insight will be the unveiling of what is already lying within the revelation we possess, not a new revelation coming from

---

[39]See Wright, *New Testament and the People of God*, pp. 307-20.
[40]Clark Pinnock, *Flame of Love: A Theology of the Holy Spirit* (Downers Grove, Ill.: InterVarsity Press, 1996), p. 209.

outside of what God disclosed of Himself through Israel and Jesus.[41] This means not that God cannot be known in ways apart from Jesus but that the revelation of God in Christ is definitive for human knowledge of God.[42]

Hence, Jesus Christ is a "subversive memory" that challenges all of our a priori assertions about God.[43] God has revealed Himself fully in Christ. Our understanding of that revelation is far from complete; in fact, it may be far less than what it will be someday. For if "all that the Father has" belongs in truth to Jesus (Jn 16:15), then the scope of the Spirit's work in illuminating that revelation is as wide as the cosmos itself.[44] Yet the revelation itself is God's conclusive demonstration of His character and being and is therefore the great standard against which all other ideas about God must be measured.

[41]Gavin D'Costa, "Revelation and Revelations: Discerning God in Other Religions: Beyond a Static Valuation," *Modern Theology* 10 (April 1994): 168-69.

[42]See Richard Bauckham, "Jesus the Revelation of God," in *Divine Revelation,* ed. Paul Avis (Grand Rapids, Mich.: Eerdmans, 1997), pp. 174-200.

[43]Alister McGrath, *The Genesis of Doctrine: A Study in the Foundation of Doctrinal Criticism* (Oxford: Blackwell, 1990), p. 175.

[44]Newbigin, *Gospel in a Pluralist Society,* pp. 78-79.

3

BIBLICAL
|SUGGESTIONS|

Now THAT WE HAVE SKETCHED AN OUTLINE OF WHAT IT MEANS TO speak of revelation, we will look more particularly in this chapter at the *biblical* evidence for revelation in religions outside the Judeo-Christian tradition. We shall see that the Bible contains hints and suggestions that God has given knowledge of Himself to people and traditions outside the Hebrew and Christian traditions. Three things must be said at the outset. First, revelation, as was discussed in the last chapter, may involve not doctrine or historical event but inner experience or new awareness.[1] Second, the evidence is not proof; just as with other Christian teachings that are still debated within the church—such as predestination, the role of women, church government, the gifts of the Spirit—Scripture contains examples and commentary that point more implicitly than explicitly to definite doctrines. On each of these contested issues, there are two or more

---

[1]Of course, the inner experience or new awareness usually leads, after reflection, to what we could call doctrine.

positions held by Christian thinkers who can point with greater or lesser cogency to biblical data for support. In this case, I think there is enough by way of hint and suggestion in Scripture that one can say there is biblical support for the notion that God has given revelation of aspects of His Person and ways to people outside Israel and the church. The evidence is neither overwhelming nor crystal clear, but it is sufficient to make a claim for revelation in the religions biblically *plausible*.

Third, by knowledge of God among the Gentiles (for our purposes this includes not only non-Jews in the Old Testament era but also non-Christians in general) I do not mean *saving* knowledge. The question of salvation among the religions is beyond the scope of this book. I mean simply that there is scriptural evidence that God has given knowledge of some aspects of His Person and work to people who were or are neither Jews nor Christians. This knowledge may or may not have led to salvation. The traditional distinction between general and special revelation has shown that many can have knowledge of God without experiencing salvation. There were also occasions when God's people in Scripture *learned* things about God from the Gentiles.

God Wants the Gentiles to Know Him

A recurring theme in the Old Testament is that Yahweh desires for all the world to know that He is the Lord. It is prominent even in the story of the exodus, in which God is concerned not only with redeeming His own people but also with displaying His glory to everyone else—particularly the Egyptians. In other words, He is intent on showing His salvation not only to the Jews but also to their captors: "I will harden Pharaoh's heart, and he will pursue [the Israelites], so that I will gain glory for myself over Pharaoh and all his army; and the Egyptians shall know that I am the LORD" (Ex 14:4; cf. v. 18). Hence, in the greatest act of salvation of the pre-Christian era, God wanted not only to save the Jews but also to reveal to the Gentiles His own identity.

The theme surfaces again in the prophets, particularly in Isaiah and Ezekiel. In Isaiah 37, King Hezekiah prays that Yahweh will save Judah from capture by the Assyrian king Sennacherib: "So now, O LORD our God, save us from his hand, so that all the kingdoms of the earth may know that you alone are the LORD" (Is 37:20). Hezekiah suggests that it is God's desire for all the kingdoms of the world to know Him, or at least to acknowledge His sovereignty, and that an answer to his prayer will fulfill that desire. Later, Isaiah foretells a time when all people together will see the glory of the Lord, and the suffering servant will bring light and justice to the nations (Is 40:5; 42:1; 49:6). God's punishment of Zion's oppressors will show "all flesh" that the Mighty One of Jacob is her savior and redeemer (Is 49:26). Both Isaiah and Jeremiah proclaim that the nations shall come to the light of Jerusalem and gather before the throne of the Lord (Is 60:3; 66:18-19; Jer 1:5; 3:17).

Ezekiel addresses the nations more specifically on this score. In general, he announces, God wants His name not to be profaned among the nations; He desires to manifest His holiness in the sight of the nations and for all flesh to know that He is the Lord (Ezek 20:9, 14, 22, 41; 21:5). More directly, He declares that through His chastisements the following peoples will discover that He alone is God: the Ammonites, Moabites, Philistines, residents of Tyre and Sidon, and the Egyptians (Ezek 25:5, 11, 17; 26:6; 28:23; 29:6, 8, 16; 30:19, 26; 32:15). He tells Gog, the ruler and general of Magog's forces,[2] that He will use him to invade Israel "so that the nations may know me, when through you, O Gog, I display my holiness before their eyes" (Ezek 38:16). In the same chapter God adds that He will also destroy Gog, and that even that destruction "will display my greatness and my holiness and make myself known in the

---

[2]"Gog and Magog appear [to be] transhistorical, though the name Gog may derive from the name of the Lydian ruler Gyges" (David L. Petersen, notes to Ezek 20, *HarperCollins Study Bible* [New York: HarperCollins, 1993]).

eyes of many nations. Then they shall know that I am the LORD" (Ezek 38:23).

We are shown through these passages, then, that the history of redemption in the Old Testament is not simply a story of God's raising up and delivering a people for Himself through Israel; it is that, of course, but it is not conducted in utter disregard for the nations that surrounded Israel. God was also intent on making Himself known to those surrounding peoples. It is beyond the scope of this book to understand why God was doing this—that is, what relation this demonstration had to God's salvation of Israel and whether this meant that salvation was available for any of these surrounding peoples. It is clear, however, that God intended not only to raise up and save a people known as the Jews but also to make known His name and glory to Gentiles throughout the ancient Near East. This means that some Gentiles outside of Israel came to know something of the true God through what God did in and through Israel.[3]

The New Testament also contains intimations that God wants to reveal Himself to men and women outside the orbit of the Christian revelation. In the last chapter I noted that Romans 1—2 and other biblical texts point to "general" revelation in nature and conscience. Acts 14:17 states that God witnesses to Himself through the blessings of nature and food: "He has not left himself without a witness in doing good—giving you rains from heaven and fruitful seasons, and filling you with food and your hearts with joy." God is portrayed by

---

[3]Some have suggested that Amos 9:7 speaks of peoples other than Israel being elected: "Are you not like the Ethiopians to me, O people of Israel? says the LORD. Did I not bring Israel up from the land of Egypt, and the Philistines from Caphtor and the Arameans from Kir?" See, e.g., George A. Lindbeck, *The Nature of Doctrine: Religion and Theology in a Postliberal Age* (Philadelphia: Westminster Press, 1984), p. 54. But there is no mention of election in this passage. Shalom M. Paul argues in *Amos* (Minneapolis: Augsburg Fortress, 1991) that the intent is to disabuse the Israelites of cocky self-assurance based on their divine election. Amos's point is that Israel's election does not depend on the exodus: other nations have been delivered by God, and they too have been destroyed. Exodus is no guarantee of protection from judgment. See also James Luther Mays, *Amos: A Commentary* (Philadelphia: Westminster Press, 1969).

Scripture as wanting to reveal Himself in ways not connected to the history of Israel or Christ. These ways of revelation seem to spring from a desire to make Himself known even to people who have not heard of the revelation in Israel and Christ.

Knowledge of God Outside the Hebrew and Christian Traditions

If Scripture suggests that God *desires* all the world to know Him, it also indicates that people outside the Jewish and Christian churches[4] *have* known Him—or at least some aspects of His Person and character. For example, the early pages of the Bible contain the remarkable story of Melchizedek, a Canaanite priest-king who is shown to have known the true God apart from the revelation given to Abraham (Gen 14:17-24). Melchizedek, whom the author of Genesis calls the king of Salem (identified with Jerusalem in Ps 76:3), brought bread and wine to Abram after his victory over Chedorlaomer and his allies. The text says that Melchizedek was a priest of El Elyon (roughly translated "God Most High"), a Canaanite deity whose identity here is curiously merged with Abram's God.

Melchizedek blessed Abram by El Elyon and said El Elyon is maker of heaven and earth (Gen 14:19). Then Melchizedek blessed El Elyon and declared that El Elyon had delivered Abram's enemies into his hand (v. 20). Abram thereupon tithed to Melchizedek. When another figure in the story, the king of Sodom, offered to Abram the spoils taken from the defeated armies, Abram refused with these intriguing words: "I have sworn to the LORD [Yahweh], God Most High [El Elyon], maker of heaven and earth, that I would not take a thread or a sandal-thong or anything that is yours, so that you might not say, 'I have made Abram rich'" (vv. 21-23).

Notice what Abram has done in these words: he has identified

---

[4]Following a custom in the Reformed tradition, I refer to ancient Israel as God's church. Calvin and his followers taught that God established one covenant with His people, starting with Israel and continuing in the Christian era.

Yahweh with El Elyon in two ways. He has conjoined the two names in a gesture that suggests they point to the same God, and—as if it were not completely clear—he has given Melchizedek's description of El Elyon to Yahweh: maker of heaven and earth. Claus Westermann argues that both Abram's acceptance of Melchizedek's blessing and his tithe to the Canaanite priest indicate that Abram acknowledged the legitimacy of Melchizedek's priesthood and sanctuary.[5]

Melchizdek, then, is represented as worshiping the true God under the name of a Canaanite deity. Another way of putting this is to say that Melchizedek had knowledge of the true God despite all appearances of *not* having received revelation from the Hebrews. This is not to suggest that Melchizedek's beliefs about God were the same as Abram's, and it certainly does not imply that all Canaanite beliefs about El Elyon were accurate. But the text *does* seem to imply that Melchizedek had some sort of knowledge of the God who manifested Himself as the Holy One of Israel. It means that true knowledge of God came to Melchizedek apart from revelation given through the Abrahamic lineage.

The Old Testament is replete with Gentiles who knew something of the true God. For example, after the (third) plague of gnats, Pharaoh's magicians told Pharaoh, "This is the finger of God!" (Ex 8:19). There is no indication that they had saving knowledge of God, but the text states that they recognized at this point that He, and not some other agent, was at work. Although the New Testament condemns Balaam's errors (2 Pet 2:15; Jude 11), the Old Testament historian records that Balaam made accurate prophecies of the future of Israel, presumably under the inspiration of the Holy Spirit (Num 24). Rahab the Canaanite prostitute recognized that the God of the Israelites was the true God and became an example of faith for Jewish Christians in the New Testament era (Josh 2:10-11; Heb 11:31).

---

[5]Claus Westermann, *Genesis: A Practical Commentary* (Grand Rapids, Mich.: Eerdmans, 1987), p. 115.

King Huram of Tyre told Solomon that he knew it was the God of Israel who made the heaven and the earth (2 Chron 2:11-12). Other people outside the Jewish tradition who knew and sometimes "walked with" the true God were Abel, Enoch, Noah, Job, Abimelech, Jethro, Ruth, Naaman and the Queen of Sheba.

The Old Testament is also run through with a red thread of foreign officials recognizing the sovereignty of the God of Israel. Pharaoh, for example, more than once acknowledged that he had sinned against Yahweh (Ex 9:27; 10:16). After Naaman's healing he confessed, "Now I know that there is no God in all the earth except in Israel" (2 Kings 5:15). Nebuchadnezzar made a similar confession after Daniel interpreted his dream and then again after Sahdrach, Meshach and Abednego emerged unscathed from the fiery furnace. When he regained his sanity after mental illness, he again testified to the sovereignty of the God of Israel (Dan 2:46-47; 3:28; 4:34-37). When Daniel was saved from the lions, Darius issued a decree commanding "all peoples and nations . . . throughout the whole world" to tremble before and fear the God of Daniel: "For he is the living God, enduring forever. His kingdom shall never be destroyed, and his dominion has no end. He delivers and rescues, he works signs and wonders in heaven and on earth; for he has saved Daniel from the power of the lions" (Dan 6:25-27).

Now some of this knowledge of God by Gentiles came from encounters with Yahweh, the God of Israel, so it does not count as knowledge coming from outside the Jewish tradition. But like general revelation, it shows that there is true knowledge of God outside the sphere of special revelation. Many of these people, like the Pharaoh's magicians and Balaam, apparently never came to a saving knowledge of Yahweh; nonetheless they knew something about the true God. What they knew was not part of general revelation since it was not given to all, nor was it special revelation since it usually[6] did

---

[6]For some like Rahab, however, it may have provided salvation.

not point to salvation. But it was true knowledge of the true God given by God directly or through an encounter with God's works.

The New Testament adds an intriguing twist. John indicates cryptically that the second person of the Trinity is responsible for knowledge of God given to Gentiles and non-Christians: "What has come into being in him was life, and the life was the light of all people" (Jn 1:3-4). If all human beings have been given light by Christ, then knowledge of God that they possess would presumably be included in that light. He goes on to claim that all true enlightenment—which must include that of pagans since it is said to come to "everyone"—comes from Christ: "The true light, which enlightens everyone, was coming into the world" (Jn 1:9).

This means that Christ gave true knowledge of God to Epimenides and Aratus, the sixth- and third-century B.C. poets whom Paul quoted approvingly at Athens: "'In him we live and move and have our being'; as even some of your own poets have said, 'For we too are his offspring'" (Acts 17:28). If nothing else, this passage shows that for Luke and Paul these secular poets possessed religious truth. They knew something about the true God, and according to John, this knowledge was mediated to Epimenides and Aratus by Christ.

God's People Learn from Those Outside the Jewish and Christian Churches

So far we have seen not only that God wanted Gentiles and non-Christians to know Him but that some actually did come to know certain aspects of His Person and character. Some came to this knowledge independently of Israel and the church while others came to see something of God through God's dealings with Israel. Two Hellenistic poets are said to have known something true about God, and there is no indication that they had any knowledge of the Jewish tradition. These individuals may not all have had saving knowledge of God, but their knowledge was to some degree *true* knowledge. They had come to know something true about Yahweh. In this last section of this chapter I want to show that some of God's people in the Bible learned from pagans things that helped them better understand God's revelation through the Jewish and Christian churches.

Much of the religion of the patriarchs, for example, was shared by their compatriots in the ancient Near East. In fact, "there was not much in the world-view of the patriarchs and their families that differentiated them from the common ancient Near Eastern culture of the day."[7] This is not by itself proof that the patriarchs borrowed their religious ideas from their pagan[8] neighbors, but there is evidence that God used pagan religion as a background from which to teach His people about true religion.

For example, in the massive polytheistic systems of the ancient world the great cosmic deities, while respected and worshiped in national and royal contexts, "had little personal contact with the common people." In Mesopotamia in the first part of the second millennium B.C. people began to relate to minor deities who were thought of as "personal gods" that took interest in a family or individual. While the personal deity was not worshiped exclusively, most individual and family worship was devoted to it. Some scholars believe that Abraham's first responses to Yahweh may have taken place in this context—"Abraham may have viewed Yahweh as a personal god that was willing to become his 'divine sponsor.'"[9] The point is not that Yahweh took on all the characteristics of these personal gods but that Abra-

---

[7] John H. Walton and Victor H. Matthews, *The IVP Bible Background Commentary: Genesis—Deuteronomy* (Downers Grove, Ill.: InterVarsity Press, 1997), p. 15.

[8] In this book *pagan* and *heathen* will be used interchangeably to refer to people who were or are neither Jewish nor Christian. Nothing demeaning is intended by the use of these terms.

[9] The quotations in this paragraph are taken from a discussion of Abraham's religion in Walton and Matthews, *IVP Bible Background Commentary*, pp. 36-37. For further discussion of the influence of ancient Near Eastern culture on the Old Testament, see W. Robertson Smith, *Lectures on the Religion of the Semites*, 2nd ed. (London, 1894); Meredith G. Kline,

ham may have used this religious framework to understand Yahweh and that Yahweh in turn may have used and then adapted this framework to teach Abraham truths about Himself.

The smoking firepot and blazing torch in Genesis 15 and the practice of circumcision are more examples from the patriarchal period. Mesopotamian religious rituals already used sacred torches and censers in rites of initiation and purification; torches and ovens represented deities. Circumcision was practiced widely in the ancient Near East as a rite of puberty, fertility or marriage. Once again, the point is that God used common cultural (and religious!) practices to teach new religious concepts about Himself and His ways with His people.[10] There were symbols in these pagan practices and beliefs that God used to teach new truths, albeit by transmuting the old beliefs and practices. Yet the fact remains that God's people learned things about the true God from those who had not received the fullest revelation (at the time) about that God.

Even God's names in the Bible bear mute witness to this phenomenon of learning from pagans things about the true God. The Hebrews appropriated the Semitic name *El* for God, perhaps from the Canaanites, while the New Testament authors used the Greek term *theos*. The *El* of the sixth-century B.C. history of Phoenicia by Sanchuniathon was a fierce warrior god—in most respects unlike Yahweh, but like Yahweh a god of battles.[11] The Hellenistic *theos* was often understood to be a single godhead behind many names and mythologies or an impersonal One behind all that is.[12] The

---

Treaty of the Great King (Grand Rapids, Mich.: Eerdmans, 1963); Jack Finnegan, *Myth and Mystery: An Introduction to the Pagan Religions of the Biblical World* (Grand Rapids, Mich.: Baker, 1989); James B. Pritchard, ed. *Ancient Near Eastern Texts Relating to the Old Testament*, 3rd ed. (Princeton, N.J.: Princeton University Press, 1969).

[10]Walton and Matthews, *IVP Bible Background Commentary*, pp. 42, 44.

[11]Patrick D. Miller Jr., *The Divine Warrior in Early Israel* (Cambridge, Mass.: Harvard University Press, 1973).

[12]See "Theos," in *New International Dictionary of New Testament Theology*, ed. Colin Brown (Grand Rapids, Mich.: Zondervan, 1976), 2:66-67.

New Testament's *theos* is the epitome and source of personhood, unlike its Hellenistic counterpart, but like its namesake it is the ground and force behind everything that exists. My point is that even when a word is borrowed and invested with new meaning, it seems impossible to strip the word of every last bit of old meaning or context. For Christians who believe that God's Spirit superintended the entire process of Scripture writing, which included the use of language and stories used to describe other gods, this is neither surprising nor theologically problematic. It simply means that God used all of the biblical authors' influences to reveal aspects of His being and work.

It should be clear by now that the biblical authors were not always concerned about the religious or moral character of those from whom they learned. Balaam spoke the truth about the future of Israel despite his becoming a symbol of avarice and idolatry. Neco, the king of Egypt, was never distinguished by moral or religious virtue. Yet the Bible says that God spoke through Neco and was displeased that Josiah did not listen to the word of the Lord that came through this pagan king (2 Chron 35:20-27).

Although there is no clear proof, evidence exists that the author of Psalm 104 may have learned from the Egyptian hymn of Amenhotep IV (Akhenaten, early fourteenth century B.C.). This is a hymn of praise to the deity that is manifested by Aten, the sun disk. It is a remarkable example of monotheism, made all the more remarkable by its presence in a long history of ancient Egyptian polytheisms. Perhaps for this reason it vanished as soon as its progenitor died. But it contains remarkable parallels to Psalm 104. Both speak of God sending rain to water the earth and satisfy the beasts of the field and birds of the air, of the earth returning to darkness and lions emerging when the sun retires, of God's manifold works fulfilling the divine will, of ships and fish sporting in the oceans before God, of humans getting their food from God, and of all creaturely life depending on the divine spirit.[13]

Scholars debate the connection between the Aten hymn and Psalm 104. Some argue that the differences are more striking than the similarities. For example, the Aten hymn portrays night and the lions as almost enemies of human beings, while the psalmist sees them as "fellow-pensioners."[14] The elements that are similar are arranged in different order in each poem, and some of the most vivid images (Aten's care for the embryo of the baby in the womb and the chick in the egg) are missing from the Hebrew stanzas. Others postulate that both poems share a common background, noting general similarities with other Egyptian sun hymns and a Mesopotamian hymn to Shamash. Many believe that there was a chronological and cultural bridge between the texts—that the Aten hymn was known to Israel via Canaanite, specifically Phoenician, translations and adaptations.[15]

One of two possibilities seems likely: either these ideas were common to the ancient Near East and the psalmist used them, under the inspiration of the Holy Spirit, to describe Yahweh's providence, or there was direct borrowing from the Egyptian hymn. In either case non-Hebrew sources influenced the Hebrew writer in ways that eloquently depicted God's loving care for His creatures. This is part of the larger pattern apparent in revelation—God's use of non-Hebrew and non-Christian cultures to make Himself known to the biblical authors. As C. S. Lewis expressed it, "It is

---

[13]For Akhenaten's hymn, see "The Hymn to the Aton," in *An Anthology of Texts and Pictures,* vol. 1 of *The Ancient Near East,* ed. James B. Pritchard (Princeton, N.J.: Princeton University Press, 1958), pp. 226-30.

[14]C. S. Lewis, *Reflections on the Psalms* (Glasgow: Fontana, 1958), p. 76.

[15]See A. Barucq, *L'expression de la louange divine et de la prière dans la Bible et en Égypte,* Bibliotheque d'Étude 33 (Cairo: Institut Français d'Archeologie Orientale, 1962); K.-H. Bernhardt, "Amenhophis IV and Psalm 104," *Mitteilungen des Instituts für Oreintforschung* 15 (1969): 193-206; P. C. Craigie, "The Comparison of Hebrew Poetry: Psalm 104 in the Light of Egyptian and Ugaritic Poetry," *Semitics* 4 (1974): 10-21; G. Nagel, "À propos des rapports du Psaume 104 avec les textes Égyptiens," in *Festschrift A. Bertholet,* ed. W. Baumgartner et al. (Tübingen: Mohr, 1950); Leslie C. Allen, *Psalms 101—150,* Word Biblical Commentary 21 (Waco, Tex.: Word, 1983), pp. 28-31.

conceivable that ideas derived from Akhenaten's system formed part of that Egyptian 'wisdom' in which Moses was bred. Whatever was true in Akhenaten's creed came to him, in some mode or other, as all truth comes to all men, from God. There is no reason why traditions descending from Akhenaten should not have been among the instruments which God used in making Himself known to Moses."[16]

Proverbs 22:17—24:22 is another example of an Old Testament text that many scholars think was influenced by a non-Hebrew tradition. According to James D. G. Dunn, "it is well-known" that this text is "most probably drawn" from an earlier Egyptian wisdom tradition known as the *Teaching of Amenemope*.[17] There are "striking similarities" in both structure and subject matter. Both consist of thirty precepts or exhortations. The preamble of the Proverbs passage appears in a different form in the conclusion of *Amenemope*. More than a few exhortations use the same images. For example, Proverbs 23:4-5 ("Do not wear yourself out to get rich. . . . When your eyes light upon [riches], it is gone; for suddenly it takes wings to itself, flying like an eagle toward heaven") is matched by parts of the seventh chapter of *Amenemope* ("Cast not thy heart in pursuit of riches. . . . [Or] they have made themselves wings like geese and are flown away to the heavens").[18] R. B. Y. Scott says there is no way to prove direct literary dependence of the Proverbs text on the (probably) earlier Egyptian text, but he thinks that the profession of scribe in that era was international and that scribes probably were trained in a wide range of wisdom writings. If the Hebrew scribe did not have the Egyptian text before him or was not recalling it from mem-

---

[16]Lewis, *Reflections*, p. 74. Lewis refers to the Jewish (and early Christian) tradition that Moses "was instructed in all the wisdom of the Egyptians" (Acts 7:22).

[17]James D. G. Dunn, "Biblical Concepts of Revelation," in *Divine Revelation*, ed. Paul Avis (Grand Rapids, Mich.: Eerdmans, 1997), p. 7.

[18]"The Instruction of Amen-em-opet," in *An Anthology of Texts and Pictures*, vol. 1 of *The Ancient Near East*, ed. James B. Pritchard (Princeton, N.J.: Princeton University Press, 1958), pp. 237-43.

ory, he probably was calling upon a tradition that was international rather than merely Hebrew.[19]

We see a similar pattern in the New Testament. On several occasions Jesus praised the faith of pagans and urged Jews to learn from these pagan examples. He commended two pagans on his visit to Nazareth, whose citizens rejected His claim to be the servant of the Lord of the later Isaiah passages (Lk 4:14-30; cf. Is 58:6; 61:1-2). "Is not this Joseph's son?" they asked skeptically (Lk 4:22). They demanded that He do miracles as He had done in Capernaum (Lk 4:23). Jesus replied, "Truly I tell you, no prophet is accepted in the prophet's hometown. But the truth is, there were many widows in Israel in the time of Elijah, when the heaven was shut up three years and six months, and there was a severe famine over all the land; yet Elijah was sent to none of them except to a widow at Zarephath in Sidon" (Lk 4:24-26).

Zarephath was on the Phoenician coast south of Sidon, in the heartland of the Baal cult (1 Kings 16:31). The woman had only a handful of meal, but when Elijah commanded her to make a cake out of it, she proceeded to bake, trusting Elijah's promise that God would miraculously multiply the meal (1 Kings 17:1-16). Of course, she was also desperate and had nothing to lose since she and her son were doomed to die soon with or without the handful of meal. But Jesus commended her nonetheless, because of her faith in Elijah's word, which was the word of the Lord. She had less evidence for faith than the residents of Nazareth had but believed that God was speaking and could be trusted.

Then Jesus pointed to another pagan exemplar of faith, Naaman the Syrian general, who trusted Elisha's word from God that he would be cured of his leprosy if he would dip himself in the Jordan River (2 Kings 5:1-14). Jesus said, "There were also many lep-

---

[19]R. B. Y. Scott, *The Anchor Bible: Proverbs and Ecclesiastes* (Garden City, N.Y.: Doubleday, 1965), pp. 20-21.

ers in Israel in the time of the prophet Elisha, and none of them was cleansed except Naaman the Syrian" (Lk 4:27). Jesus suggested that Naaman the pagan had more faith than his Jewish contemporaries and that his boyhood Jewish neighbors would do well to learn from this heathen. From the context it also appears that Jesus was contrasting Naaman's humility (doing what at first he considered ridiculous) with Nazareth's pride. Jesus' reference to the "oppressed" and "blind" (Lk 4:18) suggested that His hearers needed to acknowledge their sins and need for help. But in their rage they refused to humble themselves and instead drove Jesus out of town (Lk 4:28-29).

Most readers of the New Testament are also familiar with the story of the centurion who sought healing for his slave (Lk 7:1-10). When Jesus came near, the Roman soldier sent friends to tell Jesus not to bother coming any farther because he was confident Jesus could heal his slave from a distance merely by uttering a word. Jesus was "amazed" by this faith response and told His hearers, "I tell you, not even in Israel have I found such faith" (Lk 7:9).

This is a third instance, then, when Jesus praised the religious example of a pagan and suggested that Jews could learn from the example. I would take this one step further and say that the Gospel writers imply that we Christians can also learn from these pagans.

Am I minimizing the centurion's faith, however, by calling him a pagan? After all, he had faith in Jesus. In this case he recognized Jesus' authority. And he, like Cornelius in Acts (10:2, 22), was a friend of the Jews who "feared" God. As a Roman officer, however, he was not permitted by Rome to undergo circumcision as a convert. Jesus Himself placed him outside the Jewish community ("not even in Israel have I found such faith"). And all we know from the text is that the centurion had faith that Jesus could heal. As far as we can tell, the centurion may have known Jesus only as a miracleworker. There were others in this part of the world whom people believed capable of such things;[20] there is no evidence that the centurion knew anything more about Jesus than that He was a worker of such wonders. Hence it is likely that the centurion knew little more than his other pagan neighbors and acquaintances knew about Jesus—which further accentuates Jesus' (and Luke's) admonition that we should learn from this one who was neither Jew nor (yet) Christian.

On at least three other occasions Jesus lauded the example of "heathen." Jesus celebrated the faith of the Canaanite woman in Matthew 15:21-28, recommended the ethical behavior of the Good Samaritan (Lk 10:25-37), and pointed out that "a foreigner" was the only leper among ten to "return and give praise to God" (Lk 17:18). In all three instances Jesus applauded the acts of faith made by people who were not yet inside the Jewish or Christian circles of faith and recommended that His hearers learn from their example.[21]

Peter also seems to have learned from the religious experience of someone who had not yet been introduced to the gospel. He appears to have learned something new and profound about God from what he observed God to be doing in and for Cornelius before Cornelius heard about Jesus. When he heard that Cornelius had heard from an angel to come to his (Peter's) house, Peter's eyes were suddenly opened to God's ways with the Gentiles: "[Now] I truly understand that God shows no partiality, but in every nation anyone who fears him and does what is right is acceptable to him" (Acts 10:34-35).

Cornelius, like the Roman centurion of Luke 7, was one of the Gentiles to whom Luke several times referred as seekers who feared or worshiped God (Acts 13:16, 26; 16:14; 18:7) but may not have become converts to Judaism. In any event, Cornelius had never

---

[20]See Acts 8:9-11.
[21]Like the centurion, the Canaanite woman appears to have known nothing about Jesus except that He was a healer. Jesus praised the persistence and humility that she showed in her faith.

heard of Jesus when he had the experience with the angel that led Peter to understand God's work of redemption in a completely new way. Later, when Cornelius heard the gospel and the Holy Spirit "fell upon all who heard the word" with him, Peter understood even more about this work of redemption (Acts 10:44-48). But the initial revelation came while Cornelius was still in his pre-Christian state—that is, while Cornelius was either technically a pagan or at the very most a Jewish proselyte. A Christian (Peter) was learning religious truth from someone who had not yet received the gospel. And in this case, as for the exemplars whom Jesus commended, God's people were learning from those outside their traditions things that helped them better understand their own revelation. Jesus used pagans to teach His would-be disciples about faith, and Peter learned from a Gentile that Christ's mission extended to the Gentiles.

There is less evidence of this pattern in the Pauline writings. As Terence Paige has observed, Paul was schooled in the philosophical currents of his age but was not as concerned as other thinkers such as Philo to reconcile his message with contemporary philosophy. He proclaimed that the gospel was the only means to divine wisdom (1 Cor 1:21; 2:6-16; Eph 1:15-18). While his writings resonate with certain Stoic and Cynic themes, there are profound differences on the nature of God and the human self. For Stoics, for example, self-sufficiency (*autarkēs*) comes from resolution of the will, while for Paul it springs from assurance of God's favor and presence. Cynic boldness was based on self-confidence and independence, but Paul's boldness was rooted in a sense of God's calling.[22]

On the other hand, it would be a docetic mistake to conclude that Paul's thinking about God was not shaped in part by his cultural milieu—or, to put it more theologically—that God did not use Paul's

---

[22]Terence P. Paige, "Philosophy," in *Dictionary of Paul and His Letters*, ed. Gerald F. Hawthorne and Ralph P. Martin (Downers Grove, Ill.: InterVarsity Press, 1993), pp. 713-18.

cultural background and intellectual training to help shape his inspired insights. In his important study *Paul and the Popular Philosophers,* Abraham J. Malherbe argues that Paul and Epictetus sound remarkably similar at points because they both depended on a common tradition of (Stoic) rhetoric and reasoning. Paul, in fact, appropriated the style and commonplaces of his philosophical contemporaries; for example, he used the Stoic and Cynic traditions to describe his battles with his opponents at Corinth.[23] It is now a commonplace that the use of a tradition's symbols and reasoning to talk about God, self or world will shape the way God, self and world are seen. There can be little doubt, then, that God used Paul's culture to shape Paul's presentation of God's self-revelation. Hence, while Paul was unique (*Paulus christianus*) he was also *Paulus hellenisticus.* Malherbe reminds us, "After all, like Tennyson's Ulysses, and like the eclectic Plutarch or Musonius, we are part of all we have met. So was Paul."[24]

Now the reader can see more clearly why I said at the beginning of this chapter that it contains evidence but not hard proof. Most of the New Testament examples I have cited come from encounters with Jesus or preaching about Jesus. They are not examples of knowledge about God gained from sources completely disconnected from Jewish or Christian communities. Yet they demonstrate that Jesus and Paul believed Christians could learn about God from individuals who knew little or nothing about the Christ.

These, then, are some of the biblical passages that suggest that the notion of God's people learning about God from those outside their traditions (in ways that help them better understand their own revelation) is not a phenomenon foreign to the Bible. I will turn in the next chapter to a more systematic and theological understanding of how to place this notion within our fuller understanding of God and redemption.

---

[23]Abraham J. Malherbe, *Paul and the Popular Philosophers* (Minneapolis: Fortress, 1989), esp. chaps. 2 and 3.
[24]Ibid., p. 9.

4

THEOLOGICAL
[CONSIDERATIONS]

Is THERE REVELATION FROM GOD IN NON-CHRISTIAN RELIGIONS?
There is no simple answer to this question. One must first say that
there is no direct continuity from the religions to Christ. They are
not beginnings or foundations of which Christ is the completion or
superstructure. There may be lines of continuity between a non-
Christian religion whose method of religious advancement is human
effort and a particular construal of Christianity in which salvation is
earned by human striving, but this is a version of Christianity that
Christ repudiated. As Lesslie Newbigin has observed, non-Christian
religions represent goals and methods too foreign to Christ for there
to be any direct line of continuity. They face in different directions,
ask different questions and look for different kinds of religious ful-
fillments. In Rudolf Otto's words, they turn on different axes. Therefore a person who is religious is not necessarily closer to God than a
person who is nonreligious. The gospel is not the end or culmina-
tion of the religions, as if a person could move logically (in religious

terms) from one of the religions to Christ and His church.[1] There is radical discontinuity between the religions and the Christ: Christ is a Being before whom all other beings and manifestations of God are separated by an infinite qualitative difference. There may exist revelations *from* God in other religions, but only in the religion of the Christ is there the revelation *of* God as incarnate in Jesus of Nazareth.[2]

At the same time, Newbigin insisted, an objective observer must concede that there is real experience of God outside Christianity. When Paul looked back on his pre-Christian past, he saw God at work in his life before his conversion. New Christians who have converted from other religions sense that the same God was working on them in the days of their pre-Christian wrestlings. While their conversion to Christ is a real and radical repentance, that conversion (from all their pre-Christian past) does not deny God's activity in that past.[3] All their pre-Christian religious experience is seen differently now that they see through Christ, yet some of that experience was genuine encounter with God. God was not without witnesses when people did not know Him as revealed in Jesus Christ.

There are also some religions that teach a way of approaching God that resembles what Christians mean by grace. In Hinduism's *bhakti* movement and in Mahayana Buddhism, devotees believe they reach the divine by a gift of the deity. (Krishna is the most popular Hindu deity who saves by grace, and Amitabha Buddha the best-known Buddhist divinity.) The notion of salvation by a gift of the divine is very similar to the Christian notion of grace, but there are significant differences. In neither of these traditions is the absolute holiness of the divine depicted with such clarity as in the Christian

---

[1]Lesslie Newbigin, *The Finality of Christ* (London: SCM Press, 1969), p. 44.

[2]This is a variation on a distinction from Alister McGrath, *A Passion for Truth: The Intellectual Coherence of Evangelicalism* (Downers Grove, Ill.: InterVarsity Press, 1996), p. 36. Later in this chapter I will suggest that in some of the religions there are "revealed types," but only in Christian faith is there fully manifest special revelation.

[3]Newbigin, *Finality of Christ*, pp. 59-60.

tradition; and while the gift of salvation is given by the Hindu and Buddhist deities somewhat gratuitously, the God of Jesus confers the gift only at infinite cost to Himself.

Therefore, the relationship between believers' pre-Christian and Christian experiences is a double (if you will, dialectical) one. There is both discontinuity and continuity. Another way of putting it is to say that there is radical but not total discontinuity. Perhaps we could compare this complex relationship to that between imagining and experiencing the taste of a mango. Before I spent a year on the Mexican border in the Rio Grande Valley of Texas, people had told me that mango meat was slimy in texture and its taste very sweet, something like the combination of a ripe peach and a very ripe plum. That description gave me a certain idea of what mangoes might taste like. But when I actually sank my teeth into a mango, I discovered that its taste was finally indescribable because it was unique—unlike (in an absolute sense) anything I had ever tasted. Yet in a relative sense, it was *something* like what I had imagined—at least insofar as it was very sweet and slimy. So it was both *like* what I had imagined and very *unlike* what I had imagined—radical but not total discontinuity.

Or, to try it another way (and perhaps better, because it involves persons), there is the difference between experiencing a person as a child and experiencing that same person as an adult. When we know a child, we know (something of) the person behind (as it were) the child. If for some reason we leave that child and upon returning thirty years later take time to get to know the adult, we find that the adult is a completely different person from the child we knew thirty years before. Different in every way, and yet (almost inexplicably) the same person—radical but not total discontinuity.

Both of these illustrations are poor analogies, but it would be difficult—in fact impossible—to find an apt analogy for what has no parallels in human experience: encountering the living God. There is no truly similar set of phenomena to those involved with experiencing God in different religions. So, as in all talk about God, while there is no univocal knowledge of God, we are not left with only equivocal language. There is analogical knowledge, although all our analogies are imperfect.[4]

A Christian theology of the Holy Spirit can help us understand that imperfect knowledge. Curiously, it is an aspect of that theology that for centuries has been dismissed as restricted to the arcane discussions of professional theologians—the *filioque* controversy—that sheds light on the question of truth in the religions. This began when the Western church added *filioque* (from the Son) to the Nicene Creed (in 589 and then again in 1017), asserting that the Spirit proceeds not only from the Father but also from the Son. The Eastern church protested not only that this was a politically imperialistic act (since the West acted unilaterally, ignoring protests from the East) but also that it subordinated the Spirit to the Son in a way that restricted the freedom of the Spirit and detracted from the harmony of the Trinity.

There are some biblical grounds for *filioque*. It was Christ who poured out the Spirit upon the church (Acts 2:33), and Christ did indeed say in John 15:26 that He would send the Spirit. But the same verse says that while Jesus would send (*pempsō*) the Spirit from the Father, the Spirit of truth proceeds (*ekporeuetai*) from the Father. Hence both East and West can appeal to the biblical text. But the use of *filioque* can also lead to a misunderstanding that relates to the religions, as Clark Pinnock has pointed out. It can suggest to the worshiper "that Spirit is not the gift of the Father to creation universally but a gift confined to the sphere of the Son and even the sphere of the church. It could give the impression that the Spirit is not present in the whole world but limited to Christian territories."[5] But in fact the Spirit unfolded the creation at the beginning (Gen 1:2), gives life to all creatures (Jn 6:63; Ps 104:30; Acts 17:25), infuses

---

[4]Thomas Aquinas *Summa Theologiae* 1a.13.5; see also Brian Davies, *The Thought of Thomas Aquinas* (Oxford: Clarendon, 1992), pp. 70-75.

[5]Clark Pinnock, *Flame of Love: A Theology of the Holy Spirit* (Downers Grove, Ill.: InterVarsity Press, 1996), p. 196.

the world with love and flies on the air (Job 12:10; 33:4), and is omnipresent throughout the cosmos (Ps 139:7). In the words of the Nicene Creed, He is the "Lord and giver of life"—words that rightly suggest that the Spirit is active in all the world through all of history.

Gavin D'Costa points out that the doctrine of the Holy Spirit allows us to relate the particularity of Christ to the entire history of humankind. That is, we cannot divorce our knowledge of God from the story of Jesus, but our reading of that story is transformed and challenged in the light of what we see the Holy Spirit doing in the world religions. Jesus is *totus Deus* but not *totum Dei*. He is wholly God but not all of God. Hence, while He is normative for our knowledge of God—all that we think we learn about God from other sources must be related to the revelation of Christ—He is not exclusive or absolute in revealing God. Christ is our norm for understanding God, but He is not a static norm; the norm (our understanding of Christ) is transformed and enriched by the guiding/declaring/judging function of the Holy Spirit.[6]

In other words, Christ is the unique revelation of God. But the Holy Spirit is ever at work, as He was in the history of Israel before Jesus, to give understanding of the God Who was to send the Messiah and then to give understanding of the Messiah Himself. He continues to give the church insight into the meaning of the Messiah—and some of those insights may come from reflection upon what the Spirit is doing in and with people outside Israel and the Christian church.

Prominent theologians in the early church came to similar conclusions. Justin Martyr wrote that *semina Verbi* (seeds of the Word) implanted in all human beings enabled ancient pagan authors to see spiritual realities but "darkly." As a result Christ was known in part, even by Socrates.[7] Clement of Alexandria taught that ancient philos-

---

[6]Gavin D'Costa, "Christ, the Trinity, and Religious Plurality," in *Christian Uniqueness Reconsidered: The Myth of a Pluralistic Theology of Religions,* ed. Gavin D'Costa (Maryknoll, N.Y.: Orbis, 1992), pp. 18-19, 23.
[7]Justin *First Apology* 46; *Second Apology* 8, 10.

ophers were influenced by the Holy Spirit, so the best Greeks knew God indirectly through their own philosophical *preparatio euangelii*. Philosophy was a schoolmaster for the Greeks as the law was for Jews.[8] Although Augustine tended to exclude pagans from the kingdom of God, he nevertheless saw God at work wherever he found truth, even if it came from the mouth or pen of pagans.[9]

I find the work of Jonathan Edwards, the great eighteenth-century American theologian, most suggestive for considering this question. Two concepts that Edwards worked out at length have import for our understanding of truth in the religions: covenant and typology. First I will unpack Edwards's understanding of the relation between the two biblical covenants and draw out the implications of this relation for the religions. Then I will proceed to his conception of typology.

Covenants and the Religions

John Calvin and his successors had departed from the Lutheran bipolar separation of law and gospel (which at the popular level sometimes divorced the Jewish Old Testament from the Christian New Testament) by proposing that the two covenants—Jewish and Christian—were simply two "modes of dispensation" of "one and the same" covenant.[10] Edwards's concept was not remarkably different from that of his predecessors among the Puritans and Reformed, but his was among the more subtly delineated.

Edwards followed Calvin and his heirs by portraying the two cov-

---

[8]Clement of Alexandria *Exhortation to the Heathen*, in Ante-Nicene Fathers, chaps. 6-7; *Stromata* 1.5, 17-20; 6.6-7, 17.

[9]Augustine *Confessions* 5.24; *On Nature and Grace*, in *Basic Writings*, chap. 2. Augustine *tended* to exclude pagans from the church, but he left the door open at points. In *The City of God*, for example, he wrote that the story of Job, who was not a Jew, teaches us that "it was divinely provided, that from this one case we might know that among other nations also there might be men pertaining to the spiritual Jerusalem who have lived according to God and have pleased Him" (*City of God*, trans. Marcus Dods [New York: Modern Library, 1950], 18.47 [p. 658]).

[10]Calvin *Institutes* 2.10.2.

enants (the Jewish "covenant of works" and the Christian "covenant of grace")[11] as different but integrally related modes of a single plan of redemption. He used an anatomical image to represent the relation between the two. Drawing on the distinction between the "cortex" ("shell" or "husk") of an organ and its "medulla" (central parts or "nucleus"), he played on the contrasts between outer versus inner and letter versus spirit. The covenant of works was the cortex or shell, which "envelops" the medulla of the "gospel" or covenant of grace. The first is comparable to the letter of the law, whose true meaning is communicated obscurely and indirectly, while the second may be likened to the spirit of the law, delivered more simply and directly.[12]

---

[11]By the covenant of works Edwards meant generally what he learned from the Westminster Confession and its interpreters, who drew a distinction between "the covenant of works made with Adam and his posterity on the condition of perfect obedience and the covenant of grace made with believers, offering the gift of salvation on the condition of faith in [Christ]" (William Klempa, "The Concept of the Covenant in Sixteenth- and Seventeenth-Century Continental and British Reformed Theology," in *Major Themes in the Reformed Tradition*, ed. Donald K. McKim [Grand Rapids, Mich.: Eerdmans, 1992], p. 95). See also Calvin *Institutes* 2.11.1-8; 2.10.1-6; Heinrich Heppe, *Reformed Dogmatics Set Out and Illustrated from the Sources* (Grand Rapids, Mich.: Baker, 1978), chaps.13-16. In Misc. 1353 Edwards wrote that the covenant of works was "proposed" to Israel in the wilderness, but only as a goad to lead her to the covenant of grace, which alone was "established." Grace was the "kernel" contained within the "shell" of works.

[12]The cortex actually consisted of two covenants, the covenant of works (which God established with Adam and his posterity) and the national covenant (which God "made with external Israel or the seed of Abraham"). The national covenant is "an appendage" to the covenant of works that typifies or foreshadows the covenant of grace and is therefore "subservient" and "subordinate" to the covenant of grace. All of its institutions were external and point to the internal spirit of the covenant of grace. Hence it consisted of an "external temporal society . . . an external earthly countrey . . . an external carnal priesthood . . . a worldly sanctuary . . . carnal sacrifices; an external altar; an external holy of holies, & an external mercy seat . . . external conformity to the law of God, an outward conformity to the moral law, and a conformity to an external and carnal law." Even pardon and sanctification were external: "freedom from guilt as it excluded from external priviledges, and a sanctification that consisted in the purifying of the flesh, delivering from carnal pollutions, & qualifying for carnal priviledges" (Misc. 1353). For a full explication of the meaning and dynamics of Edwards's understanding of national covenant, see McDermott, *One Holy and Happy Society* (University Park, Penn.: Penn State Press, 1992), pp. 11-36.

If the covenant of works was the outer shell containing an inner core of grace, it was also a means God used to secure the end of grace in biblical times. Edwards saw the same pattern working in his own day: just as the covenant of works was "proposed" to Israel in the wilderness, "the same is now proposed in the course of a sinner's convictions in these days." Sinners are first confronted with God's demands in the covenant of works, and only by trying to meet those demands do they discover their inability and need for grace.[13] Hence the history of covenants in the work of redemption is reproduced in the religious psychology of the person coming to faith.

Edwards believed that this pattern is by design, not by default. It is God's method to use veils to protect the inner pearls of the gospel from being trampled by reprobate swine. The cortex of the covenant of works is at once the means to lead the elect into the nucleus *and* God's manner of hiding the inner mystery from the carelessly carnal who do not deserve to see it. God uses the cortex to blind the minds of the proud and to serve as an occasion for their self-righteousness.[14]

This is one way of explaining why in the Old Testament the gospel is imperfectly and seldom revealed but is demonstrated fully and directly in the New Testament. The people of God in the old dispensation "could not bear" a clear revelation of the covenant of grace because they were not convinced of their inability to establish their own righteousness, just as sinners of Edwards's day did not know their own sin and so could not appreciate the covenant of grace.

Therefore the Ten Commandments had the appearance of a covenant of works in order to teach the Israelites their inability to keep it. Yet the commandments also revealed, albeit indirectly, the covenant of grace, since their true intent was to establish the covenant of grace. This is evident from internal clues, according to Edwards.

---

[13]Edwards, Misc. 1353.
[14]Ibid.

First, they are called "tables of the covenant," which suggested God's initiative in choosing Israel. In fact, He chose to be "married" to Israel and unilaterally constructed a covenant by which to effect the relationship. Further, Edwards wrote, the preface indicated that God had already become their God and redeemer before they had shown whether they would obey. So the commandments were instructions on how to cleave to and trust a heavenly spouse, not terms that had to be fulfilled before a marriage would begin. Edwards claimed that in the ancient world a god was not only an object of reverence and ritual observance but also (and "especially") an object of trust and source of defense and salvation.

In addition, Edwards pointed out, God in the Ten Commandments proclaimed that He shows mercy to thousands (in the second commandment) and ordered the Decalogue to be covered by the mercy seat in the wilderness tabernacle. Finally, "these ten commandments . . . were seal'd with the blood of the sacrifice, which typified the blood of [Christ]." The mention of sacrifice demonstrated that God's relationship to His people was based not on human obedience but on divine mercy.

The true basis of God's relationship to humans was demonstrated but nevertheless "insinuated to [Israel] & proposed under covert" because of Israel's spiritual immaturity. Edwards used the metaphor of human development, referring to the Old Testament period as the childhood of the race. God's people ("the church") under the first covenant were still in an "ignorant and infantile state."[15] Hence it was for pedagogical purposes that God taught people to make sacrifices for their sins. Edwards explained that this primitive idea was used to teach respect for God's law and authority. If they had been permitted to "fly to God's mercy" with a simple display of repentance, they would have learned to despise and take for granted God's holy majesty. But the requirement of sacrifice for sin showed

---

[15]Edwards, Misc. 439; cf. also Misc. 1354, 250, 994.

them that there is no pardon without satisfaction, that sin must be suffered for, and that God hates sin and trespasses against his authority. This taught them a proper trust in God's mercy and an accurate view of God's majesty and jealousy, "which is the exercise of the same disposition of mind as is exercised in actually believing on Christ crucified, and is the same sort of act."[16] According to Edwards, then, the first covenant could produce the same saving disposition that was produced by the second covenant.

Another reason that grace was not revealed more directly was that Christ and His kingdom had not yet been revealed fully. God's hatred for sin had not been illustrated in the sufferings of the Messiah and His promises of eternal punishment for the wicked. In the absence of these clear demonstrations, Israel needed tangible and severe punishments in order to maintain "the honor of the divine greatness & majesty & the dread of his spotless holiness." This was the reason God kept His people at a distance and used graphic and brutal punishments in the Old Testament but allowed the saints of the New Testament to converse with Him "most freely and intimately."[17]

Because of these differences, expectations were different under the two covenants. Since we are in the new dispensation, we have greater obligations. Because our revelations are much clearer, we are bound to duties from which saints in the old dispensation were free.[18] In fact, we are to love God "vastly more" and "in an unspeakably higher degree" because of the new manifestations God has given of Himself. But we are also beneficiaries of "higher exercises of love to God" than Adam and Eve enjoyed and "higher degrees of spiritual joys."[19] Therefore Old Testament saints were not as accountable. Many things that would have been innocent in Adam's day would be exceedingly sinful for us. Adam might have been

---

[16]Edwards, Misc. 326.
[17]Edwards, Misc. 440.
[18]Edwards, Misc. 439.
[19]Edwards, Misc. 894.

"earthly minded in a sense wherein it would be corrupt and abominable in Christians to be [in Edwards's day]."[20]

Yet, this difference notwithstanding, the two covenants actually are different phases or ways of performing a single covenant. As Edwards put it early in his career, "The gospel was preached to the Jews under a veil."[21] The process of conversion for Jews in the Old Testament was the same as that for Christians in the New Testament. They were "convinced so much of their wickedness that they trusted to nothing but the mere mercy of God." The same was true for the antediluvians, and indeed for all those who lived since "the beginning of the world." Even the rate of conversion was the same. There were wicked and godly then, and conversions were just as frequent then as in Edwards's day.[22] Christ saved the Old Testament saints just as He saved their cohorts in the New Testament, and they believed in Christ, but under the name of the "angel of the Lord" or "messenger of the covenant."[23] In fact, Christ appeared to Old Testament Jews; Moses saw His back parts on Mount Sinai, and He appeared in human form to the seventy elders (Ex 24:9-11) as well as to Joshua, Gideon and Manoah. For that matter, every time God was said to have manifested Himself to humans in a voice or in some other tangible form, it was always through the second person of the Trinity.[24]

Though the two covenants had two federal heads, Adam and Christ, and one was a "dead" way but the other "living," "in strictness of speech" they were not two but one. For they shared the same

---

[20]Ibid.

[21]Jonathan Edwards, "Profitable Hearers of the Word," in *Sermons and Discourses 1723-1729*, ed. Kenneth P. Minkema, vol. 14 of *The Works of Jonathan Edwards* (New Haven, Conn.: Yale University Press, 1997), p. 247.

[22]Edwards, Misc. 39.

[23]Edwards, Misc. 1283; "Controversies Notebook," Edwards Papers, Beinecke Rare Book and Manuscript Library, Yale University, p. 213.

[24]Jonathan Edwards, *A History of the Work of Redemption*, ed. John F. Wilson (New Haven, Conn.: Yale University Press, 1989), pp. 197, 131.

mediator, the same salvation (which means the same calling, justification, adoption, sanctification and glory), and the same medium of salvation: the incarnation, suffering, righteousness and intercession of Christ. The Holy Spirit was the same person applying Christ's redemption in both dispensations, and the method of obtaining salvation was the same—faith and repentance. The external means (the word of God and ordinances such as prayer and praise, sabbath and sacraments) were not different. Nor were the benefits (God's Spirit by God's mere mercy and by a divine person—the angel of the Lord or Mediator) and future blessings different. For both covenants, the condition was faith in the Son of God as Mediator, expressed with the same spirit of repentance and humility. This is why all parts of the Old Testament point to the future coming of Christ. In sum, the religion of the church of Israel is "essentially the same religion with that of the Christian church."[25]

We cannot say the same for religions outside the orbit of Judaism and Christianity. Far from being "essentially the same," their conceptions of God, the human self and salvation are often radically at odds with their counterparts in Christian revelation. Nevertheless, Edwards's reflections on the covenants contain some pointers that can help us with our consideration of truth in the religions. First, they suggest that it is within God's providential designs to reveal His truth sometimes obscurely, partially and indirectly. The biblical story of the covenants suggests that not all peoples are equal in stages of spiritual development. God is the Great Pedagogue Who unveils His truths at different levels and to different degrees depending on the spiritual receptivity and maturity of His pupils. Just as Jesus used parables to close some eyes and open others, God uses veils to protect His pearls from being trampled by swine. Salvation by works might sometimes have to be suggested at the surface level of a text in order to teach human inability, which may be implied at a deeper

---

[25]Edwards, Misc. 35, 875, 1353; Edwards, *History of the Work of Redemption*, pp. 283, 443.

level of understanding of a text. Or, in order to protect God's majesty, graphic displays of God's power and ferocity may have to be shown in religions that do not know of God's holiness revealed in Christ. One thinks of Islam, which emphasizes God's justice and transcendence and has little conception of the kind of intimacy with God that Jesus modeled. Just as Old Testament sacrifices were necessary to prepare a people for the revelation of Christ, some of the religions may contain revelations of aspects of God's person and character comparable to what was revealed at some stages of the Old Testament period. And in some way that only the future will reveal, some of the religions may be providential preparations for future peoples to receive the full revelation of God in Christ. This does not mean that there is direct continuity from the religions to Christ, but it does mean that the religions may be used by God to prepare their devotees to understand and receive Christ—just as the practice of animal sacrifice instituted by Yahweh (and copied by nearly every world religion thereafter) prepared the Jews to be able to understand and receive Christ as Lamb of God that takes away their sins.

One also learns from the biblical covenants that the Holy Spirit is at work revealing God even when the name of Christ is not known. The hope of a Messiah was only dimly known to some Old Testament saints and probably completely unknown to others. Yet they clearly had some knowledge of the living God. One thinks of Mahayana Buddhism and Hindu *bhakti,* both of which teach that human merit is not sufficient to reach God. Neither teach the radical notion of grace that is taught in the Christian revelation, but *something* of God's gracious character is unveiled in these other religions that know next to nothing of the Jesus of the Gospels.

Finally, we can infer that if there were different expectations for Old Testament saints under a different dispensation with different degrees of revelation, we should not dismiss other religions as completely lacking revelation merely because they make different requirements of their adherents. In fact we might *expect* there to be different requirements where lesser degrees of revelation have been given.

Typology

Edwards's second theological concept with significant implications for our discussion is typology. By that he meant a system of representation by which God points human beings to spiritual realities. For centuries Christians had seen in the Old Testament "types" that pointed to New Testament "antitypes"; the exodus, for example, was a type of Christ's liberation of sinners, and David's sufferings in the Psalms were types of Christ's sufferings in the passion. Edwards endorsed this traditional reading but pushed it beyond its traditional limits, arguing that God's typology extended to nature and history—and, I would add, the history of religions.

Edwards justified this extensive reading by appeals to the Bible. The Old Testament, he insisted, is full of evidence that the biblical authors believed God had filled the world with types. The bowing down of the sheaves of Joseph's brothers toward Joseph's sheaf in a dream foreshadowed their literal bowing toward him. Pharaoh's dream of fat and gaunt cows truly predicted fat and lean years. Daniel's four beasts forecast the rise of four pagan empires. All the Hebrew prophets' prophecies were fulfilled.

Paul was more explicit. He declared unequivocally in Galatians 4:21-31 that the story of Abraham's two sons was an allegory for the two covenants. Paul also wrote in 1 Corinthians that the Old Testament admonition not to muzzle an ox was "indeed written for our sake " (1 Cor 9:9-10) and that the stories of the Israelites' idolatry in the wilderness were to serve "as examples [*tupoi*]" (1 Cor 10:6). Edwards took these passages to be confirmation that all the history of the Old Testament was intended to be typical of spiritual things.

Edwards also believed that Scripture endorses a system of types in nature. When Jesus proclaimed He was the true light and true bread and true vine, He implied that all lights and breads and vines are pointers to, or types of, their antitypes in Jesus. Paul did the same for seed and sowing in springtime when he used them in 1 Corinthians 15 to argue for the resurrection of bodies. Unless God intended seed and planting to be types of spiritual realities, Paul's arguments would not make sense: "If the sowing of seed and its springtime were not designedly ordered to have an agreeableness to the resurrection, there could be no sort of argument in that which the Apostle alleges, either to argue the resurrection itself or the manner of it, either its certainty or probability or possibility."[26]

Scripture also suggests that human institutions can be typical of things in the spiritual world. In Ephesians 5 Paul tells us marriage was instituted by God to typify the relationship between Christ and the church. Paul's point was not that Christ's relationship to the church can tell us things about marriage, or simply that marriage can tell us things about Christ and the church, but that God established the human institution of marriage for the express purpose of signifying a relationship in the spiritual world.

C. S. Lewis articulated a typological vision of history and religion not unlike Edwards's. Lewis spoke in terms of a principle whereby the Higher comes down to include what is lower or less.

> Thus solid bodies exemplify many truths of plane geometry, but plane figures no truths of solid geometry: many inorganic propositions are true of organisms but no organic propositions are true of minerals; Montaigne became kittenish with his kitten but she never talked philosophy to him. Everywhere the great enters the little—its power to do so is almost the test of its greatness.[27]

An example perhaps closer to home is our own human composition. Mind operates in, and controls, the matter of the human body.

---

[26]Jonathan Edwards, *Images of Divine Things*, in *Typological Writings*, ed. Wallace E. Anderson and Mason I. Lowance Jr., vol. 11 in *The Works of Jonathan Edwards* (New Haven, Conn.: Yale University Press, 1993), no. 7.

[27]C. S. Lewis, "Miracles," in *The Best of C. S. Lewis* (Grand Rapids, Mich.: Baker, 1969), p. 309.

The higher principle of intelligence somehow—mysteriously—suffuses and directs the activity of atoms and molecules at the same time that it cannot be separated from those molecules. Lewis observes that this is a miracle comparable to the incarnation. Both are inexplicable fusions of spirit (or mind) and matter. If we can accept the former mystery, there is no reason why the latter could not be. But the point most relevant to our discussion is what Lewis calls "vicariousness," which he asserts "is the very idiom of the reality [God] has created." The higher reality is present more dimly and less substantially in lower levels of being. In nature we find signs (Edwards would say "types") of the divine. The higher is in the lower. Lewis writes, "In science we have been reading only the notes to a poem; in Christianity we find the poem itself."[28] Both Edwards and Lewis would add that in the religions can be found notes to the poem of Christianity.

Edwards also believed that God had planted types of true religion even in religious systems that were finally false. God outwitted the devil, he suggested, by using diabolically deceptive religion to teach what is true. For example, the practice of human sacrifice was the result of the devil's mimickry of the animal sacrifice that God had instituted after the Fall.

Sacrifice was taught not by the light of nature but by God's express commandment immediately after he revealed the covenant of grace in Genesis 3:15: "I will put enmity between you and the woman, and between your offspring and hers; he will strike your head, and you will strike his heel." The skins with which God clothed the first couple in Genesis 3:21 were taken from animals sacrificed by God, who taught them thereby that only the righteousness of Christ won by his sacrifice could cover their sins.[29]

Edwards insisted that animal sacrifice, the main type of Christ in

---

[28]Ibid.
[29]Edwards, *History of the Work of Redemption*, pp. 134-36.

the Old Testament but revealed to all the Gentiles, taught the necessity of propitiatory sacrifice to atone for sin. Imitating this divine type, the devil led the Gentiles to sacrifice human beings, even their own sons. Satan believed he had "promote[d] his own interests," outsmarting God; but God outflanked the devil. He permitted this diabolical deception because through it "the devil prepared the Gentile world for receiving . . . this human sacrifice, Jesus Christ." Similarly, the devil induced human beings to worship idols and think that the Gentile deities were united to their images. But God used this deception as well for his own purposes, to prepare the Gentile mind for the concept of incarnation, perfectly realized in Christ: "And so indeed was [the] heathenish doctrines of deities' being united to images and the heathenish fables of heroes being begotten [by] gods, a preparation for their receiving the doctrine of the incarnation, of the Deity's dwelling in a human [body], and the Son of God's being conceived in the womb of a virgin by the power of the Spirit of [God]."[30]

Twice, then, in the history of religions, God used false religion to teach the true. In each case the devil's machinations were overruled ironically by divine wisdom. Practices considered by all Jews and Christians to be abominable—human sacrifice and idol worship—were transposed by a divine stratagem into pedagogical devices to prepare the Gentile world for true religion. In both cases God used non-Christian religions typologically to point to Christian truths.

The implications of this typological way of looking at reality are fairly clear. If there are types of true religion in the midst of religions that contain falsehood, and if these types are divinely implanted, then there is revelation from God even in the midst of religious error. The revelation may be shadowy rather than clear and incomplete rather than full, but it can be divine revelation nonetheless. I am not concerned in this book with whether these types or shadows can lead to

---

[30]Edwards, Misc. 307.

salvation, or even whether Gentiles can understand these types. In fact, I shall argue in the next section that it makes theological sense for Gentiles *not* to understand the full (Christian) meaning of these types in the religions. But the point I want to make in this section is that Edwards's development of typology shows us a way theologically to affirm the possibility of revelation from God in religions outside the Judeo-Christian tradition. For reasons we do not fully understand, God sometimes plants within the religions types of His fuller Christian realities.

Barth's Parables of the Kingdom

Jonathan Edwards never developed the implications of his musings on the religions. He believed that there was revelation in the religions because of borrowings from the Jews and traditions passed down to the fathers of the nations through Adam and Noah and their progeny. These revelations demonstrated that God did not abandon the Gentiles to ignorance of the divine being and nature. But Edwards never had much hope for the salvation of the heathen and did not suggest directly that Christians could learn from the Gentiles.[31]

Edwards was not the only modern Reformed thinker, however, who believed that God has revealed Himself outside the church of Jesus Christ. Even Karl Barth, who is better known for his denial of true religion outside of Christianity, believed that there are revelations *extra muros ecclesiae* [outside the walls of the church] that are "quite real." In *Church Dogmatics*, Barth wrote, "We recognize that the fact that Jesus Christ is the one Word of God does not mean that in the Bible, the Church and the world there are not other words which are quite notable in their way. Other lights which are quite clear and *other revelations* which are quite real" (emphasis added). Barth added that the possibility of this makes theological sense if we

---

[31]For more on Edwards and the religions, see Gerald McDermott, *Jonathan Edwards Confronts the Gods: Christian Theology, Enlightenment Religion, and Non-Christian Faiths* (New York: Oxford University Press, 2000).

affirm that the whole world is under the lordship of God, Who is free to attest Himself as He pleases. "Why should not the world have its varied prophets and apostles in different degrees?"[32]

Barth said that these little lights or "flickerings" must not be mistaken for the one true light and must be measured by the final radiance of Christ. But these truths are "worth something," and we must "take note of them." They are parables of the kingdom of Heaven in a history outside of *Heilsgeschichte* [the history of salvation] that can be tested in three ways. First, their messages must be harmonized with the whole context of the biblical message. Second, they must coincide with the dogma and confessions of the Church, and third, they ought to bear fruit, summoning their bearers to faith and repentance.[33]

A foremost Barth interpreter has recently explained that Barth not only recognized the value of "truths" coming from outside the church but also used them to his own advantage. In order to use these concepts, however, Barth had to "shatter" and "recast" them. For example, Barth took the idea of being, which for the Greeks meant a lifeless and inert entity, and recast it in terms of an "acting subject" Who is God always living and acting. Barth also took the modern existential idea of nothingness and reconfigured it in terms of the biblical idea of chaos. He thereby denied to nothingness the status of ultimate reality and intensified its evil character as that which disrupts and threatens the good creation. Apparently Barth felt that "while we can learn from these concepts, we cannot credit them with having adequately depicted reality." Barth even reworked Jewish theologian Martin Buber's idea of "I and Thou." All doctrines coming from outside biblical revelation had to be reconstructed critically.[34]

---

[32]Karl Barth, *Church Dogmatics*, IV/3, trans. G. W. Bromiley (Edinburgh: T & T Clark, 1961), p. 97.

[33]Ibid., pp. 155, 126-28.

[34]George Hunsinger, *How to Read Karl Barth: The Shape of His Theology* (New York: Oxford University Press, 1991), pp. 61-62.

Once More: Revelation in the Religions

Is there revelation in the religions? Until this point I have argued that it is not a simple question but that the notion has been hinted or explicitly claimed by leading orthodox Christian theologians. It is time for me to go on record and make the same claim: there is revelation from God—of a sort—in at least some of the religions. Before I explain what I mean by "of a sort," I must say first that Scripture contains evidence (some of which I described in chapter three) that God has revealed Himself to those outside Israel and the church. Much of this revelation is what theologians have called "general revelation"—"that divine disclosure to all persons at all times and places by which one comes to know that God is, and what he is like."[35] The psalmist, for example, claims that "the heavens are telling the glory of God" (Ps 19:1). Isaiah predicts that all the world will see God's glory when God returns to Judah (Is 40:5). Paul testifies that all human beings have known God, even when they suppress the truth, because God's eternal power and divine nature have been understood and seen through the things God made (Rom 1:20). Paul also explains that God has implanted His law in every human conscience (Rom 2:14-15), and he specifically refers to those "without the law"—those whom we say are outside Israel and the church. Luke suggests that through the gifts of rain and food and simple human pleasures something of God is revealed to human beings (Acts 14:17).

Therefore, while some have debated the purpose of general revelation (recall the discussion of Barth in chapter two), most theologians have agreed that there is revelation of God to those outside Israel and the church. The biblical evidence is fairly clear. More debatable and contentious is the question of whether some of this revelation has come through non-Christian or non-Jewish *faith com-*

---

[35]Bruce Demarest, "General Revelation," in *Evangelical Dictionary of Theology,* ed. Walter A. Elwell (Grand Rapids, Mich.: Baker, 1984), p. 944.

munities (religions). I think there is biblical evidence for this as well. Melchizedek was a priest of the Canaanite religion, and his worship of the true God used the name of the Canaanite deity. It would be difficult to argue that his encounter with God was not mediated at least in part by his Canaanite religion. When Melchizedek refers to Abram's God as *El Elyon* (the Canaanite deity translated as "God Most High"), he suggests that his understanding of God's transcendence had been delivered or at least shaped in part by the Canaanite religious tradition.

Job's encounter with and understandings of God were also delivered and shaped by religious traditions outside Israel. So were the encounters and understandings of God by Balaam, who, though a false prophet condemned by New Testament writers, nevertheless was used by the Holy Spirit to deliver true prophecies (a form of revelation!) about Israel. We do not know if Epimenides and Aratus, the two Greek poets whom Paul quoted in Athens to teach his audience something about the true God (Acts 17:28), were members of what we would call "religious" communities, but they represent Greek literary and philosophical traditions that traded in religious understandings of ultimate reality. Once again, it is probable that other traditions are mediating religious truth.

But when does religious truth become revelation? In other words, what is the difference between human insight and revelation from God—particularly if the insight is remarkably different from what is available in the surrounding culture and apparently similar to truths found in Scripture? The Bible talks about a higher wisdom, given by God (Job 28; Mt 11:25; 1 Cor 2:13). However, as James D. G. Dunn has written, neither the Old Testament nor Jesus clearly distinguishes between human wisdom and divinely given wisdom—especially when the two seem to coincide.[36] Yet when those outside

---

[36]James D. G. Dunn, "Biblical Concepts of Revelation," in *Divine Revelation*, ed. Paul Avis (Grand Rapids, Mich.: Eerdmans, 1997), p. 8.

Israel and the church display knowledge of God in accord with Christian faith, theologians typically say such knowledge has come by general *revelation*. This includes such disparate phenomena as moral consciousness, appreciation for the abundance of nature's provisions, recognition of God acting in history, insightful lessons about right living, prophecy as inspired speech, dreams and visions.[37] If all these can be revelation, it is difficult to know how one could say that religious truth in accord with Christian faith and markedly different from common cultural views must be merely human insight.

It is especially difficult to dismiss this truth as merely human insight because the distinction between human insight and divinely given truth seems to assume an epistemological God-of-the-gaps. God seems involved in knowledge of Himself only in extraordinary situations. In ordinary life, recognizing God's identity would appear, by this distinction, to be an autonomous activity completely removed from grace.

Hence this distinction also seems to presume a limited view of God's sovereignty. If there is knowledge of God that can be gained by human insight alone, God would seem to be uninvolved. There is a sphere, this presumption suggests, of human knowing in which human beings by their own unaided powers speculate (accurately) about the divine so that there is a way apart from God to come to know the true God. Then there is a special sphere, rare and extraordinary, in which God enters the picture and communicates awareness of His person and nature. God apparently is not the source and sustainer of all being and knowing: He is not the sovereign lord of

---

[37]See, for example, Dunn, "Biblical Concepts of Revelation," and the articles entitled "Revelation" and "General Revelation" in the *New Dictionary of Theology*, ed. Sinclair Ferguson, David Wright and J. I. Packer (Leicester: Inter-Varsity Press, 1988), in the *Evangelical Dictionary of Theology*, ed. Walter A. Elwell (Grand Rapids, Mich.: Baker, 1984), and in *The Westminster Dictionary of Theology*, ed. Alan Richardson and John Bowden (Philadelphia: Westminster Press, 1983). See also Bruce Demarest, *General Revelation: Historical Views and Contemporary Issues* (Grand Rapids, Mich.: Zondervan, 1982), pp. 227-47.

all history but a deistic deity occasionally intervening in human affairs. God is not the foundation and fountain of all being and beauty, the Glorious One "in whom we live and move and have our being," but a cause agent who operates on us from the outside of our own autonomous spheres.

This notion of some true awareness of God coming from mere human insight does not seem to me to cohere with the biblical portrait of the sovereign God. All recognition of the identity of the true God comes only from God. It is a participation in God's own self-knowledge. But, to return to my earlier question, what sort of revelation is it when a religion presents an aspect of the identity of the true God? For example, Mahayana Buddhists and Hindu *bhaktas* teach variations on the theme of grace—the idea that human beings are accepted by the divine on the basis of divine love rather than human effort.[38] In an earlier chapter I suggested that this is not "special revelation," because it does not go so far as to reveal salvation through Jesus Christ. Neither is it "general revelation," because it is not an idea ordinarily available to all human beings. Then what kind of revelation is it?

I would suggest that these are "revealed types" akin to the types that Jonathan Edwards found in many world religions and the "good dreams" and "great stories" that C. S. Lewis saw scattered throughout the myths of the world.[39] Edwards suggested that animal sacrifices, found in almost all world religions, were "shadows" or "images" of Jesus' great and final sacrifice that would eliminate the need for all subsequent sacrifices. Even idol worship and human sacrifice were hints of the incarnation and the Father's sacrifice of the Son. While

---

[38]As I have stated earlier, the grace taught by these communities is not the same as the grace shown by the God of Jesus Christ. Humans are sometimes expected to do something to merit this grace, and the Hindu and Buddhist deities do not manifest the holiness of the God of Israel. Hence the grace is not as costly as for the Christian Trinity. Nevertheless, the basic idea of divine love overruling legal demands is present.

[39]See C. S. Lewis, *Mere Christianity* (New York: Macmillan, 1967), bk. 2, chap. 3; *Miracles*, chap. 14; and *The Problem of Pain* (New York: Macmillan, 1962), chap. 6.

each of these pagan practices pictured divine realities in distorted (and sometimes horrific) fashion, they nevertheless contained enough truth to point truly to aspects of God's triune identity. Furthermore, they were not merely human insights but developments (albeit twisted and broken) of original perceptions granted by God Himself.

The word *type* is used purposely to recall the types of Christ found in the Jewish covenant. The Old Testament types reveal Christ obscurely, partially and indirectly—but nevertheless truly—in times and places where Christ's name was not known. They contain developments and applications of divine imperatives that sometimes confound and horrify, such as Joshua's extermination of what seem to be innocent women and children. So if the types in the religions give only broken and partially distorted access to divine realities, they are similar to Old Testament types—which point to truth but sometimes obscurely.

This is not to equate the Christian Scriptures, which contain types, with other scriptures that may contain types. The Bible is in a different category of revelation from that of the religions since it alone mediates the reality of the triune God as incarnate in Jesus of Nazareth. But the Bible itself suggests that there are "little lights" in the religions that help illuminate the realities that the Light of the World more clearly displays. Indeed, as Edwards has argued, it suggests that all the world is full of types that point to the triune God— just as traditional theology has claimed that all the world is full of general revelation. My claim is that among the religions are scattered promises of God in Christ and that these promises are revealed types planted there by the triune God.[40]

Why Would God Provide Such Types?

If it makes theological sense for God to reveal something of His

---

[40]For a fuller argument for the world as full of types, see McDermott, *Jonathan Edwards Confronts the Gods*, chap. 6.

nature and ways to people outside the circles of Christian and Jewish faith, the next question concerns purpose. Why would God do such a thing? The purpose most commonly discussed is salvation. Perhaps God might use this revelation, however incomplete, to save those who have not heard rightly about Jesus. As I explained early in this book, many good theologians have discussed this possibility. Even Jonathan Edwards concluded in the eighteenth century that God might use this "inspiration," as he called it, to make people more interested in what God had revealed to the Jews and better prepared to receive the gospel when it would be (later) preached to them. This inspiration may also be used, he added, to confer "great benefit" to the souls of those who receive the revelation.[41]

Others have suggested that other revelations are part of God's beneficent purposes to bless human beings during their earthly lives, whatever their religious choices. Joseph DiNoia writes that the religions foster the development of a supportive social climate, while Clark Pinnock states that they help make human life more decent and so may be seen as God's gifts of common grace.[42] God provides not only rain and sun and food to all but also the comfort and direction of a sense of the divine presence. This is not to imply that there are not demonic and destructive elements in the religions but only to say that in the midst of error there is truth that enlightens and helps.

Perhaps a more interesting question, however, and one more relevant to this discussion, is what help these types can be to Christians. Francis Clooney testifies that exploring the faith of others (in his case, certain Hindus) and pondering what might be true in those

---

[41]Edwards, Misc. 1162. A fourth reason Edwards listed was confirmation to Christians of the "great truths of Christianity."

[42]Joseph DiNoia, "The Universality of Salvation and the Diversity of Religious Aims," *World Mission* (Winter 1981-1982): 12; Clark Pinnock, *A Wideness in God's Mercy: The Finality of Jesus Christ in a World of Religions* (Grand Rapids, Mich.: Zondervan, 1992), p. 121.

faiths helps him restate more effectively his own Christian faith.[43] A theologian who likes Edwards's conclusion that there is no independent substance may be better able to articulate that theological position after reading the Buddhist thinker Nagarjuna, who came to the same conclusion.

Others have argued that seeing truth in other religions can remind Christians of the best of their faith and help them sharpen their thinking about those truths.[44] For example, the apophatic strain in Theravada Buddhism may remind us Christians of our own tendency toward anthropomorphism. That is, Buddhists recognize the inadequacy of the human mind to grasp ultimate realities in their own being—something that good Christian theologians also recognize though they sometimes need reminding.

Or we may see an illustration of a Christian principle in someone of another religion. Martin Luther King Jr., for instance, worked out his philosophy of nonviolent resistance by studying Gandhi's methods, which were influenced in turn by the Sermon on the Mount. King may not have learned the concept originally from Gandhi, but Gandhi helped him understand how such a principle could be practiced in a movement for social change. For both Gandhi and King, nonviolence was not simply a strategy to achieve desired ends but the embodiment of religious principles.

In an important recent book, George Lindbeck has gone further by suggesting that Christians can learn from other religions new truths of which Christians were not formerly aware. Partly false religions, he argues, may contain truths of an important but subordinate nature that are not initially present in the highest religion (which for him is Christianity) and can therefore enrich it. Hence other religions may contain realities and truths of which Christianity

---

[43]Francis X. Clooney, *Theology After Vedanta: An Experiment in Comparative Theology* (Albany, N.Y.: SUNY Press, 1993), pp. 8-9.

[44]Keith Ward, *Religion and Revelation: A Theology of Revelation in the World's Religions* (Oxford: Clarendon, 1994), p. 335.

to this point knows nothing and by which it could be greatly enriched. Other religions can teach Christians just as geocentrists taught heliocentrists certain things even though the latter knew the former were wrong in their overall interpretation of the data.[45]

I would add that the Christian doctrine of objective revelation (having been finalized with the closure of the biblical canon) puts limits on how this is to be interpreted. Christian orthodoxy has always believed that God's final and complete revelation was made in Christ, as that revelation was expressed in the Old and New Testaments. Therefore "new truths" must be new understandings of that revelation rather than ideas that go beyond what is already contained or suggested in that revelation. Consequently, revelation in the religions may give Christians new ideas about how to better understand the Christian revelation, and these ideas may have never been thought by Christians in the previous history of the church—or at least by those who have left written remains. It stands to reason that if this is a revelation of an infinite God, our understanding of the revelation of that God is still only a fraction of what is possible. So one would expect the church to continue to grow in understanding of that revelation, perhaps aided by revelations God has provided outside the church. Yet if this revelation in Christ is God's provision to make His people "thoroughly equipped" (2 Tim 3:17 NIV) and is God's last word "in these last days" (Heb 1:2), there cannot be new truth that is not already contained—if hidden to this point—in it. The religions may therefore contain types that help us better understand Christian revelation, but they will not tell us new truths that subvert what God has revealed in Christ.

Truths that Christians learn from the religions may not always be apparent to practitioners of those religions. Just as Christians saw more in Judaism than Pharisees did, Christians can see things in

---

[45]George A. Lindbeck, *The Nature of Doctrine: Religion and Theology in a Postliberal Age* (Philadelphia: Westminster Press, 1984), pp. 49, 54, 67. Geocentrism and heliocentrism are the beliefs, respectively, that the earth and sun are the center of the cosmos.

other religions that devotees of the religions have missed. D'Costa says this is a consequence of human and divine freedom. God remains hidden even within His revelation, as He was initially hidden from the disciples at Emmaus (Lk 24:13-16). Revelation can therefore remain within a religion as a partly or even totally concealed revelation. It might not be apparent to insiders in the religion, or even to outsiders, without the work of the Holy Spirit.[46]

This applies also to the Christian faith, whose theology is continually developing as the Spirit increases the church's understanding through the ages. The Spirit has revealed to the church in the last two centuries implications of the gospel for slavery and women that were not seen by most in the church in the first eighteen centuries of its history. We now believe that the Spirit gave the church understanding of what was implicit in the gospel but remained hidden for centuries. There is no reason to think that there is not more truth and understanding of Christ and the biblical revelation yet to be illuminated by the Spirit, and perhaps aided by insights from other religions.

Finally, the religions can be used by the Spirit to induce repentance and awareness of God's judgment. D'Costa and others who have worked in missions warn that other religionists can show Christians—if they are open to it—the poverty of their own commitment. Christians may also see or hear God in the encounter. According to D'Costa, there is always a moment in mission when the Christian realizes that the evangelized may already implicitly or explicitly know God and that from this one the Christian may learn and hear God's word, as Peter learned from Cornelius and

---

[46]Gavin D'Costa, "Revelation and Revelations: Discerning God in Other Religions: Beyond a Static Valuation," *Modern Theology* 10 (April 1994): 171-72. See also Pinnock, *Wideness in God's Mercy,* p. 183; S. Mark Heim, *Salvations: Truth and Difference in Religion* (Maryknoll, N.Y.: Orbis, 1995), p. 48. Even apart from the Spirit it is apparent to students of culture that some cultures may be better understood, in a certain sense, by others than by themselves. Alisdair MacIntyre, "Rationality and the Explanation of Action," in *Against the Self-Images of the Age* (London: Duckworth, 1971), pp. 244-59.

heard God's word through him.[47]

Having explored both the biblical evidence for, and the theological sense in, the notion that Christians can learn from other religions, I will look briefly in the next chapter at key moments in the history of Christian thought when leading Christian thinkers were influenced by non-Christian thought in ways that helped them better understand the Christian revelation. In other words, what this book proposes is not something new but a pattern that has continued since the beginning.

---

[47]D'Costa, "Revelation and Revelations," p. 173.

5

AN OLD PATTERN

Christian Theologians
|Who Plundered the Egyptians|

A LITTLE MORE THAN SIXTEEN HUNDRED YEARS AGO A THIRTY-TWO-year-old professor of rhetoric who believed in Christ but could not commit because of sexual lust was sitting in a garden in Milan. When a little child's voice singing a song (*Tolle lege*, "pick up and read") moved him to pick up a book of Paul's letters, open it at random and read the passage on which his eyes first alit, Augustine's sexual addiction was broken. Paul's words were "Let us live honorably as in the day, not in reveling and drunkenness, not in debauchery and licentiousness, not in quarreling and jealousy. Instead, put on the Lord Jesus Christ, and make no provision for the flesh, to gratify its desires" (Rom 13:13-14). In a moment was born, as it were, a theological mind that would become the greatest influence on Christian thought in the history of the church.

Saint Augustine
Most of us know this story, but how many know that Augustine's

insights into Christ were aided in part by a pagan named Plotinus? I have noted in previous chapters how thinkers as diverse as the psalmist and Karl Barth have used traditions from outside Jewish and Christian thought to help refine and articulate biblical truth. In this chapter I will consider some of the greatest theologians in the church who have done something similar.[1] "A part of [his] pagan past was still alive in Augustine," for example, "stimulating his finest thought, and challenging him to a continuous inner dialogue that would last up to his death."[2] For Augustine (A.D. 354-430), the pagan who came closest to Christian truth was Plato, and his interpreter Plotinus (c. A.D. 205-270) was not far behind.[3] They taught the fifth-century professor to see all things as shadowy images of invisible realities—all the world as depending for its existence on eternal principles. Augustine retired to his death with the words of Plotinus in his mind and accorded "heroic stature" even to Porphyry (c. A.D. 232-303), a Platonist critic of Christianity.[4]

Augustine accepted a "substantial proportion of Neoplatonic theology,"[5] but some of it was inconsistent with what has since become recognized as biblical thinking. The reader can see from the *Confessions*, for instance, that Augustine viewed the body as a lower part of the human self, matter as a negative influence on the human soul,

---

[1]Exodus 12:36: "The LORD had given the people favor in the sight of the Egyptians, so that they let them have what they asked. And so they plundered the Egyptians."

[2]Peter Brown, *Augustine of Hippo: A Biography* (Berkeley: University of California Press, 1967), p. 307. This means that it was not just in his Christian period that Augustine was influenced by Neo-Platonic thinking. Nor, for that matter, was Augustine the first Christian thinker to have been so influenced. Since at least as far back as Justin Martyr, Neo-Platonism had helped shape Christian theology. See A. H. Armstrong, *Christian Faith and Greek Philosophy* (London: Darton, Longman & Todd, 1960).

[3]"If, then, Plato defined the wise man as one who imitates, knows, loves this God, and who is rendered blessed through fellowship with Him in His own blessedness, why discuss with the other philosophers? It is evident that none come nearer to us than the Platonists" (Augustine *City of God* 8.5).

[4]Brown, *Augustine of Hippo*, pp. 426, 307.

[5]Henry Chadwick, "Introduction" to Augustine's *Confessions* (Oxford: Oxford University Press, 1991), p. xxiii.

changeless things and beings as preferable to those that change, and Christ as removed from time and impassible.[6] But Augustine did not merely identify Neo-Platonism and Christianity. According to Jaroslav Pelikan, the bishop of Hippo also looked to Neo-Platonism for help in clarifying enigmas of the faith.[7] For example, Neo-Platonism helped Augustine come to his understanding of evil as lacking in substance, the privation of good.[8] It gave him a way to conceive of the Fall as a turning from unity to multiplicity—from devotion to the one principle behind things to absorption in the things themselves.[9]

But Neo-Platonism also provided Augustine a powerful corrective to understandings of God that were derived more from extrabiblical traditions than from the scriptural canon. While a Manichee, Augustine had believed that the individual is entirely merged with the substance of a good God, but Neo-Platonism taught him that no individual can be identified with God and that God is utterly transcendent.[10] This understanding helped Augustine see the biblical emphasis on God's sovereignty and holiness.

It also helped him formulate his response to the Donatist controversy—a response that shaped Christianity's theology of the church ever after. In the wake of Diocletian's persecution at the beginning of the fourth century, the Donatists preached that the true church is a pure church. They refused to accept as bishop a man thought to have been consecrated by *traditores,* those who had surrendered Bibles to the authorities to be burned, and they taught that sacraments administered by men who were connected with *traditores* were invalid. Only those priests and bishops who were free of serious sin could faithfully administer the sacraments. Holiness and

---

[6]Augustine *Confessions* 7.16.22-23; 7.1.1; 7.9.14; Javoslav Pelikan, *The Emergence of the Catholic Tradition: 100-600* (Chicago: University of Chicago Press, 1971), p. 296.
[7]Pelikan, *Emergence of the Catholic Tradition,* pp. 296-97.
[8]Augustine *Confessions* 3.7.12; 7.12.18.
[9]Augustine *Confessions* 2.1.1; 10.29.40. Corresponding concepts can be found in Plotinus *Enneads* 4.3.32.20; 1.2.5.6; 6.6.1.5.
[10]Brown, *Augustine of Hippo,* pp. 99-100.

purity are essential marks of the true church.

Yet to Augustine, steeped in Neo-Platonic thought, this is a world of becoming, a hierarchy of imperfectly realized forms that depend for their quality on participation in an intelligible world of ideal forms. The universe is therefore in a constant state of dynamic tension in which imperfect forms of matter strive to realize their fixed, ideal structure, grasped by the mind alone. Hence the only purity lies in the invisible world of eternal forms, not in this visible world where we must be content with shadows and imperfection. Augustine recognized the Neo-Platonic vision as a pagan glimpse of what the biblical writers meant by a fallen world in which original sin is always with us (Rom 3:9-18, 23; 7:14-24; Phil 3:12; 1 Cor 13:9-12).[11]

Therefore, if the rites of the church are holy (and they are, according to Augustine), they are holy only by virtue of their participation in the objective holiness of Christ. The church is not subjectively holy, or holy in and of itself, because it is a broken shadow that is imperfectly striving to realize its union with Christ. But a sinful minister of Christ can nevertheless connect the believer to Christ through the sacrament because the true minister of the sacrament is Christ, who is the eternal Form, as it were, behind the human minister. Hence the church is not a company of the perfected but a community of ailing sinners engaged in a long convalescence that will terminate only in the perfected city of God in the day of resurrection. If these conclusions are biblical (and I think they are) and have helped and continue to help Christians steer a path between utopian rigorism and antinomian laxity, we may be indebted to Plotinus for helping Augustine see the implications of the biblical vision.

Thomas Aquinas
As the greatest Christian theologian ever was helped by pagan think-

---

[11]Ibid., pp. 221-22.

ing, so was the greatest theologian of the medieval period. It has become a truism that Thomas Aquinas synthesized Aristotle and the Bible, and many scholars have examined the ways in which Aristotle set the agenda and supplied the vocabulary for much of Aquinas's theology. Most conclude that Aquinas by and large Christianized Aristotle, but few if any would claim that Aristotle did not color the lens through which Aquinas looked at Christ. Therefore what I present in the next few paragraphs is not new to Aquinas experts but shows how another great Christian mind was helped by a pagan thinker to see Christian truths more clearly.

As I noted above, Platonism helped Augustine by distinguishing between seen and unseen realities. One result of this distinction between nature and its supernatural support, however, was the denigration of matter and the body—propelled in part by Plato's teaching that the body is a prison of the soul. This had obvious perils for Christian theology, at the center of which is belief in Christ's bodily resurrection. But with Aristotle's help, Thomas Aquinas played a major role in resuscitating Christian belief in the goodness of created bodies. A central feature of Aristotle's gargantuan philosophical project was the analytical understanding of what moderns call nature. Aquinas's achievement was to harmonize the Christian doctrine of creation with Aristotle's conception of the natural world. In the process Aristotle showed Aquinas that the soul, which for Plato defines the human person, is only a part of a human being and exists by nature in a body. Hence Aristotle gave Aquinas philosophical support for the biblical doctrine of the resurrection of the body—and perhaps the confidence he needed to teach a robust view of the body in an age that demeaned it.[12]

Aquinas is far better known, though, for his articulation of the relation between nature and grace. Here too Aristotle's teachings

---

[12]Timothy McDermott, *Thomas Aquinas: Selected Philosophical Writings* (New York: Oxford University Press, 1993), p. xxii.

offered assistance. The Greek philosopher showed the Christian theologian not simply that "grace perfects nature," as it is commonly interpreted, but that grace uses nature as its tool. As Aquinas scholar Timothy McDermott (no relation to me) has recently written, "Nature is a tool of grace, used to do something beyond its own powers, but only because it has its own powers to contribute." The natural world is still operative within the revealed world. "Every natural doing and every chance doing in the world and every free doing of man is a tool of the doing of God."[13]

This helps us understand how Christian realities can be interpreted both from a natural point of view as simply human phenomena, and from a revealed point of view as instances of God at work. McDermott offers two examples: sacraments and language. The Christian sacraments are not—as they were for other medieval theologians—mysterious "medicines" that act merely by God's will but "ritual religious performances akin to those of natural religion but now become tools of God." In other words, they are truly similar to the rituals of other religions and can be viewed legitimately by a scholar of religions on that level. This analysis takes nothing away from what they are on another level—the action of God in the world to mediate His presence and grace to His people.[14]

Biblical language illustrates the same principle. The religious language of Israel is both "an example of the languages men use to address and express their gods *and* God's exploiting of that example to speak about himself."[15] Words with their roots in nonbiblical culture bear new and richer flowers when they are taken up and planted afresh in a redemptive context. Each word is born again, as it were, when it is used in the new context. In both cases—sacraments and language—the same phenomenon has both a natural and revealed face. Nature is real, is created by God and is the tool through which

---

[13]Ibid., pp. xxviii, xxx.
[14]Ibid., p. xx.
[15]Ibid., p. xxvii.

God shows not only that nature is real and good but that there is something beyond it. Aristotle's magisterial attention to nature helped Aquinas to see this.

Aquinas is also well known for his doctrine of analogy, and here too Aristotle was a formative influence. He was not the only influence, to be sure, but a real one nonetheless. Much of the medieval debate over language and analogy from which Aquinas learned was framed by an Aristotelian agenda and informed by Aristotle's definitions.[16] According to Brian Davies, "The notion that terms can be applied to God and to creatures analogically is one to be found in a number of thirteenth-century authors indebted, in this respect, to Aristotle."[17]

The result of Aquinas's reflection, using Aristotle, was a helpful way of understanding the kind of knowledge we gain from Scripture. Aquinas has taught us that knowledge of God gained from the Bible is not univocal—that is, it is not wholly like our knowledge of things in the world—for God is not a being or object in space and time, and creatures are composite while God is simple (has no parts). While God is immanent in the world, He also transcends creation.

Another reason that our knowledge of God is not univocal is that all of our knowledge, even about God, is mediated by our experience of things in the world. But while things in the world have causes, God has no cause. All of creation is contingent, but God alone is a necessary being. Aristotle helped Aquinas see that we

---

[16]For more on Aquinas and analogy, see Ralph M. McInerny, *The Logic of Analogy: An Interpretation of St. Thomas* (The Hague. Martinus Nijhoff, 1971), George P. Klubertanz, *St. Thomas Aquinas on Analogy: A Textual Analysis and Systematic Synthesis* (Chicago: Loyola University Press, 1960); William C. Placher, *The Domestication of Transcendence: How Modern Thinking About God Went Wrong* (Louisville: Westminster Press, 1996), pp. 27-31; David Burrell, *Aquinas: God and Action* (Notre Dame, Ind.: University of Notre Dame Press, 1979), and *Knowing the Unknowable God* (Notre Dame, Ind.: University of Notre Dame Press, 1986).

[17]Brian Davies, *The Thought of Thomas Aquinas* (Oxford: Clarendon, 1992), p. 70 n. 38.

know through our experience of things in the world. However, Aristotle assumed the world had always existed, while Aquinas insisted that both reason and revelation require belief in a cause of the universe, a creator. Because God does not depend on anything else for His being but *is* Being itself, His Being is radically different from the being of everything else, which depends on Him. Hence the words we use to describe our everyday reality cannot be applied univocally to God.

On the other hand, our knowledge of God gained from the Bible is not equivocal either. God is not wholly unlike anything else we know. That is why the biblical writers could say that God is good and assume that we can have some understanding of what that means for God. Here again Aristotle was helpful. The Greek philosopher said that a cause imparts reality to its effects. Aquinas reasoned that since God as the creator is the source or cause of goodness (and everything else), God's goodness cannot be entirely different from human goodness. Our experience of limited human goodness thus gives us a hint of what God's goodness is, even though we cannot grasp the simple perfection of God from our partial and fragmented perspective.

Aquinas did not mean that God is the infinite expansion of positive human qualities (as his doctrine of analogy is sometimes interpreted); rather he meant that God as found in Scripture defines what these terms mean. The movement of meaning starts with God and goes down, as it were, to creatures rather than from creation up to God. In Aquinas's words, terms apply to God primarily and only secondarily or derivatively to creatures.[18] So when we call God "good," we derive our understanding of good from what we see in creatures, but our reference is primarily to God because all creaturely goodness derives from God. Their goodness is but a broken and pale imitation of archetypal goodness in God.

Yet while there is similarity, there is also dissimilarity. God's good-

---

[18]Thomas Aquinas *Summa Theologiae* 1.13.7.

ness is never dependent on other things as human goodness is, and God's goodness is always pure, while human goodness is always impure. To use another example, if God is our Father because He cares for us, He is not a human being existing in space and time Who brings children into this world by sexual procreation.

Biblical language, then, is figurative and analogical. It cannot be otherwise because while God created and is in the world, He is also above it. So language about Him is neither wholly like nor wholly unlike Him. But there are genuine points of similarity. As Timothy McDermott has expressed it, "God is the doer of all perfection, the originating source of all form, so that though those forms cannot apply to him in the way that they do to creatures, nevertheless he who does wisdom must in some sense be wise, and he who does goodness must in some sense be good, and he who does existence must in some sense exist. Not in the same sense but in some analogical sense."[19]

Thanks to Aristotle, Aquinas has helped generations of Christians understand how they can talk about an infinite God using broken, finite language. In other words, he has helped the church understand how the Spirit wants us to think of what is said in Scripture about the triune God.

John Calvin
Recent study of John Calvin's intellectual context has uncovered the significant debt he owed to Renaissance humanism. William J. Bouwsma refers to the "growing recognition" that Calvin's formation and culture were those of a Renaissance humanist: "Between 1527 and 1534, at any rate, and in a more general sense all his life, Calvin inhabited the Erasmian world of thought and breathed its spiritual atmosphere; he remained in major ways always a humanist of the

---

[19]Timothy McDermott, *Summa Theologiae: A Concise Translation* (Westminster, Md.: Christian Classics, 1989), p. xlvi.

late Renaissance."[20] Latin oratory, particularly that of Cicero and
Quintilian, made a deep impression on the young French theologian. So did the work of the great humanist scholar Erasmus; in the
last French version of the *Institutes,* Calvin used a description of the
gospel particularly associated with Erasmus: "Christian philosophy."[21] Calvin's academy at Geneva offered a typical Erasmian trilin-
gual education: Latin grammar and rhetoric (Virgil and Cicero),
Greek dialectic and physics (Aristotle), and history and Hebrew.
Calvin's model for would-be pastors was "Quintilian's generally edu-
cated orator—the ideal of humanist educators everywhere."[22]
Calvin's use of the word *Institutio* (instruction, manual, summary) in
the title of his great theological treatise was reminiscent of both Lac-
tantius's *De institutione christiana* and Quintilian's *Institutio oratoria.*
The word was particularly evocative to a humanist of his era.[23]

Renaissance humanism was not strictly pagan—after all, Erasmus
was a Christian monk. But its admixture of (classical) pagan thinking helped direct Calvin to positions now recognized as sub-
Christian: his portrait of the human self as ordered hierarchically (in
contrast to the biblical view of the self as a unified whole), his
understanding of the soul as identified with the mind (we can see
Platonic thinking here coming through the Renaissance humanists)
and his tendency to represent Christianity as somewhat intellectual-
ized—probably more cerebral than its portrayal in the New Testament.[24]

At the same time, nominalist philosophy probably helped Calvin
see that reason cannot grasp the gospel, and therefore natural theology leading to the true God is virtually impossible. As I noted in
chapter two, Calvin concluded that nature's findings are so confused

---

[20]William J. Bouwsma, *John Calvin: A Sixteenth-Century Portrait* (New York: Oxford University Press, 1988), pp. 3, 13.
[21]Ibid., p. 14.
[22]Ibid.
[23]Ibid., p. 17.
[24]Ibid., pp. 88, 98.

that they lead only to the worship of an "unknown God."[25] The humanist emphasis on rhetoric probably also helped him to see the importance of preaching. Throughout his career he said that Rome underestimated the value of the spoken word and that the progress of the gospel was vitally dependent on it: "The living voice has a greater effect in exciting our attention, or at least teaches us more surely and with greater profit, than simply seeing things without oral instruction."[26] And the humanist confidence in self-reformation through human effort may have stimulated Calvin's notable formulation of what we have come to know as sanctification. (Of course Calvin Christianized this humanist strain by insisting on the futility of human effort without the work of the Spirit.)[27]

One of the most important influences of Renaissance thinkers on Calvin was their conception of oratory as deliberately attuned to the ears of the audience. Humanists recognized that the distance between one human being and another can be bridged only by the essential humanist virtue—decorum—which involves careful adaptation to one's audience for the sake of persuasion. We can see this concern in Calvin's prescription for good teaching: "A wise teacher accommodates himself to the understanding of those who must be taught. He begins with first principles in teaching the weak and ignorant and should not rise any higher than they can follow. In short he instills his teaching drop by drop, lest it overflow."[28] Calvin, who saw little difference between preaching and teaching, believed that teachers must consider the needs of the times and what is appropriate to the people.

Calvin brought this humanist training to bear on his depiction of how God teaches through Scripture. He said that just as a good human teacher adapts his teaching to the needs of his audience, God accommodates Himself to human capacity. The Holy Spirit always

---

[25]Calvin *Institutes* 3.10.1, 3.
[26]Commentary on Psalm 19:1, cited in Bouwsma, *John Calvin*, p. 158.
[27]Bouwsma, *John Calvin*, pp. 88-95.
[28]Commentary on 1 Corinthians 3:2, cited in Bouwsma, *John Calvin*, p. 116.

"accommodates itself to our infirmity," even that of "the roughest common people."[29] God stammers in Scripture, speaking "like a nurse who will not speak to a child in the same way as to a man but keeps in mind the child's capacity." This is why the Bible sometimes seems to be rude and unrefined. "God must descend to us so that we may mount to him."[30] What we read in Scripture may reflect a primitive mindset. For example, Genesis speaks of the sun and moon as two great lights in the sky, though of course the stars are really larger than the moon. For Calvin this principle of accommodation resolves the problem: "God speaks to us of these things according to how we perceive them, and not according to how they are." When the Bible speaks of God as "repenting," it is speaking "figuratively." "For had the prophets spoken without metaphors and simply narrated the things treated of by them, their words would have been frigid and inefficient, and would not have penetrated into the hearts of men." The prophets spoke rhetorically, accommodating what they said to the needs and capacities of their hearers.[31] Calvin's doctrine of accommodation has helped thousands of Christians understand how to reconcile God's concern to communicate with the Bible's occasional awkwardness, apparent discrepancies and ethical puzzles.

Calvin is yet another major Christian theologian who was helped by a pagan thinker to understand better the nature or meaning of Christian revelation. Learning from pagans in order to comprehend God's Word is therefore nothing new. So if we can learn from Plotinus, Aristotle and Cicero—and we *have,* whether we know it or not, since evangelicals talk about the church and analogy and accommodation in ways that go back to these pagan thinkers—why not from the Buddha?

---

[29]Calvin *Institutes* 4.7.5; Sermon on John 1:1-5; Sermon no. 4 on Job, cited in Bouwsma, *John Calvin,* p. 124.

[30]Sermon no. 42 on Deuteronomy, Sermon no. 16 on 2 Samuel, cited in Bouwsma, *John Calvin,* p.125.

[31]Sermon no. 34 on Job, col. 423; *Institutes* 1.17.12; Commentary on Jeremiah 49:3, cited in Placher, *Domestication of Transcendence,* p. 57.

6

BUDDHIST NO-SELF & NO-MIND

LIKE THE NAMES GIVEN TO MOST RELIGIONS, *BUDDHISM* IS PUZZLING. It seems to describe groups that are enormously contradictory. Mahayana Buddhists, for example, worship many deities, while Theravadin Buddhists are atheists for all practical purposes. Theravadins and practitioners of Zen say that we must rely on self-effort to get us to our spiritual goals, whereas Tibetan Buddhists and Mahayanists believe we can ask for grace from a Buddha or bodhisattva. Theravadins and Zennists tell us our final destination should be nirvana in which there are no ideas, beings or consciousness. But devotees of the numerous Mahayana sects look forward to Pure Lands and paradises in which they will enjoy personal communion with their deities. Because of these—and other—differences, it seems misleading to use the word *Buddhism* as if it refers to one thing. It is far better, I think, to speak of Buddhist traditions.

Different Visions

Before I discuss what some Buddhist traditions can contribute to a deeper understanding of Christian revelation, I must emphasize that the visions of reality that they produce are quite different from Christian ones. It would be the worst sort of dilettantism to suggest that the Buddha and Jesus had the same goals or had similar notions of God, self and world. Before I can even begin to talk about Buddhist insights that can open up fresh perspectives in Christian faith, I need to be quite clear on how different these faiths are.

Most important, for example, the Buddha did not know the triune God! Later Mahayana traditions came to believe in deities known as Buddhas and bodhisattvas, but Siddhartha Gotama Buddha (c. 448-386 B.C.)[1] said that he was no more than a man and that there is no creator or divine being who can help us achieve our spiritual goals. Hence Sakyamuni,[2] as the original Buddha is known by many Buddhists, said that we are to be lamps unto ourselves, but Jesus said that He was the light of the world. We are not on our own, as the Buddha suggested, but can ask for the grace of Jesus to do for us what we cannot. While Jesus emphasized moral corruption as the heart of the basic human problem (Mk 7:20-23), the Buddha's first of four noble truths taught that desire—for gratification of one's senses and one's ego—is the root of all suffering. With love one can become a bodhisattva, but only knowledge enables one to become a Buddha. Perhaps as a result, Buddhist and Christian portrayals of the spiritual ideal are curiously different: Buddhists look to a smiling Buddha seated on a lotus blossom, while Christians worship a suffering Jesus nailed to a cross. The Buddha taught his followers to escape suffering, while Jesus showed a way to conquer it by embracing it.

Although Buddhist and Christian ethics agree on important principles (that stealing, lying, the killing of innocent life, and sexual misconduct are wrong and that compassion and sympathy are

---

[1]Other chronologies assign the following dates to Buddha's life: 560-480 B.C., 566-486 B.C. and c. 448-368 B.C.; see "Buddha," in *The Oxford Dictionary of World Religions,* ed. John Bowker (New York: Oxford University Press, 1997), p. 169.
[2]*Sakyamuni* means the Wise One, or Sage, of the Sakya clan.

imperative), they differ on the relationship of ethics to ultimate reality. For Gotama Buddha and Theravadins, the ethical life is a provisional raft that takes us to the other shore of nirvana where it can then be discarded, for there differences between good and evil no longer prevail. For Christians, the distinction between right and wrong is part of the fabric of reality and will persist into eternity. Ethical differences extend to relations between the sexes. Particularly in early Buddhism one encounters the idea that one can become a Buddha only when reborn in the form of a man; not until much later did Mahayanists accept female bodhisattvas. Buddhist monasteries today dominate Theravadin life; most orders for nuns disappeared centuries ago. While Christian history contains plenty of sexism, Jesus Himself never demonized women or sexuality.[3] When compared to the rigid structure of Buddhist monasticism, which is at the heart of Theravada, Jesus' circle of disciples appears "disorderly, casual, spontaneous and free."[4]

Buddhists and Christians look at ethics differently in large part because they regard history in radically different ways. Buddhists read in the *Dhammapada* that "there is no misery like physical existence."[5] Earthly existence is necessarily a vale of tears because as long as one remains in the endless cycle of life, death and rebirth—a cycle known as *samara*—suffering is inevitable because of the desire that life in the cosmos engenders. One can escape suffering only by escaping this wearisome cycle of rebirth. So one has to break ties to this world and its routines—particularly family life and sexuality. Jesus, however, never spoke harsh words about sexual intercourse; He announced a salvation that comes not by renouncing life in the world but by trust that is lived out in loving

---

[3]It should also be stated, however, that the Buddha ordained women and, according to some legends, even his own wife, Yasodhara.
[4]Hans Küng and Heinz Bechert, *Christianity and the World Religions: Paths to Dialogue* (Maryknoll, N.Y.: Orbis, 1993), p. 344.
[5]Thomas Cleary, ed., *Dhammapada: Sayings of the Buddha* (New York: Bantam, 1995), §15.6.

commitment amid the everyday routines of worldly life. According to Him, marriage is not an impediment to spirituality but the ordinary realm in which salvation is lived out. Abstention from family and sexuality is an option, but not a higher path for the spiritual elite.

At the same time I should say that this contrast should not be drawn too sharply. At times Christian monasticism has denied the world much as its Buddhist counterpart has. Beginning with the apostle Paul (1 Cor 7), there have been many Christians who have concluded that they could find God best apart from family and sexuality. And while monasticism has been more an integral part of Theravada than of Christianity, Jesus himself chose not to marry or regard family as the center of the spiritual life (Mt 10:37; 12:49-50), and the vast majority of Buddhists enjoy the fullness of married life and participation in the secular world.

God Beyond Thoughts and Words

Once we recognize that Buddhist traditions differ from Christianity in both goals and methods, we are ready to see that nevertheless they may help us understand the reality of God in Christ more clearly. In particular, their experience of the distance between ordinary perception and reality can help check our natural presumption when talking about God.

Gotama Buddha and his successors always stressed that transcendent truth lies beyond sense perception and intellectual conception. From the standpoint of our ordinary experience and thought, final truth is what they called "empty." It cannot be filled with any of our concepts (at least with any degree of precision) because it lies beyond them. Similarly, all events and objects measured against the standard of ultimate truth are also empty, they argued, because they are limited by space and time whereas final truth transcends both categories. Hence perfect wisdom means seeing that ultimate reality is Void (*Sunya*), which means not nonexistent but beyond all powers of discrimination. The Buddha never denied the real existence of what we call final reality; he only denied the existence of a name for it.[6] For him the attempt to identify Reality with a word or concept was presumptuous—akin to anthropomorphism. He insisted we cannot penetrate ultimate reality (what Christians would call God) by exercises of will or intellectual formulas. He denied a one-to-one correspondence between thinking and being.[7]

Thomas Aquinas saw a similar disjunction between God and our thinking about God. "The mind is found to be most perfectly in possession of the knowledge of God," he asserted, "when it is recognized that His essence is above everything that the mind is capable of apprehending in this life." God is not understandable in terms taken from this world. Language about God therefore "is not confined by the meaning of our word but goes beyond it." "Therefore, the knowledge by which God is seen through creatures is not a knowledge of his essence, but a knowledge that is dark and mirrored, and from afar."[8]

Aquinas and other scholastics showed us that we know God

---

[6] Some Buddhist philosophers, however, have used the dialectic of emptiness to make a point not just about the limitations of thought and language but also about what there is (or is not) in the world. Most, at least in India, have denied the existence of an omniscient, omnipotent creator God.

[7] For some representative primary texts that illustrate this doctrine, see "Essence of the Wisdom Sutra," in *Buddhism: A Religion of Infinite Compassion: Selections from Buddhist Literature,* ed. Clarence H. Hamilton (Indianapolis: Bobbs-Merrill, 1952), pp. 113-15; Paul Reps, ed., *Zen Flesh, Zen Bones: A Collection of Zen and Pre-Zen Writings* (New York: Anchor Books/Doubleday, n.d.), esp. nos. 21, 36 and 42 in "101 Zen Stories" and nos. 1, 5 and 23 in "The Gateless Gate"; *The Platform Sutra of the Sixth Patriarch: The Text of the Tun-Huang Manuscript,* trans. Philip B. Yampolsky (New York: Columbia University Press, 1967). For a more general introduction to both early and later Buddhist writings, see E. A. Burtt, ed., *The Teachings of the Compassionate Buddha: Early Discourses, the Dhammapada, and Later Basic Writings* (New York: Signet Classics, 1955). For secondary overviews of Buddhist thought, see A. L. Herman, *An Introduction to Buddhist Thought: A Philosophical History of Indian Buddhism* (Lanham, Md.: University Press of America, 1983); and Kenneth Ch'en, *Buddhism in China: A Historical Survey* (Princeton: Princeton University Press, 1964).

[8] Thomas Aquinas *Summa Theologiae* 1a.12.13.ad 1; William C. Placher, *The Domestication*

best by the way of preeminence, which comes only after affirmation and negation. For example, we affirm that God is beauty but then deny that God is beauty in the way that we ordinarily experience beauty, for all earthly experience of beauty is only a dim and broken refraction of original Beauty, which flows like a fountain out of God, Who defines the meaning of beauty. Thus we affirm that God is beauty but only in this preeminent way: careful not to contaminate God by identifying Him with our finite creaturely standards and noting that human affirmations about God are not to be absolutized or converted into idols. Discourse about God has no terms of comparison since it is by definition unique and therefore incomparable. "Purely affirmative theology without negative theology makes God a creature of our intellects, a projection of our imagination." On the other hand, negative theology without the further turn to the way of preeminence leads to an epistemological agnosticism that denies the biblical testimony that "the Word became flesh and lived among us" (Jn 1:14).[9]

This method can also help us understand what it means to think of God as a person. Aquinas would remind us that God is not a person as we ordinarily think of persons. Buddhist thinkers would add that *none* of our ideas of personhood have exact correspondents in God. (Of course while Mahayana and Tibetan thinkers would agree that the divine is personal, Theravadins would deny the existence of any deity such as Christians profess.) Neither is God impersonal, for Jesus showed us that God incarnate is a human person. Nor is God both, since God is simple and not a composite. In some mysterious way that is beyond our grasp,

---

of Transcendence: How Modern Thinking About God Went Wrong (Louisville: Westminster Press, 1996), p. 31; *Summa Theologiae* 1a.13.5; *Commentary on the Gospel of St. John* 1:18 (no. 211), cited in Placher, *Domestication of Transcendence*, p. 31 n. 1.

[9]Küng and Bechert, *Christianity and the World Religions*, pp. 394-95. On the way of negation (apophaticism), see Jaroslav Pelikan, *The Spirit of Eastern Christendom (600-1700)*, vol. 2 in *The Christian Tradition: A History of the Development of Doctrine* (Chicago: University of Chicago Press, 1974), pp. 30-32, 54-55, 258-59, 264-70.

then, God the Person is infinitely more than we can conceive when we use that word. And He is certainly not less.

God is more because God is Wholly Other, as Karl Barth famously put it—or better yet, as God Himself told us through Isaiah: "My thoughts are not your thoughts, nor are your ways my ways. . . . As the heavens are higher than the earth, so are my ways higher than your ways and my thoughts than your thoughts" (Is 55:8-9). We evangelicals sometimes regard God idolatrously as a bigger version of ourselves. The Buddhist traditions, in a way not completely dissimilar to Barth and Isaiah, admonish us to recognize that God is qualitatively and infinitely different from us. As Scripture admonishes us, we are creatures and He is the Creator. The Zen traditions urge their devotees to stop seeing the world through the eyes of the ego-self that relates everything it sees to the self. As long as we cling to regard for self, they teach, we will not see or hear what really is. As long as we think that the world (and God, I would add) exists to gratify us, we will be blind to the world (and God). Robert E. Kennedy, a Jesuit scholar who has sought to use the insights of Zen to enrich his own Christian experience, says that this Zen teaching has helped enlarge his view of God. How could we worship a God, he asks, who pays attention to our whining? It is not God's purpose to glorify us. Unanswered prayers are therefore a glorious reminder that the world does not revolve around us and that we were created not to be served but to serve. Nature's indifference to us can be a source of joy—a wake-up call to see and hear the world as it is rather than how it relates to us.[10]

We can watch the sun rise and hear the birds sing, and groan as we listen to the cries of the wounded—without being concerned with how they affect us. Of course such selfless listening and seeing

---

[10]Robert E. Kennedy, *Zen Spirit, Christian Spirit: The Place of Zen in Christian Life* (New York: Continuum, 1995), pp. 97-98.

are possible only in part and only by grace. But without recognizing the self-interested and therefore narrow perspectives we typically use unthinkingly, we will not ask for the grace to see the world beyond our own interests. We will still be locked into our own mental constructs—seeing and hearing our own projections and missing much of what really *is*. The Buddha and his successors alert us (even more sharply than Aquinas and the scholastics) to our tendency to see and hear only what we have been accustomed to see and hear. They remind us that reality is very different from what we conceive and perceive and can prod us—if we let them—to ask for grace to see and hear like we have never done before.

Sometimes we evangelicals worship an idol and call it God. We think of Jesus as our buddy, or call God "The Big Man" or "The Man Upstairs." The Buddhist traditions can remind us that God is infinitely distant from what we claim to worship and may in fact have no relation to the object of our prayer and talk. Buddhist insights, despite falling short of the true God, can teach us reverence before the mystery of God and more respect in the face of the ultimate and ineffable in God. They can remind us that all positive statements about God are inadequate and, as Hans Küng put it, must be negated in order to be lifted up finally into the infinite: God is immeasurably ineffable, infinitely good, absolute goodness. Hence God simultaneously transcends and permeates the world and human beings; He is infinitely far and yet closer to us than we are to ourselves, "intangible yet we experience [God's] presence, present even when we experience [God's] absence." Every statement must pass though the dialectic of affirmation and negation before it can be conceived as preeminent.[11]

Contingency of World and Self
If Buddhist thinkers can help us keep our thoughts about God in per-

---

[11]Küng and Bechert, *Christianity and the World Religions*, p. 397.

spective, they also confirm the Bible's picture of this cosmos and ourselves as radically dependent on God. This is what philosophers call contingency—the notion that a thing exists not on its own but by dependence on something else. We theists may find it somewhat remarkable that the earliest Buddhist thinkers, who were atheists for all practical purposes, were convinced that nothing exists of itself but each thing is dependent on an infinite network of causation. This is entirely plausible for someone who believes in a god who created and now sustains the cosmos, as the Christian faith teaches, but it is not immediately obvious to a person who denies that any thing holds all things together, particularly before the advent of modern scientific support for the notion of things as relational.[12] Yet Buddhists have always maintained that there is no such thing as absolute independence of being. Their doctrine of "dependent origination" holds that no phenomenon in the cosmos is isolated and without cause but every phenomenon is linked with every other phenomenon. Thus there are no independent substances that exist on their own. The world is transient, ever changing, devoid of any permanent substratum.

This corroborates the biblical claim that the world is not a concatenation of self-subsisting substances but is "held together" in Christ (Col 1:17). Jonathan Edwards interpreted this to mean that things in the world are merely God's thoughts continuously recreating the reality of those things. A thing is not a substance with identity apart from everything else but is the expression of divine communication. In Samuel Johnson's words, "Things are God's words in print." The Buddha did not believe in divine communication, but he would have agreed with Edwards that no substances subsist as independent entities. Instead they find their identities in the relations between each entity and all other entities: a being is

---

[12]Because of recent developments in physics, even some materialists can now argue that no thing exists by itself but each is dependent on an infinite or near-finite network of causation. That this is so, however, makes this Buddhist notion no less helpful to Christians.

only as it is related to other things. Being is therefore relational and dynamic—it consists of a vast network of interrelations wherein every entity is related to every other. (Contrary to some interpretations, the Buddha was not a nihilist. He did not deny the existence of being but preached a middle way between being and nonbeing. His concern was to insist that our conventional understanding of substance as independent—what we normally call "being"—is illusory.)[13]

If the world is contingent, so is the human self. The Buddha is famous for *anatta,* the doctrine of no-self. By this he meant that there is no unchanging subject and nothing that is the fundament of everything else. Like everything else, the human person is purely contingent, totally dependent on the system of being, which for the Christian is sustained moment by pulsating moment sheerly by the grace of God. David Tracy regards this notion—limned by Scripture and confirmed by Buddhist writings—to be a healthy antidote to our culture's possessive individualism and its illusion of a purely autonomous, nonrelational self.[14]

Incidentally, the Japanese Pure Land school of Mahayana Buddhism contains an extraordinary testament to the radical *moral* contingency of the human ego. Shinran (1173-1262), the founder of *Jodo-Shin-shu* (Pure Land True Sect), rejected all "ways of effort" in the search for salvation and preached that we must rely on "the power of the other," which for him was Amida Buddha, who would bring to

[13]Samuel Johnson, *Technologia sive Technometria,* in *Samuel Johnson, President of King's College: His Career and Writings,* ed. Herbert Schneider and Carol Schneider (New York: Columbia University Press, 1929), 2:67. See Johnathan Edwards, "Of Atoms," in *Scientific and Philosophical Writings* (New Haven, Conn.: Yale University Press, 1980), p. 215. On Edwards's ontology, see Stephen H. Daniel, *The Philosophy of Jonathan Edwards: A Study in Divine Semiotics* (Bloomington: Indiana University Press, 1994), esp. chap. 3. On the Buddha's ontology and reputed nihilism, see Raimundo Pannikar, *The Silence of God: The Answer of the Buddha,* trans. Robert R. Barr (Maryknoll, N.Y.: Orbis, 1989), pp. 23, 28, 55-56.

[14]David Tracy, *Dialogue with the Other: The Inter-Religious Dialogue* (Grand Rapids, Mich.: Eerdmans, 1990), pp. 76-77.

his Pure Land all those who have faith in his power. Shinran's conviction of underlying sin in all human beings is reminiscent of Paul or Augustine:

> In their outward seeming are all men diligent and truth speaking,
> But in their souls are greed and anger and unjust deceitfulness.
> And in their flesh do lying and cunning triumph.[15]

His despair over the inner corruption of even his outward righteousness seems to be an Asian translation of Isaiah: "Even my righteous deeds, being mingled with this poison, must be named the deeds of deceitfulness. . . . I, whose mind is filled with cunning and deceit as the poison of reptiles, am impotent to practice righteous deeds."[16] And his hope for divine mercy reads like a line from Martin Luther:

> There is no mercy in my soul. The good of my fellow man is not dear in
>   mine eyes.
> If it were not for the Ark of Mercy,
> The divine promise of the Infinite Wisdom,
> How should I cross the Ocean of Misery?[17]

Buddhist thinkers do not add qualitatively to the biblical view of self and world, but they confirm and sharpen biblical claims about the radical contingency of the created order. Use of their deliberations may help remind Christians of a doctrine that is often neglected in the West, even in the church. And they show us that God has given significant truth to non-Christians.

The Mystery of the Ordinary
C. S. Lewis once wrote, "Earth, I think, will not be found by anyone

---

[15]"Shinran's Confession," in *Buddhism: A Religion of Infinite Compassion: Selections from Buddhist Literature,* ed. Clarence H. Hamilton (Indianapolis: Bobbs-Merrill, 1952), pp. 141-42.
[16]Ibid.
[17]Ibid.

to be in the end a very distinct place. I think earth, if chosen instead of Heaven, will turn out to have been, all along, only a region in Hell: and earth, if put second to Heaven, to have been from the beginning a part of Heaven itself."[18]

Seeing heaven in earthly, daily existence is the achievement of Chinese Buddhism. Indian Buddhists tended to withdraw from the external world, ignore outside influences and try to unite with the Infinite by seeking intellectual illumination. The Chinese Ch'an school (which, when later transported to Japan, became known as Zen), however, taught that one can find Ultimate Reality in every little detail of ordinary life. There is no need to withdraw from the world but every need to learn to see the Reality that always stands before us. Although later Zen would emphasize the need to sit in meditation, Hui-Neng (638-713), the Sixth Patriarch and one of the most important Ch'an teachers, said that sitting is useless unless one learns to see the world as it is, which can be done in the midst of one's daily activities.

Thirteen hundred years later Lin Yutang commented on what he learned from this Ch'an tradition:

> [Ch'an] comes to "rest" in the simple, everyday living, regarding it as a blessed gift, and enjoying every moment of it. I would call it gratitude for living, a form of Oriental existentialism. There is a sense of the mystery of the mere act of living. . . . A Chinese [Ch'an] poet exclaims, "It is a miracle—I am drawing water from a well!" This is typical of the [Ch'an] life as it ought to be lived. It is a miracle that a cowboy sits on a buffalo's back at sunset on his way home. It is a miracle that flies swarm and weeds grow and a man drinks a cup of water, knowing not what water is, nor what a cup is, and not even what he himself is. All life and all living are miracles. One becomes a poet as the plowman wipes the sweat off his brow and feels the cooling breeze upon his head, or, as Tao Yuan-ming records almost with ecstasy about a walk in the field at dawn, "The morning dew wets the skirts of my gown."[19]

---

[18]C. S. Lewis, *The Great Divorce* (New York: Macmillan, 1945), preface.
[19]Lin Yutang, *From Pagan to Christian* (London: Beinemann, 1960), p. 170.

This notion that the mystery of God is to be found in all of creation and history is not foreign to Christianity. But neither is it common. Edwards wrote about it, but his bold speculation that has since been called "panentheism" (God is in everything but is also separate from the creation) was criticized in the nineteenth century as heretical. It was not, and it is illustrative of the legitimate fear that many Christians have had over the centuries of an Emerson-like pantheism that identifies God with the cosmos, thus stripping the word *god* of transcendence and personhood.

We need not assume, however, that talk of God in all of nature and history is necessarily pantheistic. Hui-Neng may not have believed in a personal and transcendent God, but the biblical writers certainly did, and they proposed just the notion that I am describing. Paul, for example, suggested that Christ is the cosmic glue or energy that holds all things together (Col 1:17) and that God superintends every event that a Christian experiences so that it works for that person's eventual good (Rom 8:28; 1 Cor 3:21). Jesus said that every hair on our heads is numbered and that not a sparrow falls to the ground apart from God's will (Mt 10:29-30). Edwards took these and other passages to mean that not an atom (we might say subatomic particle) moves apart from God's sovereign direction. H. Richard Niebuhr, a disciple of Edwards and perhaps America's most influential theologian in this century, applied these suggestions to a general view of providence. He argued for an understanding of life as a continual call to see God in both critical and mundane moments.

> At the critical junctures in the history of Israel and of the early Christian community, the decisive question men raised was not "What is the goal?" nor yet "What is the law?" but "What is happening?" and then "What is the fitting response to what is happening?" When an Isaiah counsels his people, he does not remind them of the law they are required to obey nor yet of the goal toward which they are directed but calls to their attention the intentions of God present in hiddenness in the actions of Israel's enemies. The question he

and his peers raise in every critical moment is about the interpretation of what is going on, whether what is happening be, immediately considered, a drought or the invasion of a foreign army, or the fall of a great empire. Israel is the people that is to see and understand the action of God in *everything that happens* and to make a fitting reply. So it is in the New Testament also. The God to whom Jesus points is not the commander who gives laws but the doer of small and of mighty deeds, the creator of sparrows and clother of lilies, the ultimate giver of blindness and of sight, the ruler whose rule is hidden in the manifold activities of plural agencies but is yet in a way visible to those who know how to interpret the signs of the times.[20]

Niebuhr was more interested in seeing God in the critical moments of life and less concerned with the reality of God in and behind every moment. But his writings nevertheless echo the biblical view that every moment has in some sense been created by God—even while God uses creatures who freely ignore and disobey Him. And he suggests that we humans typically miss this—just as Hui-Neng suggested that we are ordinarily blind to the mystery of ordinary moments. Once more, C. S. Lewis is helpful. When we die, he said, we will not say,

Lord, I could never have guessed how beautiful you are.
We will not say that. Rather, we will say,
So it was you all along.
Everyone I ever loved, it was you.
Everyone who ever loved me, it was you.
Everything decent or fine that ever happened to me,
everything that made me reach out and try to be better,
it was you all along.[21]

Of course, if God is sovereign over *every* thing, and not just the good things, then God was also present in and at least indirectly related to even those bad things. As Job asked his wife after they

---

[20]H. Richard Niebuhr, *The Responsible Self: An Essay in Christian Moral Philosophy* (New York: Harper & Row, 1963), p. 67 (emphasis added).
[21]Cited in Kennedy, *Zen Spirit, Christian Spirit*, p. 59.

had lost their children and wealth, "Shall we receive the good at the hand of God, and not receive the bad?" (Job 2:10) But we do not have to determine God's relation to evil[22] to be able to experience the holiness of the ordinary, of which the Bible speaks and which Chinese Buddhism explored at considerable length (though without recognizing the true origin of that holiness).

To recognize the mystery in the ordinary is to see life as the Hebrews saw it—a life of primary, not secondary, causes. If their armies were defeated in battle, it was God who defeated them, not the incompetence of their generals. If their crops failed, it was because God had sent a drought. Their view of life, as Anthony De Mello has observed, was unbalanced by its neglect of secondary causes. But our focus on secondary causes—the aspirin cured my headache and God had nothing to do with it—to the exclusion of primary is also unbalanced. The truth is that God cured my headache through the aspirin tablet.[23]

Strangely, to see God in the ordinary is easy. By that I mean we do not have to wait for a flash of mystical intuition, or vision, or hope that we hear a voice. We can see God right in front of us, right now. If what the Bible says about creation and providence is true, then we can take seriously De Mello's suggestion that God is right here right now:

> One needs to do so little, really, to *experience God.* All one needs to do is quieten yourself, become still—and become aware of the feel of your hand. Be aware of the sensations in your hand. . . . There you have God, living and working in you, touching you, intensely near you. . . . Feel him. Experience him!
>
> Most people look upon an experience like this as far too pedestrian. Surely there is more to the experience of God than just the simple feel of the sensations

---

[22]An excellent guide to answering this question is John G. Stackhouse Jr., *Can God Be Trusted?* (New York: Oxford University Press, 1998).

[23]Anthony De Mello, *Sadhana: A Way to God* (New York: Image, 1978), p. 49. I do not agree with all of De Mello's interpretations of Asian religions, but in this respect I find him insightful.

of one's right hand! They are like the Jews who were straining their eyes toward the future in expectation of a glorious, sensational Messiah, while all along the Messiah was beside them in the form of a man called Jesus of Nazareth. . . .

You wish to see God? Look at the face of the man next to you. You want to hear him? Listen to the cry of a baby, the loud laughter at a party, the wind rustling in the trees.[24]

This is another example of how a different religious tradition can open up for us truths in Christ that were previously hidden to us. Isolated Christians had known of this, and a few had written of it, but in ways that have gone largely unnoticed. Christian attention to the Ch'an and Zen traditions in the last several decades has helped some believers reappropriate dimensions of Christian revelation that for centuries have remained buried.

The Compulsive Clinging of the Old Man

George Marsden, Mark Noll and others have shown us how the Enlightenment played a role in the formation of the contemporary evangelical mind.[25] As a result, American evangelical understanding of both salvation and sanctification has tended to emphasize belief and practice rather than shared spiritual life. Yet Jesus and Paul were Semitic thinkers for whom mysticism (direct experience with divine reality) played a far larger role than it does for most evangelicals. Hence we evangelicals have a more difficult time understanding His prayer that we be "in us [the Father and the Son]" (Jn 17:21) and Paul's declaration that we have been crucified in Christ (Rom 6:6) than Paul's teaching that all humans beings have sinned (Rom 3:23) and James's command that we care for orphans and widows (Rom 1:27). We are more comfortable with an Anselmian legal model for

---

[24]Ibid., p. 46.
[25]See, for example, George M. Marsden, "The Evangelical Love Affair with Enlightenment Science," in *Understanding Fundamentalism and Evangelicalism* (Grand Rapids, Mich.: Eerdmans, 1991), pp. 122-52; Mark A. Noll, *The Scandal of the Evangelical Mind* (Grand Rapids, Mich.: Eerdmans, 1994), pp. 59-108.

grace (forgiveness granted by a judge because the debt has been paid) than an Augustinian medical model (grace is medicine for a sick soul). For this reason Asian religious thinking, in which mysticism is more common and central, may help us evangelicals better understand Jesus, Paul and other biblical subjects and writers.

I have found, for example, that Buddhist doctrine has helped me understand more clearly the Pauline concept of "the old man" and, theologically, what Luther meant by the self being *curvatus in se* (curved back into itself). For Buddhists, the essence of the human condition is what they call "desire," by which they mean an obsessive clinging to the ego's thoughts and wishes. It is an expression of the assertive, demanding me in each of us that sees itself as the center and interprets everything in terms of itself. Rather than seeing things as they are—apart from the observer's ego—the "old man" in the observer sees each thing only as it relates to the observer. Instead of seeing the lilies of the field (Mt 6:28) as they truly are—creations of God that neither toil nor spin for their clothing—we typically project onto them our desires or aversions, our nostalgic emotions, our utilitarian purposes, so that they are not seen as they are in themselves—what Buddhists call their "suchness"—but as something else (perhaps bothersome blemishes on our otherwise-green lawns that we feel compelled to mow down). We regard external reality as functions of ourselves, existing to serve "me." As the German philosopher Immanuel Kant would say, we look upon other persons and things not as ends in themselves but as means to the end of serving us.

Clinging stubbornly to our own desires, therefore, keeps us from seeing things and people as they really are. As Emerson said, we bring back from the Indies only what we take to the Indies.[26] We see only what we have been accustomed to see. Our egoistic

---

[26]Cited in Dom Aelred Graham, *Zen Catholicism* (1963; reprint, New York: Crossroad, 1994), p. 47.

clinging also prevents us from hearing the true sounds of reality. We anticipate what we will say next instead of listening to what our conversation partner has just said. It is hard for us to live in the present—listening to the present moment—instead of the past or future. As D. H. Lawrence said, "Few people live on the spot where they are."[27]

The old man's clinging to its interests and ideas is particularly evident when power is involved. We crave positions of power when we have not attained them, or cling nervously to them if they are threatened. The "pride of life" (1 Jn 2:16 KJV) is another kind of clinging—to the security of being respected by others. We want too much to be saluted in the marketplace and to sit in the first seats at the synagogues and in places of honor at banquets.

As Kierkegaard suggested, even morality can be a clinging to a set of notions that blocks our way to the real God. The Danish philosopher said that our ethical convictions can prevent us from ascending to the highest stage of the religious life by blinding us to the utter individuality of a relationship to the true God.[28] Jesus intimated that our conventional moral categories can keep us from seeing the spiritual truth at hand. He asked the rich young ruler why he asked about goodness and said that only God is good. (In other words, the young man's conception of goodness was askew and kept him from recognizing the One he was addressing.) He warned his disciples not to judge, lest they be judged, and admonished the Pharisees not to cast a stone at the adulterous woman unless they were without sin. In both cases self-righteous moral judgments prevented the participants from seeing what was really going on. Religious ideas can do the same thing, as Karl Barth argued, because of our tendency to replace God with ideas about

---

[27]Cited in Graham, *Zen Catholicism*, p. 50. This and the following paragraph are indebted to Graham, *Zen Catholicism*, pp. 47-53.

[28]Søren Kierkegaard, *Fear and Trembling,* ed. Howard Hong and Edna Hong (Princeton: Princeton University Press, 1983), pp. 54-55.

the divine that seem easier to handle. For example, spiritual self-discipline can lead to a comforting self-righteousness in the face of God's real judgment of our sin. All of these ways of clinging to the ego's false perceptions round out the picture of what Paul called "the old man."

Sitting on the Cross

What does it mean to "*put off* the old man" (Col 3:9; Eph 4:22)? Here again Buddhist understandings are helpful. If the old man is a kind of clinging, then putting it off means letting go—of our own self-interest and ideas about how things ought to be done. This is akin to what the old Zen masters meant when they said, "If you see the Buddha, kill him!" Our own ideas coming from the selfish ego, even when about morality and religion, are destructive and so need to be crucified—or better, let go.

Paul presents Christ's incarnation and sacrifice as a self-emptying or letting go. The Greek word for this is *kenosis*, which means "making empty." Christ "emptied himself" of His divine form—at least the kind that would be immediately apparent to human creatures—and allowed Himself to be taken as a slave (Phil 2:7). As a result, He was killed on a cross. The Father did a similar self-emptying or letting go: He surrendered His Son to the humiliation of human existence and the pain of death by crucifixion because "God so loved the world that he gave his only son" (Jn 3:16).

Paul showed a similar letting go in his ministry to the Corinthians. He writes that when he first came to them he resolved to let go of eloquence and human wisdom in order to rely only on "Christ and him crucified" (1 Cor 2:1-2). This was risky in a culture that prized skillful rhetoric and the latest philosophy. Because he wanted the Corinthians to experience only the "power of God," he deliberately chose not to use "wise and persuasive" words or "human wisdom" (vv. 4-5).

What does it mean for us to let go? First, I think, it means letting go of our presumption that we know the way. We should confess something like the following, "Lord, I do not know who I really am. Scripture says that my true self is hidden in Christ (Col 3:3), and at this point I am still searching for it. I am far from experiencing the reality of the risen Christ within me. Show me what that means, where it is, who I am."

Second, letting go does not mean seeking to put the right thoughts in the brain or mustering up the right faith. Nor does it mean withdrawing from the world as if God cannot be found in the world—although it sometimes helps to find a quiet place to focus the mind and heart. Evangelicals tend to think of letting go as a disciplined and determined following or imitation of Christ, as if it were a simple act of the will to be exercised. But the realities of Romans 7 ought to convince us that apart from grace the will is impotent. Instead it is a kind of self-forgetfulness that comes only by the prior breath of the Spirit and focuses not on the desires of the self but on Christ Himself. It is not a doing but a kind of being that results from an inner transformation.

Genuine dying with Christ is a letting go that allows the life of Christ to mysteriously rise up within us. It is the losing of our lives that results in finding our true lives (Lk 17:33). The following excerpt of a letter from the abbot of a Catholic monastery to a young Christian friend at a Zen Buddhist monastery illustrates how Buddhist concepts can help illuminate the mystical dimension of what Paul meant by dying with Christ.

> To sit in zazen [the term for sitting in Zen meditation] is an expression of the reality of your inmost being as a man in whom Jesus Christ is present on the cross and risen. It is a marvelous way of identifying yourself with that interior reality. In zazen you sit down on the cross with Jesus and identify with his willingness to die on the cross, i.e., you affirm your determination to die to the ego-self so that you can live the risen life of Jesus which has already been given you, but which is still secret because of the life of the ego. To sit is to allow the life of Christ to rise up quietly within you. Thus the very position itself is an

affirmation of your willingness to be on the cross with Christ, to share his dying, which was really a death for you, and to wait for his resurrection within you.[29]

Finding the True Self

If we let go of our egoistic desires and thoughts, we will be ready for Christ to rise within us. Buddhists talk about seeing our original face and finding the Buddha within. The Sixth Patriarch in the Ch'an tradition said that once we make that discovery, we will experience reality naturally. There will be no special searching for it, no need for calculated effort. The mind will operate spontaneously, and we will experience ultimate reality without any mediation.[30]

This manner of being is analogous to what Paul meant by life in the Spirit, but it is one that we Enlightenment-influenced evangelicals (along with most other Westerners) have a hard time imagining. Just as Zen Buddhists say *satori* (awakening or enlightenment) will open our eyes to our original face or true self, so too letting go of the old man will open the way for finding *our* true self, which according to Colossians is "hidden with Christ in God" (Col 3:3).

This new and true self does not cling to itself but, as Thomas Merton put it, functions *from* God and *for* others. The ego is no longer the principle of the self's deepest actions, which now proceed from Christ within. In satori, Buddhists say a person experiences "no-self," a state in which one regards the self not as ultimate but as indissolubly connected with everything else and at the disposal of all.[31] For Christians, the new self also draws its being from outside itself and is also directed outside itself, but not simply

---

[29]David G. Hackett, *The Silent Dialogue: Zen Letters to a Trappist Monk* (New York: Continuum, 1996), p. 51.

[30]Wing-tsit Chan, ed. and trans., *The Platform Scripture: The Basic Classic of Zen Buddhism* (New York: St. John's University Press, 1963), pp. 2-3.

[31]Thomas Merton, *Zen and the Birds of Appetite* (Boston: Shambhala, 1993), p. 51. Other books that I have found helpful include William Johnston, *The Mirror Mind: Spirituality and Transformation* (San Francisco: Harper and Row, 1981); John B. Cobb and Christo-

because of its structural connection with everything else. Christ is the principle of the new self, and the peak of religious experience is the awareness of mystical union: "it is no longer I [the Greek word here is *ego*] who live, but it is Christ who lives in me" (Gal 2:20).

The cheerful and almost carefree spontaneity with which Zen masters describe the satori experience is akin to what Paul meant by living in the Spirit (Rom 8). It is a life free from fear or anxious deliberation over what and how to act. Luther said it is *sua sponte* (on its own): it allows us to live no longer in ourselves but in God, doing justice and good (nearly) automatically. It is the life Augustine had in mind when he encouraged us, "*Ama et fac quod vis*" (Love and do what you like). It is the disappearance of the self-conscious "me" before the full realization of the unselfconscious "I." It is the life of the new self that is being progressively found and experienced by the breath of the Holy Spirit. It enables us to reach a measure of what Buddhists call seeing and hearing without emotional attachment. Christian revelation does not demonize the emotions (as Buddhists tend to), but it agrees with Buddhists that emotions are often rooted in the ego and distort one's vision and hearing. Therefore, looking at Buddhist satori can help us better understand the sort of freedom that the New Testament says comes from the Spirit of God.

Two Final Notes

In this chapter I have explored some preliminary ways in which reflection on Buddhist thinking and practice can help evangelicals

---

pher Ives, eds., *The Emptying God: A Buddhist-Jewish-Christian Conversation* (Maryknoll, N.Y.: Orbis, 1990); William Johnston, *The Still Point: Reflections on Zen and Christian Mysticism* (New York: Fordham University Press, 1970); Naomi Burton et al., eds., *The Asian Journal of Thomas Merton* (New York: New Directions, 1975); Thomas Merton, *Mystics and Zen Masters* (New York: Farrar, Strauss and Giroux, 1967); and Leo D. Lefebure, *The Buddha and the Christ: Explorations in Buddhist and Christian Dialogue* (Maryknoll, N.Y.: Orbis, 1993).

better understand Christian revelation. Buddhists can help us guard against the presumption that our thoughts can capture God's being; they can help sharpen our understanding of the radical contingency of all the created order; they can refresh our sense of awe before the mystery of every moment; and they can help us comprehend both our fallen nature and how the life of Christ transcends it. All of these insights, while related to what Christians have already known, nevertheless develop and provide new perspectives. Pursued further, they can contribute to new understanding and experience of God's revelation in Christ. In closing, I want to mention very briefly two more contributions Buddhists can make.

First, their meditation techniques can teach Christians how to relax, be calm, think in a deeper way, dispose themselves to receive God's love and grace, and pray with not just the mind but the body as well. (We can use these techniques without buying into an accompanying metaphysics.) These techniques can teach us about prayer beyond images and words and the prayer that is watching and listening. They can help push us to seek the fullness of life in the Spirit, where we get (some measure of) freedom from self in self-forgetfulness.

Second, Buddhists remind us that there are still plenty of serious thinkers who question the presumption of radical postmodernists that we can never know anything outside our own heads. For example, Madhyamika, a distinguished tradition in Buddhist philosophy, seeks to escape views and theories in order to observe the nature of things without viewpoints. I think postmodernism is correct when it declares that there is no pure experience but only interpreted experience. Unlike Buddhists, evangelicals believe in original sin, and this involves among other things noetic consequences. This means that sin affects our thinking and that there will be no sinless thinking this side of the eschaton, which also means that seeing without viewpoints is a chimera.

Yet if Buddhists are quixotic in their hope for intellectual purity this side of nirvana, they are not wrong in claiming the possibility of real freedom from distortion. In this they agree with Christians, but of course the latter say that that freedom will always be partial, as through a glass darkly. We will always know only in part. But that part is still precious: there *is* revelation from God, which means we can know something about what is outside of our heads. We are not doomed to eternal agnosticism.

7

A DAOIST THEOLOGY
⌐OF CAMOUFLAGE⌐

J UST AS THERE IS NO ONE THING CALLED BUDDHISM, THERE IS NO ONE
thing called Daoism. The two most important Daoist ways of looking at the world—religious Daoism and philosophical Daoism—
could hardly be more different. Religious Daoists believe in gods
with saving power, sinful human nature, and redemption from guilt
and sin by means of prayer, penance, alchemy and other rituals of
personal religion. They seek immortality. Philosophical Daoists, on
the other hand, are atheists who do not believe in life after death.
Like Theravadin Buddhists, they aim to penetrate surface appearances in order to get at the hidden Reality that animates the cosmos.
They call this the Dao (Chinese for "way"). The two forms of Daoism
are not completely disconnected, however; in fact, seeds for religious Daoism can be found in the earliest Daoist text, the *Dao-de-
jing* (*Tao Te Ching,* c. fourth century B.C.).[1]

---

[1]*Tao Te Ching,* trans. Thomas Cleary, in *The Essential Tao* (San Francisco: HarperSanFrancisco, 1993). One can see the basis for religious Daoism's pursuit of immortality in chaps.
16 and 50. (References to this document will henceforth be to chapters, not pages. In references to these texts I use the Wade-Giles Romanization in order to identify my sources;

In this chapter I will focus on philosophical Daoism, which is more familiar to the West through the *Dao-de-jing* and *Zhuang-zi* (Chuang Tzu). These texts could be called examples of an Asian wisdom literature, analogous to the Hebrew wisdom literature found in biblical books like Proverbs. While there are many similarities in both form and content between Hebrew wisdom and (this) Chinese wisdom, the Christian reader may be struck nonetheless by the differences between this Asian wisdom and the wisdom of Jesus (1 Cor 1:30). Lao-zi (Lao Tzu; sixth century B.C.)[2] and Zhuang-zi (Chuang Tzu; c. 370-286 B.C.), the supposed authors of the two texts I just mentioned, stood in opposition to the cultures of their day, as Jesus did, but only in Jesus did this opposition take a deadly turn. Jesus' wisdom went far beyond a way of seeing Ultimate Reality as something requiring resignation and accommodation—as Lao-zi and Zhuang-zi suggested—a way that could minimize suffering and might indeed help one to escape suffering. Jesus said that Ultimate Reality was finally personal and took up suffering into itself. God is a Person, He demonstrated, Who does not stand at a distance while we suffer but comes down and enters into our suffering with us. In fact God Himself suffered the ultimate evil of death and somehow overcame it, and promises to take us up into the victory. This is a new wisdom that eclipses and transcends the old wisdom of Proverbs, Lao-zi and Zhuang-zi.

everywhere else I have used Pinyin.) For further study in philosophical Daoism, see Burton Watson, trans., *Chuang-tzu: Basic Writings* (New York: Columbia University Press, 1964); Wig-tsit Chan, trans. and comp., *A Source Book in Chinese Philosophy* (Princeton: Princeton University Press, 1963); Herlee G. Creel, *What Is Taoism? and Other Studies in Chinese Cultural History* (Chicago: University of Chicago Press, 1970); Max Kaltenmark, *Lao Tzu and Taoism* (Stanford: Stanford University Press, 1969). In this chapter my translations are from the Cleary edition, *The Essential Tao*, because it is the most accessible to nonspecialists and contains all of the *Tao Te Ching* and the inner chapters of the *Chuang Tzu*.

[2]Scholars debate the dates and even existence of Lao-zi. Those who hold the *Dao-de-jing* to have been written in the fourth to third centuries B.C. contend that the book is simply a compendium of wise sayings dating back to the sixth century but set down in writing two to three centuries later.

But if Jesus' eschatological promise opens up a future never imagined by the author of Proverbs, the insights of Proverbs into human relationships and ambitions are valuable nonetheless. I have drawn a similar conclusion about the Asian wisdom of Lao-zi and Zhuang-zi. The latter two thinkers provide (at times) profound insight into the ironies and paradoxes of human existence that the Bible also reveals. Christians often have a difficult time understanding these paradoxes and sometimes entirely miss the divine Reality behind the ironies of their lives. Because of the nature of paradoxes, many will never be understood completely—at least this side of eternity. But paradoxes are often easier to handle if we know they are somehow connected to divine purposes.

This is where I find Lao-zi and Zhuang-zi helpful. They use fresh and vivid images to remind Christians of biblical truths that are often missed but that can greatly enrich our experience once we see them. Or they have a way of illustrating and confirming biblical propositions that may not become real until additional insight uncovers them. But they do not simply remind us of what we already know. When I look at these truths after learning from Lao-zi and Zhuang-zi, I find that I see these once-familiar truths in now-unfamiliar ways.

God in Camouflage

Lao-zi and Zhuang-zi remind us that God often works in camouflage. God's presence and wisdom are often taken to be God's absence and foolishness. The *Dao-de-jing* talks not about a personal God but about an impersonal Dao that animates and pervades and drives all things. Yet it insists that reality is not what it seems and that wisdom is often mistaken for its opposite: "The greatest cleverness appears like stupidity; the greatest eloquence seems like stuttering."[3] Paul said that the message of the cross is foolishness to

---

[3]Cited in Lin Yutang, *From Pagan to Christian* (London: Beinemann, 1960), p. 118.

those who are perishing;[4] Lao-zi echoed his thought, saying that to the unenlightened "the Way of illumination seems dark, the Way of advancement seems retiring . . . higher virtue seems empty, great purity seems ignominious, broad virtue seems insufficient, constructive virtue seems careless."[5]

If for Lao-zi true wisdom is not as it is conventionally conceived, true virtue is even more dissimilar. The world, and in fact most religions, think of virtue as an activity of doing, working and striving. Most think of it as a self-conscious cultivation of good actions and motives directed toward the accumulation of good deeds. Even evangelicals, despite protestations that works do not save, seem to demonstrate the opposite conviction by their nervous attention to religious rules. Those convinced that nothing they could do can redeem them nevertheless often live out their lives as if their God is a distant deist deity that has left its creatures on their own to follow its commandments. "Life in the Spirit" is little more than a mantra used to remind them of their future destiny; few have any sense of its everyday reality.

Strangely, these philosophical Daoist thinkers who lived some centuries before Christ and did not seem to know a personal God can help evangelicals regain (or see for the first time) what it means for the Spirit of their God to be a living reality in a life of faith. The door that can open up that understanding is a baffling concept called *wu-wei*, which is Chinese for "not doing." In one sense it means exactly what it says, that one is not to do or act but is to wait for the Dao to act. All of our action will lead to counterproductive results and only gum up the works we are trying to set free: "Those who contrive [this roughly means 'trying by one's own ingenuity to effect a result before watching and waiting for what the situation or Nature itself will make clear is the best way'] spoil it; those who

---

[4]1 Corinthians 1:18.
[5]*Tao Te Ching*, p. 41.

cling [to their own ideas of what is best without waiting to consider other ideas and ways that may be better] lose it. Thus sages contrive nothing, and so spoil nothing. They cling to nothing, and so lose nothing. . . . Thus sages want to have no wants; they do not value goods hard to get."[6]

Those who wait for the Dao (the Daoist correlate to the Christian God) may find their initial expectations unfulfilled but better results in the long run. "Because of this sages never do great things; that is why they can fulfill their greatness."[7] They realize that those who attempt things by their own power and ideas do not "manage to finish." So they are effective without being coercive and refuse the temptation to grab power selfishly.[8] Since they have learned that the Dao has its own way and time that alone will produce the best results, they are flexible and yielding when they confront obstacles. They know that "nothing in the world is more flexible and yielding than water. Yet when it attacks the firm and the strong, none can withstand it."[9] This means not that one should always retreat before obstacles but that one should trust in the wisdom and way of the Dao to deal with an obstacle most effectively. Sometimes what seems to be an obstacle may in fact be a blessing.

The other meaning of *wu-wei* or nonaction may be easier for evangelicals to understand: not the absence of action but acting without attachment to the action itself. This is a life that is devoted not to the accumulation of virtue and merit but to union with the Dao (for Christians, Christ). It is the recognition that we should act not according to a self-conscious mode of deliberation (*What commandment should I now obey?*) but according to the spontaneous mode of living in the Spirit, which is the life of Christ Himself (*What are you doing, Jesus?*).

---

[6]Ibid., p. 64.
[7]Ibid., p. 63.
[8]Ibid., pp. 29-30.
[9]Ibid., p. 78.

Zhuang-zi describes a way of self-forgetfulness that is uncannily similar to the Pauline life in the Spirit: "The man in whom Dao acts without impediment harms no other being by his actions. Yet he does not know himself to be 'kind,' to be 'gentle.' He does not bother with his own interests and does not despise others who do. He does not struggle to make money and does not make a virtue of poverty. He goes his way without relying on others and does not pride himself on walking alone."[10] Zhuang-zi lacks the profound theological mysticism of Paul, but he captures a similar spiritual liberty. For him, as for Paul, the life of virtue is not the result of calculation but a product of spiritual union. For Zhuang-zi, the great person is not the one who has self-consciously built a storehouse of merit and virtue but the one in whom the Dao moves "without impediment." He is a "man of Dao."[11]

This is a way analogous to the "life of faith" that the New Testament describes and perhaps a way for us to reconnect to a life of faith that has gone stale. It is concentration not on "the good" but on the Dao (for Christians, Christ). It is the grace that appears when we stop acting and plotting and let God be God in our lives. Zhuang-zi creates an Asian painting of being and walking in the Spirit, a life whose goal is union not doing.

In Zhuang-zi's words, it is the cosmic humility of the person who realizes the nothingness of the self and becomes forgetful of that self as though it were "like a dry tree stump" or "dead ashes."[12] Sages "know themselves but do not see themselves."[13] In other words, they are not obsessed with themselves and their own spiritual progress but recognize their nothingness before the Dao. (The Christian analogue would be the disciples who forget self and are in

---

[10]*Chuang Tzu* 17.3, in Thomas Merton, *The Way of Chuang Tzu* (Boston: Shambhala, 1992), pp. 137-38.
[11]*Chuang Tzu* 17.3; Merton, *The Way of Chuang Tzu*, p. 26.
[12]Merton, *The Way of Chuang Tzu*, p. 31.
[13]*Tao Te Ching*, p. 72.

love with the One Who mysteriously fills them and lives through them.) They realize that virtue comes more from believing the good than from trying to produce it by self-effort. They have come to understand with Zhuang-zi that "you never find happiness until you stop looking for it."[14] He found that when he stopped trying to be happy, suddenly "right" and "wrong" became apparent with no effort. Happiness also came, but only as a byproduct of union with the Dao. People of Spirit therefore are unconcerned with whether people like or dislike them, respect them or not. "For where there are many men, there are also many opinions and little agreement. There is nothing to be gained from the support of a lot of nitwits who are doomed to end up in a fight with each other." Hence they "imitate the fish that swims unconcerned, surrounded by a friendly element, and minding its own business."[15]

Lao-zi and Zhuang-zi explained that the self-forgetfulness that results from union with the Dao frees us from the terrible demands of the ego. If we allow the Spirit to live through us, we do not have to obey the ego's urgings to be first and to be recognized. The result, the Chinese sages promised, is a kind of fulfillment never possible when the selfish ego is in charge: Heaven and earth are everlasting because they "do not foster themselves; that is why they can live forever. For this reason sages put themselves last, and they were first; they excluded themselves, and they survived. Was it not by their very selflessness that they managed to fulfill themselves?"[16]

The result of ignoring the ego's demands and yielding to the Dao is the very irony Jesus pointed to when he said that disciples will find themselves only if they lose themselves: "Not asserting themselves, [sages] are therefore outstanding. Not congratulating themselves, they are therefore meritorious. Not taking pride in themselves, they last long. It is just because they do not contend

---

[14]*Chuang Tzu* 18.1.
[15]Ibid., 24.12.
[16]*Tao Te Ching*, p. 7.

that no one in the world can contend with them."[17] Rather than stubbornly insist on their prerogatives and plans, they yield to the exigencies of the moment. Because of their flexibility, they flourish over the long haul. "When people are born they are supple, and when they die they are stiff. . . . Stiffness is thus a companion of death, flexibility a companion of life. . . . So the stiff and strong are below, the supple and yielding on top."[18]

Sages can flex in tough times because they see the divine in and behind all that crosses their paths. Lao-zi and Zhuang-zi gave little hint of believing that the divine was anything more than an impersonal fate, yet they insisted that its workings are good—if not for an individual at least for the community of being. Resignation therefore to what is and cannot be changed is a way to throw oneself into the abyss of goodness and to rest contented that all will be well.

> If we are delighted even to be in a human form alone, insofar as the human form changes in myriad ways, without ever an end, the enjoyment therein must be incalculable. Therefore sages will roam where nothing can get away and everything is there. For them, youth is good and so is old age; for them, the beginning is good and so is the end.[19]

But while the vast majority of the Lao-zi and Zhuang-zi texts speak of an abstract Dao, there are hints in Zhuang-zi that all that exists is good because there is a beneficent Being ordering what is. He tells a story of Tzu Lai, a man on the brink of death who explains to his family, "What makes my life good is also what makes my death good. . . . Now if you consider the universe as a great forge and the creator as a great smith, what could happen that would not be all right? I go to sleep relaxed and perk up when I wake."[20]

As evangelicals we would not want to adopt philosophical Daoist

---

[17]Ibid., p. 22.
[18]Ibid., p. 76.
[19]*Chuang Tzu*, "Inner Chapters," chap. 6, in *The Essential Tao*, trans. Thomas Cleary (San Francisco: HarperSanFrancisco, 1993), p. 110.
[20]Ibid.

cosmology or theology. We know because of Jesus Christ that Ultimate Reality is personal and that therefore providence comes from a
loving heart and not from cold fate. Yet if Daoist thinkers could find
contentment by trusting in the workings of an unfeeling Dao, how
much should we be able to trust in a God Who has shown His care
by suffering for us? Jesus said that we can learn from pagans who
trusted in a God they knew imperfectly; so we may also be able to
learn something about trusting God's sovereignty from Daoists who
trust in the ultimately beneficent workings of the cosmos.

God's Paradoxical Ways

If philosophical Daoists can show us something about what Jesus
and Paul meant by mystical union, they can also help us understand
the biblical paradox that God produces strength through human
weakness. We know from Scripture that God wanted Gideon to
become weakened before He would use him and that God refused
to heal Paul of his thorn in the flesh because it was only through
weakness that Paul could experience Christ's power.[21] But most of
us are a long way from comprehending what all this means, or from
realizing its reality in our lives. Lao-zi may help us begin to
approach this mystery. If he did not understand precisely what Paul
meant (and he certainly had no explicit knowledge of the Jesus
Christ who revealed this to Paul), he at least was familiar with the
paradoxical pattern that puzzled Paul. He was intrigued by the way
in which weakness and lack of assertion lead to strength and domi-
nance.

By a "mysterious power," he observed, there is a "producing without possessing, doing without presuming, growing without domi-
neering."[22] In spite of apparent inaction, action is produced:

The Way is always uncontrived, yet there's nothing it doesn't do. . . . By not

---

[21]Judges 7; 2 Corinthians 12:5-10.
[22]*Tao Te Ching*, p. 10.

wanting, there is calm, and the world will straighten itself. . . . Higher virtue is uncontrived, and there is no way to contrive it. . . . Nobility is rooted in humility, loftiness is based on lowliness. That is why noble people refer to themselves as alone, lacking and unworthy.[23]

Paradoxically, where there is nothing there is value: "When the potter's wheel makes a pot, the use of the pot is precisely where there is nothing. When you open doors and windows for a room, it is where there is nothing that they are useful to a room."[24]

Therefore the way to rise higher is to take the low, humble approach: "The reason why rivers and seas can be lords of the hundred valleys is that they lower themselves to them well. . . . So when sages wish to rise above people, they lower themselves in their speech. When they want to precede people, they go after them in status. . . .Because they do not contend, no one in the world can contend with them."[25]

The paradox works the other way, too. Not only does strength grow out of weakness and honor from humility, but weakness results from arrogant strength: "Should you want to weaken something, you must deliberately let it grow strong. Should you want to eliminate something, you must deliberately allow it to flourish." Apparently Lao-zi had observed a nearly invariable rule that "those who assert themselves are not illustrious; those who glorify themselves have no merit, those who are proud of themselves do not last."[26] Lao-zi concluded in words similar to Paul's: "Weakness overcomes strength."[27]

By their plain but vivid images, Lao-zi and Zhuang-zi help us see the presence of this paradoxical way in which the world works under God's providence: strength is nurtured by and arises from

---

[23]Ibid., p. 37.
[24]Ibid., p. 11.
[25]Ibid., p. 66.
[26]Ibid., pp. 24, 35.
[27]Cited in Lin Yutang, *From Pagan to Christian*, p. 125.

weakness; something great is made by things considered less than nothing. But if Chinese wisdom shows us the prevalence and reality of this pattern, only Jewish and Christian wisdom explains to us *why* the world works like this. With characteristic profundity Paul says,

> God chose what is foolish in the world to shame the wise; God chose what is weak in the world to shame the strong; God chose what is low and despised in the world, things that are not, to reduce to nothing things that are, *so that no one might boast in the presence of God.*[28]

According to Paul, things work paradoxically not because of an impersonal law such as karma or an abstract order called Dao but because of a personal God Who wants to humble the arrogant and show all creatures their absolute dependence on Him. Jonathan Edwards added that God often permits calamity to come to His saints when in their greatest glory and prosperity so that they might not trust in things of this world—even spiritual success. Great calamity struck the Old Testament church at its apex of glory in the reigns of David and Solomon: David's adultery and murder, the rape and treachery committed by David's sons Amnon and Absalom, and then Solomon's idolatry and the division of the kingdom. Similarly, after the early church's triumph under Constantine, the Arian heresy arose and worldliness grew in the church. According to Edwards, God permits this pattern in order "to stain the pride of all glory (Is 23:9) and that his people may not lift themselves up against him, that he alone may be exalted."[29]

> Tis often God's manner to bring some grievous calamity on his saints, especially when they have received the greatest lights and joys, and have been most exalted with smiles of heaven upon them, as Jacob was made lame when admitted to so extraordinary a privilege as wrestling with God, and overcoming him, and so obtaining the blessing. . . . Sometimes extraordinary

---

[28]1 Corinthians 1:27-29 (emphasis added).
[29]Jonathan Edwards, *Notes on Scripture* (New Haven, Conn.: Yale University Press, 1998), p. 292.

light and comfort is given to fit for great calamities, and sometimes for death, which God brings soon after such things. So when God gives his own people great temporal prosperity, he is wont to bring with it some calamity to [e]clipse it, to keep them [from] being exalted in their prosperity and trusting in it.[30]

Paul experienced the reality of this paradox when he was afflicted with what was probably a physical illness in Galatia fourteen years before he wrote his second letter to Corinth. He says it brought him contempt and scorn—enough so that he prayed three times for it to be removed. After the third time, Christ spoke to him, "My grace is sufficient for you, for power is made perfect in weakness." In other words, Christ Jesus did not want Paul to be (physically) healed, because the Lord had a greater, spiritual healing in store for him, one in which Paul would experience the power of Christ: "So, I will boast all the more gladly of my weaknesses, so that the power of Christ may dwell in me" (2 Cor 12:9).

Curiously, God did not even want to remove what Paul said was a "messenger of Satan" (2 Cor 12:7). How about that for a paradox! God *wanted* Paul to have and keep something from Satan (!) for His own inscrutable purposes. As in the story of Job, God apparently uses the devil's works to fulfill God's larger purposes. God uses evil to fashion good. Thus Paul could say, "Therefore I am content with weaknesses, insults, hardships, persecutions, and calamaties for the sake of Christ; for whenever I am weak, then I am strong" (2 Cor 12:10).

More to the point for this discussion, however, God wanted Paul to remain weak because (apparently) only in weakness could Paul experience Christ's grace and power. This is the paradox that the Daoists knew and Paul illustrated. It is especially meaningful for me. Since I was a boy I have been afflicted with a stutter that has brought me much frustration, anger and shame. For years I prayed for relief,

---

[30]Ibid.

had demons cast out of me and received words of faith that I was healed. I received significant help about ten years ago from the best stuttering clinic in the world, but I still struggle. I still feel weak and powerless from time to time. Daoist writings resonate with me in part because of their recognition that fullness lies somehow within emptiness and strength somehow emerges from weakness. I have experienced that dynamic so many times that I have lost count. Paul's writings have helped me immeasurably by showing me *why* God might have allowed me to continue to suffer, and for that reason they have proved far more valuable than Lao-zi and Zhuang-zi. But the latter thinkers have deepened my conviction about the reality of this divine dynamic and have helped me to see that this is a principle of the cosmos that applies far beyond the walls of the visible body of Christ. They have also helped me to see that this principle applies to far more in my life than my speech problem. My stuttering is a type, if you will, of the human condition; just as I often feel helpless and realize that only the continuous exertion of divine power and grace can enable me to speak, so are we all helpless in every other part of our lives. If we think we can breathe and act on our own, we are as blind to reality as when I speak fluently and suddenly think I am cured. At those points we may benefit from listening to early Chinese wisdom.

8

THE CONFUCIAN
COMMITMENT
|TO VIRTUE|

CONFUCIUS (KONG FU-ZI; 551-479 B.C.) HAS GOTTEN A BAD RAP
from conservative Christians since the beginning of the nineteenth
century. After the European Enlightenment and even Jonathan Edwards lionized him in the eighteenth century, evangelicals turned
against the Chinese sage, dismissing him as an unbeliever who had a
hopelessly optimistic view of human nature.[1]

As in most religious polemic, there was a grain of truth in their
charges. Confucius was far more interested in human morality than
in theology, and the tradition associated with his name developed an
anthropology based on the essential goodness of human nature.

---

[1]See Gerald McDermott, *Jonathan Edwards Confronts the Gods* (New York: Oxford University Press, 2000), chap. 12. For good introductions to the Confucian tradition, see Ch'u
Chai and Winberg Chai, *Confucianism* (Woodbury, N.Y.: Barron's Educational Series,
1973); Fung Yu-Lan, *A Short History of Chinese Philosophy*, ed. Derk Bodde (New York:
Free Press, 1948). For the story of the first meeting between Christianity and Confucianism, see John D. Young, *Confucianism and Christianity: The First Encounter* (Hong Kong:
Hong Kong University Press, 1983).

However, Confucius himself was convinced of the reality of the divine world, and his *Analects* contain a far more ambiguous conception of humanity than these allegations suggest. For Master Kong, as the Chinese called him (Confucius is the Latin rendering devised by early Jesuit missionaries), Heaven was the author of his virtue and object of his prayers.[2] He felt understood by Heaven alone and regarded the success of his cultural efforts as dependent on Heaven's sovereign ordering.[3] He stood in awe of Heaven's decrees and considered the movements of nature to be under its control.[4] While Confucius treated Heaven as something of a personal god, for Mencius (Meng-zi; 371-289 B.C.), the next-greatest teacher in the Confucian tradition, Heaven was more immanent and impersonal.[5] But even Mencius said that Heaven reveals itself through acts and deeds, decreeing things to happen in the absence of human agency.[6]

The Confucian tradition has been known for its sanguine estimate of human nature; indeed, Mencius was responsible for a continuing strain in Chinese thought that emphasizes the essential goodness of humanity.[7] But at the same time the Confucian tradition has distinguished between human potentiality and actuality: while humanity's essential nature may be good, its track record is stained disproportionately with evil. Confucius himself is reported to have said that he had never met a man who had seen his own errors and taken himself to task.[8] Nor had he met a man who was as fond of

---

[2]Confucius, *The Analects*, trans. and ed. D. C. Lau (Hammondsworth: Penguin, 1979), 7.23; 3.13; 7.35.

[3]Ibid., 14.35; 9.5.

[4]Ibid., 16.8; 10.25.

[5]Julia Ching, in Julia Ching and Hans Küng, *Christianity and Chinese Religions* (New York: Doubleday, 1989), p. 72. For an intriguing comparison between Mencius and Aquinas on virtue and courage, see Lee H. Yearley, *Mencius and Aquinas: Theories of Virtue and Conceptions of Courage* (Albany, N.Y.: SUNY Press, 1990).

[6]*Mencius*, trans. and ed. D. C. Lau (Hammondsworth: Penguin, 1970), V A.5; V A.6.

[7]Chai and Chai, *Confucianism*, p. 51.

[8]*Analects* 5.27.

virtue *(de)* as he was of beauty in women, or anyone who was eager to learn, or any person who practiced what was right.[9] Even Mencius, who is known for his doctrine of the essential goodness of human nature, said that the Way *(Dao)* is like a wide road that is not at all difficult to find. But the trouble with people is that they do not look for it.[10]

On closer inspection, the Confucian doctrine of human nature emphasizes potential rather than actual goodness. It affirms that human beings are born with four "germs" of virtue—benevolence, a sense of duty, an inclination to show respect and the ability to distinguish right from wrong.[11] But according to Mencius, this means only that a person is *capable* of *becoming* good and that when people become bad it is not because of their native endowment.[12] The Christian is reminded by these words of James's admonition that when we sin we should blame not God or original nature but our own desire (Jas 1:13-16). Neo-Confucians spoke of two sides to human nature—a heavenly essential nature that is good and a physical or existential nature than can be either good or bad.[13] At no time did the Confucian tradition approach the Christian notion of an essential fallen nature or the pervasive influence of sin in all human action and being, but the Confucian emphasis on potential goodness that is never fully actualized comes close to the Christian idea of the image of God in humans that has been marred by sin. For both traditions, human nature is neither essentially good nor totally bad. So while they differ on their estimates of the nature of the human, the differences are not as sharp as many Christians have believed.

---

[9]Ibid., 9.18; 11.7; 16.11.
[10]*Mencius* VI B.2.
[11]Ibid., II A.6.
[12]Ibid.
[13]Ching and Küng, *Christianity and Chinese Religions,* p. 116.

China's Categorical Imperative

Confucius and his tradition are of far more importance for evangelicals, however, than the similarity of their teachings to certain Christian beliefs. Of much greater significance is its single-minded devotion to virtue. Confucius and Mencius taught commitment to truth and right so radical that it would embarrass many evangelicals by comparison.[14] The Chinese sages found joy in following the Way even when it spelled poverty, suffering and death. Virtue was to be pursued for its intrinsic worth, not for any external reward. In a day when American evangelicalism is inebriated on the wines of materialism and success, these Chinese teachers offer a (pagan) detox program. They can help us recover a Christian (indeed, evangelical!) tradition that has long since been lost to American Christian consciousness—the Edwardsean tradition of disinterested benevolence.

In Edwards's theological masterpiece *The Religious Affections,* his second reliable ("positive") sign of true religion is attraction to God and God's ways for their own sake ("the first objective ground of gracious affections is the transcendently excellent and amiable nature of divine things, as they are in themselves; and not any conceived relation they bear to self, or self-interest").[15] In other words, true spirituality is not rooted in self-interest. Natural love, or love of this world, is based on what returns I will get for my love. But Jesus, Edwards pointed out, suggested that supernaturally inspired love is oblivious to its returns: "If you love those who love you, what credit is that to you? For even sinners love those who love them" (Lk 6:32). When Satan suggested to God that Job was good

---

[14]Of course to some extent I am here comparing apples and oranges; Christian teachers have also taught single-minded devotion to duty, and some Confucianists might say the typical Confucianist is just as compromised as the typical evangelical. They might also concede that just as much Christian passion devolves over time into formalism, so too some Confucian dedication to virtue has become formalistic propriety.

[15]Jonathan Edwards, *The Religious Affections* (New Haven, Conn.: Yale University Press, 1959), p. 240.

only because God had bribed him with riches and the comforts of family life, God took up Satan's challenge. He agreed to let Satan take away all that Job had, in the hope of proving that Job's faith was *not* based simply on self-interest. Notice the intriguing implication—God conceded Satan's assumption that spirituality based only on self-interest is worthless.

Edwards said that the primary reason saints love God is not the benefits that will accrue but the shining magnificence, beauty and glories of God as He is in Himself. They are attracted to God's Son, God's works and God's ways, particularly the beauty of God's plan for the salvation of sinful human beings. Benefits come to saints from God, but only after and as a fruit of their first being drawn to God by a vision and taste of God and His ways as they are in and of themselves.[16] Immanuel Kant's categorical imperative is similar: the inner principle of human morality is the unconditional rule that we should act only on the maxim that we can will as a universal law. We are not to ask about consequences either for ourselves or others; we are only to determine to obey this duty. Thus Kantian ethics is called nonconsequentialism.

Now there are significant differences between Edwards and Kant. Kant believed that attention to rewards would undermine ethical seriousness, while Edwards saw nothing wrong with consideration of one's heavenly rewards during the process of sanctification as long as one's relationship to God is based primarily on the beauty of the Godhead. But both agreed with the Confucian tradition that we should do good not so much because of benefits we will thereby receive but because the Good has prior claims on us. Implicit in the writings of Confucius and Mencius is the notion that we will receive inner satisfaction from following the Way even when following means suffering but that principal attention to any

---

[16]See Gerald R. McDermott, *Seeing God: Twelve Reliable Signs of True Spirituality* (Downers Grove, Ill.: InterVarsity Press, 1995), chap. 8.

rewards besides that inner satisfaction will corrupt our following. This is akin to the corruption of religion that, in C. S. Lewis's words, takes place when we pursue not God but the thrill that God brings. It "is the first and deadly error, which appears on every level of life and is equally deadly on all, turning religion into a self-caressing luxury and love into auto-eroticism."[17]

The first months or perhaps year of Lewis's Christian experience were without any belief in a future life. It would strike many evangelicals as strange that Lewis considered it one of "my greatest mercies" to attempt obedience "without even raising that question."[18]

> My training was like that of the Jews, to whom He revealed Himself centuries before there was a whisper of anything better (or worse) beyond the grave than shadowy and featureless *Sheol*. . . . I had been brought up to believe that goodness was goodness only if it were disinterested, and that any hope of reward or fear of punishment contaminated the will. If I was wrong in this (the question is really much more complicated than I then perceived) my error was most tenderly allowed for. I was afraid that threats or promises would demoralise me; no threats or promises were made. The commands were inexorable, but they were backed by no "sanctions." God was to be obeyed simply because he was God. Long since, through the gods of Asgard, and later through the notion of the Absolute, He had taught me how a thing can be revered not for what it can do to us but for what it is in itself. That is why, though it was a terror, it was no surprise to learn that God is to be obeyed because of what He is in Himself. If you ask why we should obey God, in the last resort the answer is, "I am." To know God is to know that our obedience is due to Him. In His nature His sovereignty *de jure* is revealed.[19]

Lewis went on to say that to think of heaven and hell as anything other than the presence or absence of God (in other words, as reward or punishment for certain kinds of life on earth) is to corrupt

---

[17]C. S. Lewis, *Surprised by Joy: The Shape of My Early Life* (London: Geoffrey Bles, 1955), p. 160.
[18]Ibid., p. 217.
[19]Ibid., p. 218.

the doctrine of both "and corrupts us while we so think of them."[20]

So while neither Edwards nor Lewis discounts entirely the notion of rewards as motivation for the ethical life, both dismiss it as corrupting if it is the principal framework on which the ethical life is constructed. Confucius and Mencius provide us with vivid illustrations of that principle. They were dedicated to the life that looks neither to right nor left but only straight ahead to the Way. It is happy with eating coarse rice and drinking only water if that is all that is provided by following the Way, for it is concerned not with profit but with what is right.[21] It seeks neither a full belly nor a comfortable home but is worried about the Way rather than poverty.[22] Sages cannot be led into excesses when wealthy and honored, or deflected from their purposes when poor and obscure.[23] Nor can they be made to compromise principle before superior force.[24] Hence the virtuous never abandon righteousness (yi) in adversity and do not depart from the Way in success.[25] They refuse to remain in wealth or a prestigious position if either was gained in a wrong manner.[26] Even for one basketful of rice they would not bend.[27] If it had been necessary to perpetrate one wrong deed or kill one innocent person in order to gain the empire, no virtuous person would consent to doing either.[28] True virtue (de) is unconcerned with what others think and recognizes that it is better to be disliked by bad people than to be liked by all.[29] It is ready to give up even life itself if that is necessary to follow the way of benevolence.[30]

---

[20]Ibid., p. 219.
[21]Analects 7.16; 14.12; 16.10; 19.1; 4.11.
[22]Ibid., 1.14; 15.32.
[23]Mencius III B.2.
[24]Ibid.
[25]Ibid., VII B.9.
[26]Analects 4.5.
[27]Mencius III B.4.
[28]Ibid., II A.2.
[29]Analects 12.6; 13.24.
[30]Ibid., 19.1

Confucius resigned the most prestigious position of his life because he felt that his lord's acceptance of a gift of dancing girls had compromised his integrity.[31] When he was offered another position in the state of Chen and found that the official who invited him was in rebellion against his chief, Confucius refused to become a party to the intrigue.[32] When he was traveling in southern China and his disciples realized that their master would never again have an opportunity to put his principles into practice (as a minister of state), they wanted to know how he felt. They asked him about two ancient sages who under bad kings had died of starvation. Confucius replied that they were true men—something he rarely said of anyone past or present. So a disciple asked him again, "Do you think they had any regrets?" Master K'ung responded firmly, "Why, they wanted *ren* [benevolence], and they achieved it. Why should they regret it?"[33]

Mencius told similar stories exemplifying single-minded devotion to the Good. The sage Liu Hsia Hui was one of his favorites. According to Mencius, when Liu was passed over for a position or his virtues went unnoticed, Liu harbored no grudges. Nor was he distressed in difficult circumstances, for he was content to find his happiness in following the Way of the Good.[34] Mencius said that he would not have compromised his integrity "for the sake of three ducal offices."[35]

While we moderns might find this ideal both daunting and a tad depressing, Confucius and Mencius found it a source of joy. In the *Analects*, Confucius often remarks on the joy he finds in *ren* and *yi* even when deprived of what we would now call necessities of life. One can have joy, he said, living on a bowlful of rice and a ladleful

---

[31]Ibid., 18.4.
[32]Huston Smith, *The World's Religions: Our Great Wisdom Traditions* (San Francisco: HarperSanFrancisco, 1991), p. 156.
[33]Yutang, *From Pagan to Christian*, p. 80.
[34]*Mencius* V B.1.
[35]Ibid., VII A.28.

of water in a run-down hut.[36] "In the eating of coarse rice and the drinking of water, the using of one's elbow for a pillow, joy is to be found. Wealth and rank attained through immoral means have as much to do with me as passing clouds."[37] He was described by his disciples as one who neglected his meals in a spell of work, forgot his worries when overcome by joy, and was so absorbed in the joy of the Dao that he was unaware that old age was coming on.[38] Mencius remarked that he had no greater joy than to find on self-examination that he was true to himself. A man, he said, delights in three things: that his parents are alive and his brothers well, that he is not ashamed to face Heaven or men, and that he has the most talented pupils.[39]

Zhong and Shu

If Confucianists follow the Dao for the sheer joy of it, where will the Dao take them? To *ren*, they say, which is roughly translated "benevolence or humanity" (as a quality of action). *Ren* is an effort to return to *li*, which can be rendered "ritual, custom, propriety or manners."[40] We need to return because we typically ignore the call of conscience to act with consideration of duty to others. Alan Miller has remarked that Confucius's achievement was to reinterpret *li*, which had been narrowly defined as customs at religious rituals, as an all-encompassing style of life.[41] Master Kong defined *li* as loyalty to one's heart and conscience (*zhong*) and reciprocity (*shu*). This last quality, which he said was the "single word which can be a guide to conduct throughout one's life,"[42] has been called the Negative

---

[36]*Analects* 6.11.
[37]Ibid., 7.16.
[38]Yutang, *From Pagan to Christian*, p. 70.
[39]*Mencius* VII A.4; VII A.20.
[40]Alan Miller, in Alan Miller et al., *Religions of the World* (New York: St. Martin's, 1988), p. 273.
[41]Ibid.
[42]*Analects* 15.24.

Golden Rule: do not do to others what you do not want done to yourself. Mencius put it positively: "Try your best to treat others as you would wish to be treated yourself, and you will find that this is the shortest way to benevolence."[43]

Shu leads to thinking of others, and *zhong* to knowledge of self, which will bring humility. For *zhong's* loyalty to the heart will, if rigorously applied, show the self how far it is from following the heart and conscience. Confucius never claimed to be a paragon of virtue. In fact he claimed the opposite. He had failed to cultivate virtue, he said, and refused to claim *ren* for himself.[44] He confessed that he had not practiced what he preached and exclaimed at one point, "How dare I claim to be a sage or benevolent man?"[45] In another *Analects* entry he lamented his moral inability in terms reminiscent of Paul's cry of desperation in Romans 7: "It is these things that cause me concern: failure to cultivate virtue, failure to go more deeply into what I have learned, inability, when I am told what is right, to move to where it is, and inability to reform myself when I have defects."[46]

Therefore, he advised, those pursuing *ren* should be modest and self-effacing, particularly when society is immoral.[47] They should admit their mistakes and not be afraid of mending their ways. Nor should they hide the fact that they do not know something.[48] They should constantly examine themselves for faults and opportunities to improve.[49] When others fail to appreciate them, they should worry less about what others think and more about their own moral defects:[50] "It is not the failure of others to appreciate your abilities

---

[43]*Mencius* VII A.4.
[44]*Analects* 7.3; 7.32.
[45]Ibid., 7.33; 7.34.
[46]Ibid., 7.3.
[47]Ibid., 12.20; 14.3; 15.18.
[48]*Analects* 1.8; 2.17; 9.25; 15.39; *Mencius* VI B.15.
[49]*Analects* 15.16; 15.21.
[50]Ibid., 4.14.

that should trouble you but your own lack of them."[51] The small person seeks things from others, but the superior person realizes that the most enduring prize comes from one's own character.[52] More than a century after Confucius, Mencius summed up this teaching:

> If others do not respond to your love with love, look into your own benevolence; if others do not return your courtesy, look into your own respect. In other words, look into yourself whenever you fail to achieve your purpose. When you are correct in your person, the Empire will turn to you.[53]

Because Confucian disciples realize their own moral poverty, they are teachable. They are not ashamed to seek advice of those below them in rank.[54] Confucius said that he learned from every other person: the good points he copied and the bad he tried to correct in himself.[55] He repeatedly advised his pupils to be "eager to learn," which meant constantly examining themselves and studying the ways of the Dao.[56] He said he could not help those who were not willing to engage in constant self-examination.[57]

True disciples will be in awe of the decrees of Heaven, great men and the words of the sages.[58] They will seek to gain knowledge of these by study.[59] To love benevolence without loving learning, Confucius admonished, is liable to lead to foolishness.[60] Mencius suggested that learning enables one to go after the "strayed heart" that has wandered from its moral roots.[61] Studying the works of Heaven and the words of the sages will cultivate the four germs originally

---

[51]Ibid., 14.30; 15.19.
[52]Ibid., 15.21.
[53]*Mencius* IV A.4.
[54]*Analects* 5.15.
[55]Ibid., 7.22.
[56]Ibid., 5.28; 11.7; 15.16; 15.21.
[57]Ibid., 15.16.
[58]Ibid., 16.8.
[59]Ibid., 16.9.
[60]Ibid., 17.8.
[61]*Mencius* VI A.11.

planted in the heart—benevolence, a sense of duty, an inclination to show respect and the ability to distinguish right from wrong.[62]

Final Remarks

These last words remind the Christian reader of important differences between Confucianism and the Christian faith. Confucius and Mencius believed that there is an original moral sensibility imparted to each person by Heaven. This may be analogous to Paul's divine law "written on their hearts" (Rom 2:14-15). But while they (especially Confucius) acknowledge their own failure to live by this moral sense, they have at best an undeveloped sense of the holiness of Heaven and assume a human ability to perfect the self. They listen to the ancients rather than divine revelation, tend toward misogyny[63] and lay the foundations for a rigid hierarchicalism that can stifle freedom and love. As Hans Küng has observed, Jesus went beyond the Confucian restrictions of love to family and nation; the Palestinian sage wanted to overcome flesh and blood—and gender, for that matter—distinctions.[64] Jeffrey Wattles remarks that Confucians see others as family not from their idea of Heaven but from "golden rule comparing, extending to others the consideration that the agent had for his or her own family."[65] Jesus, on the other hand, gave a theological rationale for love of others: they should be loved because they too are children of our common heavenly Father. While Confucius taught that enemies are to receive not love but correction, Jesus told his disciples they were to love their enemies because this is how God treats His enemies.[66]

With all its differences, though, I find the Confucian tradition a bracing reminder of what it means to follow the truth wherever it

---

[62]Ibid., II A.6.
[63]Analects 17.25.
[64]Küng and Ching, Christianity and Chinese Religions, p. 118; John 4:27; Matthew 12:50.
[65]Jeffrey Wattles, The Golden Rule (New York: Oxford University Press, 1996), p. 26.
[66]Analects 14.34; Matthew 4:43-45.

might lead. It gives me insight into what it would mean to be a radical disciple of Jesus. I learn from Confucius that it may mean going without some of the amenities of life I have learned to enjoy. It will mean being misunderstood and perhaps rejected by others. It means saying no to privileges and perquisites that require me to compromise my conscience.

I knew these things intellectually before I confronted Confucius and Mencius, but the Chinese sages have given them new meaning and shape. I realize with their help that the rigors of discipleship that I have partially rationalized away still await me, waiting to be experienced—and enjoyed. Confucius and Mencius are testimony from the east Asian continent that true joy comes from wholehearted commitment to the Good and the Beautiful—and, I would add, the Holy. That commitment will probably involve pain, and we Western evangelicals, in danger of losing our saltiness amidst a rushing cultural torrent of individualism and self-gratification, need to be reminded of this.

9

MUHAMMAD
& THE
⌐SIGNS OF GOD⌐

LIKE MOST AMERICANS, EVANGELICALS TEND TO FORM THEIR VIEW OF Islam on the basis of media reports of the worst excesses of the most militant Muslims. This view is largely false because it is monumentally incomplete, just as Muslim views of Christianity that are based chiefly on the Crusades and Northern Ireland are distorted.[1]

Westerners in general often have a negative view of Islam because of publicly expressed Muslim denunciations of Western culture. While some of the most volatile expressions of disdain ("America is

---

[1]I should add, however, that although most Muslims condemn the terrorism used by their militant coreligionists, there is a historical link between Islam and aggressive military and political action. Muhammad was a military and political—as well as religious—leader: he served as both prophet and commander, preacher and soldier, Imam (religious leader) and magistrate. The first community of Muslims was a socio-politico-religious amalgamation, and traditional Islam has taught that government should enforce Islamic law; this is why Islam has usually shown greater organic unity between this- and other-worldly

the Great Satan," for example)[2] speak for only a small minority of Muslims, many Muslims nevertheless regard the West with ambivalence. They appreciate and use its technology but consider Western culture to be a threat to their own culture because it represents modernization without moral control. Muslims place great emphasis on the integrity of the nuclear family and pride themselves on the stability of their families. They see our Western values of atomistic individualism and sexual permissiveness as destructive of family life. They are fully aware of America's soaring rates of divorce, abortion, pornography, crime and chemical addiction, and wonder why Americans regard Muslim culture with self-righteous disdain.

Muslims also tend to view the West, particularly the United States, as irreligious and godless because of the practice of separation of church and state. If God is sovereign over the cosmos, Muslims argue, then every aspect of life—including the state—ought to come under the rule of his laws. Islamic law *(Shari'ah)* should therefore serve as a set of fundamental principles informing the laws of every nation on earth.

More militant Muslims feel the West is out to destroy Islam. As a

---

concerns than Christianity exhibits. The Qur'an contains passages dating from the years of warfare between Muhammad and his Meccan opponents (e.g., Qur'an 9.12-13, 29) that exhort his followers to fight those who do not accept Islam. Muslim leaders ever since have exploited these passages (as well as the Islamic teaching that warriors who die in a holy war will go straight to Paradise and skip over years of suffering in a purgatory-like existence; c.f., e.g., Qur'an 3.195) when they have tried to muster a people for war. With some notable exceptions, however, most Muslims have placed more emphasis on other Qur'anic texts that maintain there is "no compulsion in religion" (Qur'an 2.256). For more on the history of Islam and conversion, see Norman Daniel, *Islam and the West* (Edinburgh: Edinburgh University Press, 1960); Byron Porter Smith, *Islam in English Literature* (Beirut: American Press, 1939); Fred McGraw Donner, *The Early Islamic Conquests* (Princeton, N.J.: Princeton University Press, 1981); M. A. Shaban, *Islamic History A.D. 600-750 (A.H. 132): A New Interpretation* (Cambridge: Cambridge University Press, 1971); Albert Hourani, *A History of the Arab Peoples* (Cambridge, Mass.: Belknap, 1991); and the more critical work by Bat Ye'or, *The Decline of Eastern Christianity Under Islam: From Jihad to Dhimmitude* (Madison, N.J.: Fairleigh Dickinson University Press, 1997).

[2]This statement was made by the Ayatollah Khomeini during the Iranian revolution of 1978-1979.

Western-educated Muslim engineer once asked me (before the recent developments in Pakistan), "Why does the United States permit India, Israel and South Africa to have nuclear weapons but not Iraq or Pakistan?" Many Muslims believe there is a Zionist-American conspiracy to reduce the Muslim nations to their former colonial status under Western control. They see Israel as America's client state and believe that the American government is controlled by Jewish lobbies.[3]

Some Surprises

Paranoia on the Muslim side is often matched by a similar paranoia among Westerners, including evangelicals. If they were to do a close study of Islam, however, most evangelicals would be surprised by what they would learn. Not only would they discover that most Muslims are as uninterested in geopolitics as most evangelicals are, but they would also learn—to the astonishment of some—that Islam, the youngest of the world's great religions, is already the second largest. According to David Barrett, 1.9 billion people in the world now call themselves disciples of Jesus, while slightly more than one billion say there is no God but Allah and Muhammad is his prophet.[4]

Islam is also the fastest growing of the major world religions. Several factors account for this—Muslims are aggressive in their evangelism, their message is simple, and they offer the politically alienated the prospect of national transformation. In America Islam

---

[3]For introductions to Islam and its views of the West, see John L. Esposito, *Islam: The Straight Path*, 3rd ed. (New York: Oxford University Press, 1998); Frederick M. Denny, *Islam and the Muslim Community* (New York: Harper and Row, 1987); Frederick M. Denny, *An Introduction to Islam* (New York: Macmillan, 1985); Jacques Jomier, *How to Understand Islam* (London: SCM Press, 1989); Mohammed Arkoun, *Rethinking Islam: Common Questions, Uncommon Answers*, ed. and trans. Robert D. Lee (Boulder, Colo.: Westview, 1994); Yvonne Haddad, *The Muslims of America* (New York: Oxford University Press, 1993).

[4]David B. Barrett and Todd M. Johnson, World Evangelization Research Center, Richmond, Virginia, telephone interview by author, 1998. These and other figures from Barrett and Johnson are for the year 2000.

particularly appeals to African Americans (a third of American Muslims are black) by portraying black Christian churches as promoters of an irrelevant, pie-in-the-sky white man's gospel. But the most significant factor in the rapid growth of Islam is birthrate. While a woman in developed countries typically bears 1.6 children during her lifetime, the average woman in the largest Muslim countries gives birth to 5.0.[5]

Many evangelicals will also be surprised to discover that most Muslims do not live in the Middle East. Eighty-one percent of this planet's Muslims live outside the Arab world, in Asia and Africa.[6] The former Soviet Union contains more than 58 million Muslims, while the Muslim population in China is estimated at 19 million. The largest Muslim populations in the world are found in south Asia (116 million in Indonesia, 150 million in Pakistan and 121 million in India). Sub-Saharan Africa is home to more than 150 million readers of the Qur'an.[7]

Most surprising to evangelicals, however, will be the extraordinary respect that Muslims hold for Jesus. He was the greatest of all the prophets, they say, until Muhammad. The Qur'an even recognizes Jesus as "Messiah," "word from God," "a Spirit from God" and the son of Mary who was "strengthened with the Holy Spirit."[8] It teaches the virgin birth (Mary is said by Muslims to have been the purest woman in all creation)[9] and accepts the historicity of all the

---

[5]*World Population Prospects 1996* (New York: United Nations, 1997), pp. 120-29.
[6]Strictly speaking, however, the Middle East is not the same as the Arab world. Iran and Turkey, for example, are part of the Middle East but are not Arab.
[7]Barrett and Johnson, World Evangelization Research Center.
[8]Qur'an 3.45; 4.171; 5.75; 2.87 (KF). For this chapter I used three different translations of the Qur'an: *The Holy Qur'an: English Translation of the Meaning and Commentary,* ed. The Presidency of Islamic Researches, IFTA (King Fahd Holy Qur'an Printing Complex, n.d.[hereafter referred to as KF]); Kenneth Cragg, *Readings in the Qur'an* (London: Collins, 1988); and Thomas Cleary, *The Essential Koran: The Heart of Islam* (San Francisco: HarperSanFrancisco, 1993). Translations are from Cleary unless designated "Cragg" or "KF" (King Fahd).
[9]Qur'an 3.42 (KF); 3.47 (KF).

gospel miracles but one—Jesus' resurrection.

Furthermore, Muslims regard the Old and New Testaments as the Word of God—with the qualification that Jews and Christians have corrupted the texts at critical points.[10] Jews perverted the original revelation, Muslims claim, by an act of communal narcissism. Jews took a message intended for every nation and turned it into an exclusive proclamation of salvation for themselves alone—that they alone are the chosen people. Although the Qur'an is silent on the issue, some Muslims believe that Jews substituted Isaac's name for Ishmael's in the book of Genesis and thus concealed for centuries the Arabian connection in the history of salvation.[11]

Christians, they believe, made the mistake of turning Jesus into a god and therefore reverting to the polytheism that Allah (lit., "the God") forbids. Most Muslims deny that Jesus was crucified; the Qur'an states that God "raised [Jesus] to himself" in a manner reminiscent of Elijah.[12] More importantly, it denies that Jesus was the Son of God, imagining that that would mean that God had engaged in sex, which is unimaginable.[13] Most important, it denies that Jesus was a savior because of its conviction that each of us must be responsible for our own sins. To imagine that someone else can save

---

[10]Qur'an 2.136 (KF).

[11]The Qur'an recognizes both Isaac and Ishmael as prophets and does not explicitly name which son Abraham was asked to sacrifice. However, the commentary of an influential English translation assigns the name Ishmael to the boy: Qur'an 37.99-111 (KF). I thank Valerie J. Hoffman for this and other important additions to this chapter.

[12]Qur'an 3.55 (KF); 4.157 (KF). While the Qur'anic text says the Jews did not kill or crucify Jesus, some Muslims concede that Jesus did in fact die, and may have been crucified—but not by Jews. See, e.g., the Egyptian Muhammad 'Abd al-Latif (Ibn al-Khatib), *Ahdah al-tafasir* (Cairo: Al-Matba'a 'l-Misriyya li Awlad Ibn al-Khatib, n.d.), commentary on Qur'an 3.54.

[13]See, e.g., Qur'an 2.116 n. (KF): "It is a derogation from the glory of Allah—in fact it is blasphemy—to say that Allah begets sons, like a man or an animal. The Christian doctrine is here emphatically repudiated. If words have any meaning, it would mean an attribution to Allah of a material nature, and of the lower animal functions of sex." Interestingly, the Qur'anic description of Jesus' conception depicts God (or an angel) blowing the Spirit into Mary's vaginal canal (21.91; 66.12)—about as crassly physical as what they (mistakenly) suppose Christians teach.

us from our sins seems to Muslims to be spiritually irresponsible. No one can receive such spiritual benefits from another.[14]

But the differences here are not as sharp as may at first appear. If Muslims deny that grace from God—a term that the Qur'an uses repeatedly—can mean (wholly) unmerited favor, they nevertheless emphasize God's mercy toward sinners. The Qur'an repeats incessantly that Allah is "most forgiving" and "most merciful."[15] At one point it says that Allah is "the best of forgivers."[16] The Muslim editor of an English translation of the Qur'an writes that "man's nature is weak, and he may have to return again and again for mercy. So long as he does it sincerely, Allah is Oft-returning, Most Merciful." He suggests that human moral weakness requires God's mercy: "for His grace helps out the sinner's shortcomings."[17] Several passages in the Qur'an itself intimate that because of that moral weakness one must trust Allah's promise of forgiveness: "Our Lord! We have indeed believed. Forgive us then our sins, and save us from the agony of the Fire."[18]

There are other indications as well that the usual Christian view of Islamic soteriology as Pelagian is misleading. Valerie J. Hoffman has noted the popular hadith (a supposed saying of the Prophet) that likens the family of the Prophet to the ark of Noah—those who cling to them are saved, and those who ignore them perish. This would suggest that while the piety of the believer plays a role in salvation, it is more the virtue of Muhammad and his family that saves those who cling to them.[19] According to Hoffman, "Despite what Christians say

---

[14]Qur'an 2.48 (KF) and passim.

[15]For example, Qur'an 4.100; 4.106 (KF); 110.3; 3.31 (KF).

[16]Qur'an 7.155.

[17]Qur'an 2.38 n. (KF).

[18]Qur'an 3.16 (KF). See also 3.160 (KF): "If Allah helps you, none can overcome you: If he forsakes you, Who is there, after that, That can help you? In Allah, then, let believers put their trust."

[19]See Valerie J. Hoffman-Ladd, "Devotion to the Prophet and His Family in Contemporary Egyptian Sufism," *International Journal of Middle East Studies* 24 (1992): 615-37, and *Sufism, Mystics and Saints in Modern Egypt* (University of South Carolina Press, 1995).

about Muslims, Muslims don't believe God will simply stack good deeds against bad—in fact, such a perspective is very frightening to Muslims, who are well aware of their faults. They tend to place their hope in God's mercy and the Prophet's intercession for them."[20]

Muslims reject the Christian doctrines of original sin and human depravity, but the Qur'anic picture of human nature is far from optimistic. Generally, human beings are depicted as "perverse and thankless."[21] Allah seems exasperated by their behavior in Surah 80: "Man—death take him! How thankless he is!"[22] Human beings are fickle and prone to naive pride: "When distress afflicts man, he invokes Us [Allah and his angels]. Yet when We accord him grace, then he says, 'This has come to me because of my *savoir faire.*' The fact, rather, is that it was a test—a fact few understand."[23]

If Muslim pessimism on the spiritual state of humanity resonates with Christian views, so do some Muslim attitudes about religious motivation. Often, as in one Qur'an quotation cited above, saints are described as those who obey Allah's commandments *in order to* merit Paradise and escape the fires of hell. But there are some important counterindications. A tradition in Sufism (a movement of Islamic mysticism) of disinterested love is similar to that which was discussed in the last chapter on Confucianism. Sufi Rabi'a al-Adawiya (d. 801) is best known for introducing in the eighth century an emphasis on love that ever after became characteristic of Sufism. In a famous poem she demonstrated that she loved God for Himself alone and not from fear of hell or hope of heaven:

> O my Lord, if I worship Thee from fear of Hell, burn me in hell, and if I worship Thee in hope of Paradise, exclude me thence, but if I worship Thee for Thine own sake, then withhold not from me Thine Eternal Beauty.[24]

---

[20]Valerie J. Hoffman, letter to author, 1999.
[21]Qur'an 14.34 (Cragg).
[22]Qur'an 80.17 (Cragg).
[23]Qur'an 39.49 (Cragg).
[24]Margaret Smith, *Rabi'a the Mystic and Her Fellow Saints in Islam* (Cambridge: Cambridge

Furthermore, in some Muslim circles there is a tradition of redemptive suffering. It is based in part on the assassination at Karbala in 680 of Muhammad's grandson Husayn, who is believed by Shi'ites (those who believe that Muhammad's son-in-law Ali, not Abu Bakr, was Muhammad's legitimate successor) to have been a "ransom for his people, for Mankind."[25] It is also derived from the remarkable life and death of Husayn ibn Mansur al-Hallaj (d. 922), who consciously identified himself with Jesus Christ. When he refused to recant his statement, "I am God" (lit. "I am truth" or "reality"), he was crucified for blasphemy. According to sympathetic interpreters, Hallaj meant by this statement not that he was the divine being but that he had annihilated his own ego so thoroughly in God that when he looked at himself he saw nothing but God. Descriptions of his death report that he approached his cross laughing, forgiving his executioners and thanking Allah that he was permitted to see "the raging fires of Thy Face." A famous Sufi hymn inspired by Hallaj begins, "Kill me, O my trustworthy friends, for in my being killed is my life."[26]

Few Muslims have rivaled Hallaj for religious intensity, but many have invoked his themes of disinterested love and redemptive suffering. Sufi literature since the ninth century has emphasized disinterested love, and Sufism has become the foundation for popular Islam all over the world. Hence many Christians may be surprised to discover these important points of contact with Muslims on what both traditions consider to be central to true piety.

Differences

For all the similarities between Islam and Christianity, there are sig-

---

University Press, 1928), p. 30, cited in Esposito, *Islam*, p. 102. For more on Rabi'a and Sufism, see Annmarie Schimmel, *Mystical Dimensions of Islam* (Chapel Hill: University of North Carolina Press, 1975).

[25]Hamadi ibn Abdullah al-Buhri, *Utenzi wa Sayedina Huseni,* as quoted in Esposito, *Islam*, p. 112.

[26]Denny, *Introduction to Islam*, pp. 260-63.

nificant differences, such as the difference between Muslim and Christian views of written revelation. This owes first to the fact that the content of the respective scriptures is strikingly different. The Qur'an is about the same length as the New Testament, but the similarities stop there. It was dictated by only one man (the New Testament was composed by many writers) and is not a book of history (as the Gospels and the Acts of the Apostles purport to be), a life of Muhammad (the Gospels aim to provide the theologically significant events of Jesus' life) or a theological treatise (as the letter to the Romans could be considered). Instead, it is a book of proclamation: God is one and sovereign; judgment is coming; we need to submit to Allah.

Muslims and Christians also have very different conceptions of the nature of scriptural inspiration. While Christians believe that the Bible is a joint product of both human and divine agency, Muslims believe their holy book contains not a shred of human influence. Christians usually want to distinguish Paul's personal writing style or cultural influences from the divine Word,[27] for example, but Muslims deny that Muhammad's personality or cultural affinities had anything to do with the words of the Qur'an. Muslims, then, accept a dictation theory of inspiration that nearly all Christians reject for their Bible. This is one reason why the Muslim community was so outraged by Salman Rushdie's *Satanic Verses*. The novel insin-

---

[27]For instance, most Christians believe that 1 Corinthians 11:5-16 contains cultural mandates about head-coverings for women, mandates that are not required of Christians in other times and cultures. Some think the passage nevertheless suggests the eternal principles, applicable to all times and places, that church unity and propriety of dress should be upheld. See Craig Keener, *The IVP Bible Background Commentary: New Testament* (Downers Grove, Ill.: InterVarsity Press, 1993), pp. 475-76, and "Man and Woman," in *Dictionary of Paul and His Letters,* ed. Gerald F. Hawthorne et al. (Downers Grove, Ill.: InterVarsity Press, 1993), pp. 585-86. Whether or not one agrees that this eternal principle is implied by the passage, or even that there is *any* eternal principle implied, Christians generally agree that the Bible contains time-bound elements that must be distinguished from what is eternal. Muslims deny that this distinction exists in the Qur'an.

uates that the Qur'an is not the Word of Allah but has been altered by either the angel Gabriel or Muhammad's followers who first recorded the revelations entrusted to the Prophet. The title is even more sinister: very early versions of the Qur'an contained verses that suggested the worship of three goddesses alongside Allah. Muhammad soon had them removed, explaining that the devil had given him disinformation. They have been known ever since in Islamic tradition as the "satanic verses."[28] So the implication of Rushdie's title is that the entire Qur'an, which for Muslims is as sacred as the person of Jesus is to Christians, has been corrupted.

Striking Lessons

If there are important disparities between Muslims and Christians on revelation, there are also some striking lessons that Christians can learn from the Islamic tradition. As with other traditions I have examined, none of the following themes is completely absent from Christian thought, but all are expressed in a distinctive way by Muslims—and these distinctives remind or inform us of things we should see in our own tradition, perhaps in a new way. I will highlight five themes: submission to God, creation as a theater of God's glory, regular and theocentric prayer, charity to the poor and the importance of faith to the public square.

1. Submission to God. Muhammad taught that the ultimate virtue is submission (the literal meaning of *Islam*) to God's will; Muhammad tells us this is the essence of true religion.[29] One's personal desires are irrelevant; one's only duty is to bend the knee in humble obedience. There is no room for the Muslim to equivocate regarding God's commands or to consider them anything but absolute, for

---

[28]Qur'an 53.19-20 (KF). After naming Lat, Uzza and Manat as three goddesses, the original text contained the following: "These are the intermediaries exalted, whose intercession is to be hoped for. Such as they do not forget." See Denny, *Introduction to Islam*, p. 72, and Salman Rushdie, *The Satanic Verses* (New York: Viking Penguin, 1989).
[29]Qur'an 3.19 (KF).

they issue from infinite wisdom, before which believers must bow in meek deference. Like many Christians, many Muslims submit for the purpose of gaining Paradise. Yet, as we have seen, there is also a rich strand in the Islamic tradition exhorting a believer to submit not because of what could be gained by submission but simply because God is God. Muslims proclaim to the world that God alone is great and rules with absolute control over every atom of the cosmos. Therefore it only makes sense for each of us to submit every detail of life to God's will as it has been revealed to the greatest and *seal* (last) of the prophets, Muhammad. To give allegiance to anything other than God—money, family, race, success or earthly life itself—is idolatry (*shirk*), the unrelieved indulgence of which will merit the boiling water and searing wind of hell.

Two stories from the ministry of Bob McCahill, a Maryknoll missionary to Bangladesh, illustrate this Muslim sense of God's absolute control over every aspect of life. When he first arrived in Bangladesh, he wondered why he so seldom heard a simple "Thank you" after helping a person in need. Then, after several years of working among the Muslim poor, he realized that the answer to his question had to do with "the centrality of Allah in the thinking of Muslim Bengalis. . . . To single out a fellow human being in order to give him or her thanks without explicitly and emphatically recognizing that Allah is the actual source of the benefit received would be unacceptable—so conscious is the grateful Muslim that every single benefit in life comes to us from the Best Giver (one of the ninety-nine descriptive names of Allah)."[30]

After a flood McCahill had an opportunity to observe the profound humility and attitude of submission that result from a sense of God's sovereignty.

After several hours in a small sailboat I arrived in Nikhli. Here I would be

---

[30]Bob McCahill, *Dialogue of Life: A Christian Among Allah's Poor* (Maryknoll, N.Y.: Orbis, 1996), p. 69.

able to see how the people in outlying areas were coping with the flood. People had evacuated their farms and homes and come to the higher ground near the bazaar. Hundreds had found shelter in a primary school. Men, women and children gathered around me, standing ankle deep in mud, to learn what their unexpected visitor had to say. They had time on their hands. Moreover, the circumstances that the flood had placed them in had made them especially sober and reflective.

"What caused the flood?" I asked.

"Flood waters came down from India" answered a man, and no one expanded on his reply. Apparently none of them understands that deforestation in the Himalayas is a precise cause.

"Who did this?" I asked.

"Allah-tallah," replied another man with respect and wonder in his tone.

"Why did He do it?" I asked.

"Who knows the mind of Allah?!" one replied. "To punish us for our sins. What else?" he added.

"Which sins?" I asked.

"For our failure to pray and to fast, mainly," responded one. He continued: "Also for cheating, stealing, robbing, and the coercing that some do. We are all paying for that."

Another man confirmed him, saying, "In a word, for our singing songs while we should have been praying and fasting."[31]

We need not agree with all of the theology implied by these statements to admire the underlying attitude of faith-filled respect for, and submission to, God. In his book *The American Religion* literary critic Harold Bloom identifies quintessential American religion as that devoted to self-affirmation and human freedom and asserts that evangelical Christianity is the most representative example of this religion. This is faith more in self than Christ, concerned more with individual expression than care for community and seeking more freedom *for* the self than freedom *from* sin.[32] Ironically, we would

---

[31]Ibid., pp. 69-70.
[32]Harold Bloom, *The American Religion: The Emergence of a Post-Christian Nation* (New York: Simon & Schuster, 1992).

say that our theology is far more accurate than that of these Bengalis, yet perhaps the attitude of their hearts is better than ours—particularly the hearts of those of us who have been captivated by Bloom's American religion. It should disturb us that evangelicals are viewed this way by folks outside the fold, and it certainly confirms the charges leveled by some of our best evangelical Jeremiahs.[33] But a look at Muslim understandings of human responsibilities to God—their theocentric dismissal of self-indulgence—may help us break free from the narcissism that threatens to overwhelm us. Attention to Islamic awe before the majesty of God may help us better appreciate the reverent fear of God with which Isaiah, Daniel and Cornelius served God.[34]

2. *Creation as a theater of God's glory.* A common theme in the Qur'an is that the creation is studded with signs of God's reality—in nature, society and the human person. This is what Calvin referred to when he said that creation is a theater of God's glory. It is also what the psalmist meant when he wrote, "The heavens are telling the glory of God; and the firmament proclaims his handiwork" (Ps 19:1). While Calvin and the psalmist speak more particularly of God's beauty and magnificence, Muhammad usually has in mind the testimonial value of the creation—to provide humankind evidence of God's existence and sovereignty. To recognize these signs for what they are is close to what faith is all about; our principal responsibility on earth is to "believe in God's signs."[35]

God's signs are everywhere, especially in nature. The Qur'an

---

[33]See especially David Wells, *No Place for Truth: or, Whatever Happened to Evangelical Theology?* (Grand Rapids, Mich.: Eerdmans, 1993); *God in the Wasteland: The Reality of Truth in a World of Fading Dreams* (Grand Rapids, Mich.: Eerdmans, 1994); and *Losing Our Virtue: Why the Church Must Recover Its Moral Vision* (Grand Rapids, Mich.: Eerdmans, 1998).
[34]At one level, the comparison I make is unfair: our worst with their best. There are plenty of worldly Muslims and plenty of dedicated evangelicals. Yet at another level, it is instructive to see living examples of the best of what another tradition offers in order to clarify our own vision when it has become muddled.
[35]Qur'an 30.53.

points to the very existence of the heavens and the earth (which philosophers have called the cosmological argument for God), the daily
alternation between light and darkness, rain that brings life out of
parched earth, the profusion of animals on the planet, lightning that
occasions both fear and hope, and the stars that guide through "the
darkness of land and of sea."[36] Perhaps because of his desert envi-
ronment, Muhammad seemed particularly struck by the miracle of
vegetation arising from lifeless sand. Like the medieval Christian
monk Brother Lawrence, who was converted upon watching the for-
saken outline of a wintry tree burst into bright springtime color,
Muhammad was amazed by the movement of life from clouds and
rain to the earth "after it has died."[37] He marveled at "the winds that
stir up a cloud" according to the divine will and divide it into pieces
when rain falls from it. Then God showers it on whomever He
will.[38] This and everything else in nature are "signs for intelligent
people" that God rules the world and will call us into judgment.[39]

Human culture is also full of signs. Ships, for example, are mar-
velous tokens of God's providence, for they are propelled by winds
that only God can send, "as bearers of glad tidings and to have you
taste of the mercy divine."[40] They sail the ocean "by the grace of
God."[41] Agriculture, which depends on God's blessing, also shows
God's bounty and therefore His rule over all.[42] Human responses to
God's miraculous interventions in history, such as Noah's ark, like-
wise demonstrate God's mercy to humankind: after egregious sin
necessitated judgment, God mercifully saved Noah and his family.[43]

---

[36]Qur'an 2.163-64; 6.97; 30.22-25; 6.97.
[37]Qur'an 2.164; Brother Lawrence of the Resurrection, *The Practice of the Presence of God*
(Mount Vernon, N.Y.: Peter Pauper Press, 1963).
[38]Qur'an 30.48.
[39]Qur'an 30.25.
[40]Qur'an 30.46.
[41]Qur'an 31.31.
[42]Qur'an 30.23; 30.46.
[43]Qur'an 33.41.

Human languages, in all their diversity and complexity, are further signs of God's existence, wisdom and power.[44] Their beauty and complexity appeared to Muhammad to be evidence of the divine reality.

Perhaps most particularly, the human person is a sign of God. The Qur'an takes special note of the human conscience as a testimony of God's moral nature, something like Paul's observation in Romans 2:14-15 that even nonbelievers respond to an innate conscience. The Qur'an also points to the variation of human "complexions" as a sign of God and to the phenomenon of human sleep![45]

Unfortunately, the Qur'an laments, most humans beings "turn away" or "repudiate" the signs because of pride or inscrutable perversity.[46] This is the basic sin of humanity, another way of naming, or perhaps the consequence of, the sin of *shirk* (idolatry): "They rejected the signs of God and took them for a joke."[47] As a result they will suffer "excruciating pain" and become "inhabitants of fire." They are "traitorous ingrates," bad examples because they "turn away" from clear proof of God's reality.[48]

3. *Regular and theocentric prayer.* Five times a day (early morning, noon, midafternoon, sunset and evening) a good Muslim washes his forearms, feet, mouth and nostrils three times before facing Mecca and reciting a memorized prayer of faith, praise and gratitude. He utters several prayers of worship and proclamations of faith, recites the first sura of the Qur'an (which praises God as creator, sustainer, gracious and merciful, and master of the day of judgment and asks for grace to help him follow the straight path), and only at the end recites a short prayer for his own personal needs.[49] This prayer is marked, then, by concentration on God's character and attributes—

---

[44]Qur'an 30.22.
[45]Ibid., 30.23.
[46]Qur'an 33.46; 3.21; 7.36 (KF); 7.177; 30.10.
[47]Qur'an 30.10.
[48]Qur'an 3.21; 31.7; 7.36; 31.32; 7.177; 33.46.
[49]Denny, *Introduction to Islam*, pp. 105-11.

not on the human self—by the notion that the principal part of prayer is not supplication but worship, and by the idea that we need to take time at regular intervals throughout the day to acknowledge God's lordship over us and the world.

Jesus said we could learn from the faith of pagans (Mt 15:21-28). Bob McCahill suggests that we can learn from the Muslim practice of regular prayer:

> One of the most edifying works for which I admire Muslims is the practice of regular prayer. I can always find Muslims who, individually or in a group, stop their other occupations in order to offer prayer at five set times between dawn and evening. Not all Muslims do so; not even a majority of the adults do so, consistently. But the ones who do pray regularly maintain among all the Muslims of their neighborhoods and villages a consciousness of the importance of prayer. It seems to me that among the five pillars of Islam (i.e., the confession of faith, prayer, almsgiving, fasting, and pilgrimage to Mecca) prayer is the one which best illustrates what Muslims think of Allah and of themselves in relation to Allah. Allah is the transcendent Creator, and they are Allah's adoring creatures.[50]

Evangelicals can be reminded by Muslim practice that the heart of prayer is worship and that a prayer life dominated by supplication is unbalanced and self-absorbed. They can also relearn from Muslims the importance of regularity in prayer and how set times can help check our inclination to forget about prayer entirely.[51]

4. *Charity to the poor.* Extraordinary emphasis is placed by the Qur'an on helping the poor. Giving to the poor is part of the short list of duties that define righteousness: "They are righteous who believe in God and the last day, and the angels and the Book, and the prophets; and who donate goods and money for love of God to

---

[50]McCahill, *Dialogue of Life,* pp. 76-78.
[51]I am not claiming that Muslims are more faithful in prayer than Christians are; they may or may not be, and I am not sure how anyone would measure that anyway. My point is that we Christians can learn from what they expect of themselves; it is a religious ideal with lessons for us.

relatives and orphans, and to the poor and wayfarer, and to the needy, and for freeing slaves; and who are constant in prayer and give alms for welfare."[52] The wicked are criticized for not honoring orphans (among the truly needy in premodern society) or encouraging each other to feed the poor.[53] Both unbelief and hypocritical religion are defined in terms of inattention to the poor: the one who repudiates (true) religion is the one who "rebuffs the orphan and does not encourage feeding the poor. So woe to those who pray without paying attention to their prayers; those who appear to pray but are depriving the needy."[54]

The importance of charity to the poor can be measured by its use as a discipline for unfulfilled oaths. The negligent party is required to "feed ten needy folk with food comparable to how you normally feed your own families, or by clothing those ten, or else liberating one captive slave."[55] The significance of charity can also be seen in Qur'anic eschatology: failing to help the unfortunate is one of the two reasons given in some texts for going to hell. In gardens of Paradise, it is said, they will ask the guilty sinners, "What has conveyed you into *Saqar* [Hell-Fire]?" and they will say, "We never prayed nor did we feed the destitute. We took our fill with the rest and it was our habit to deny the Day of Judgment, until the one certainty—death—overtook us."[56]

Like Jesus, Muhammad condemned those who gave in order to be seen. Such an approach only "nullifies" one's acts of charity, he said. In contrast, concealing one's charity will "remove some of your stains of evil."[57]

Muslims distinguish between *zakat*—which is the required 2.5 percent of one's income to be given by Sunnis (20 percent by

---

[52]Qur'an 2.177.
[53]Qur'an 89.13-14.
[54]Qur'an 107.1-7.
[55]Qur'an 5.89 (KF).
[56]Qur'an 74.42 (Cragg).
[57]Qur'an 2.264, 2.271 (KF).

Shi'ites) for alms—and charity, which is *sadaqa*. The former is a legal, obligatory act and considered part of one's service to God, in fact a technical part of worship. "Zakat . . . is more like a tax payable once a year and computed as a percentage of one's various forms of wealth."[58] One of the meanings of the word *zakat* is "purity," which suggests that money is "unclean" until the proper percentage has been donated to the Islamic community.

It is not known what percentage of Muslims pay the zakat, but it is clear that the majority of evangelicals do not tithe. To be sure, the Christian tithe (10 percent) is considerably greater than the Sunni Muslim *zakat* (2.5 percent), but we evangelicals can still learn from the Muslim conviction that money is not properly used by us until some has been given to the community. Most of us would also do well to be instructed by the Qur'an's insistence on the integral connection between faith and charity to the poor.

5. *Faith and the public square.* Finally, Islam can help us understand why there is no such thing as a naked public square. Muslims believe that the human heart is incurably religious. It will worship the true God or something else as god (*shirk*). Even the atheist is religious and worships a god—perhaps nature, or happiness, or family or self. Therefore, to speak of religion being removed from public life—which includes government—is to embrace a mythical vision of the human. It fails to recognize that when overt connection to God or morality is banned from public expression, a vacuum is created, and other gods (of race or nation or secular ideology) rush in to fill the hole.

Lamin Sanneh grew up as the son of a Muslim tribal chief in West Africa. Sanneh has since become a Christian, but he retains an acute appreciation for the integrity and percipience of Islam. More than Christians, he writes, Muslims understand that religion cannot be merely a private, subjective affair. He says that we would never want

---

[58]Denny, *Introduction to Islam*, p. 111.

to return to Christendom with its oppressive territorial system that enforces religion by coercion and does not tolerate religious diversity. But the modern Western understanding of religion as free speech with no objective foundation in truth is disastrous in both origin and consequence.

Sanneh believes that "standard Muslim sources are correct that a state that would deserve public loyalty and respect cannot be neutral with regard to moral principles; the state must in that case either cooperate with religion, or coopt and enjoin it, or worse still, proscribe it."[59]

Somehow, Sanneh argues, we must find a way between the disastrous Western status quo, which relegates religion and morality to opinion, and the theocratic pretensions of temporal Islam. The postmodern alternative could be worse in the long run. "The widespread postmodernist attitude that, since there are so many religions with a claim to truth, no one religion matters in the end, thus allowing us to ransack religions to suit our personal tastes, merely strengthens the status quo by driving religion from the public sphere into the private, with the weakening of religion going side by side with the growth of state power."[60]

Sanneh looks to the example of Václav Havel, former prisoner of conscience and recent president of the Czech Republic, who recognized what Muslims have always proclaimed, that a government without religious and moral grounding has no effective weaponry to combat absolute and oppressive human pretensions. In a 1990 address to the United States Senate, Havel contended, "The most dangerous enemy today is no longer the dark forces of totalitarianism, the various hostile and plotting mafias, but our own bad qualities. My presidential program is, therefore, to bring spirituality,

---

[59]Lamin Sanneh, "Muhammad's Significance for Christians: Biography, History, and Faith," in *Piety and Power: Muslims and Christians in West Africa* (Maryknoll, N.Y.: Orbis, 1996), p. 48.
[60]Ibid., p. 49.

moral responsibility, humaneness, and humility into politics and, in that respect, to make clear that there is something higher above us, that our deeds do not disappear into the black hole of time but are recorded somewhere and judged, that we have neither the right nor a reason to think we understand everything and that we can do everything."[61] Sanneh notes that what Havel identifies as secular self-sufficiency Muslims attack as *shirk*, the false absolutes of human idolatry. They point out, perhaps more clearly and with less hesitation, that truth is not a matter of individual conscience. It does not depend on majority assent, nor is it captive to the will of Congress or the White House.

A radical postmodernism that assumes we can know nothing outside our own heads, and therefore that no moral vision is any truer than another, has chilling implications for public life. No longer would we be able to claim that anything is morally wrong, only that some people *think* it is wrong because of the moral world in which they grew up. And that if people think something is right for them—despite centuries of moral consensus saying otherwise—then what they do is permissible.

Few today would say that these are the straits to which we have come in North America—at least in the public squares of the media, courtroom and legislatures. There is still a large consensus that agrees that rape, incest, murder and terrorism are *morally* wrong. And most are willing to say this publicly. But I see a disturbing phenomenon in my classes of middle- and upper-middle-class (largely) white Americans. I see a sizeable percentage of students who walk into my classroom as convinced moral relativists. They are fairly sure that religion and morality are simply matters of opinion and that they have their own views of these things because they have been socialized in homes and communities that have taught them these beliefs. If they had been raised elsewhere, they tell me, they

---

[61]Havel's address is cited in Sanneh, "Muhammad's Significance for Christians," p. 49.

probably would believe differently. So how can they criticize anyone who believes differently—such as headhunters who believe that cannibalism is just fine or people raised in tribes dominated by witchcraft who believe that the proper return to a death in the family is to grab an unsuspecting innocent and kill him or her?

After all, they tell me, what finally matters is the sincerity of one's own beliefs, for we cannot know what is "absolutely" or "objectively" right and wrong. So if a soldier has been raised to believe that Muslims are evil and perhaps even less than human and therefore thinks there is nothing wrong with raping Muslim women, who are we to condemn him? He acts out of the sincerity of his convictions. One fortyish woman who came of age in the 1960s told the class that while she disagreed with what the Nazis did and *personally* felt they were wrong, she could not condemn what they did if they believed they were doing the right thing.

Muslims would tell this woman that there is objective morality that exists whether or not *anyone* is sincere. The Nazis were wrong even if *all* of them thought they were right. For God is there, as Francis Schaeffer used to say,[62] and His moral law rules the world. Not only is He there, but He has made His existence and moral character known through the signs in creation. No one has any excuse for missing the signs and proceeding in life as if things were *not* clear.

We evangelicals may not want to affirm with so little qualification the clarity of the signs, but we should recognize the power of the Muslim response to moral relativism. Some are undoubtedly converting to Islam for precisely that reason: in a world that is morally confused, Islam offers simple and clear answers. But we may want to take notes from Islam about the relation of religion to public life and the answers that strong faith can give to the moral and philosophical peril that confronts us.

---

[62]Francis Schaeffer, *The God Who Is There* (Downers Grove, Ill.: InterVarsity Press, 1968).

10

IN CONCLUSION
| *Objections & Responses* |

T HIS LITTLE INTRODUCTION TO THE QUESTION OF REVELATION IN
the religions has tried to show that God has revealed some of His
truth to people and traditions outside the Jewish and Christian communities. I have discussed not only the familiar categories of general
and special revelation but also a new one—revealed types, which I
have suggested is one source of truth in the religions. Scattered
throughout history are images and shadows of the triune God, not
only in nature and conscience (general revelation) but also in religious traditions. From these we can learn things that can help us
better understand the revelation of God in Christ.

I have argued that there is both biblical and theological grounding (chapters three and four) for this notion of learning about God
from non-Christians and indeed that there is a long history of Christian thinkers doing just that (chapter five). I have also shown some
specific lessons that can be learned from some texts and traditions
outside of the Christian community (chapters six through nine). But
for some evangelicals, this will not be enough. They will have grave

reservations about a project like this one, and for good reason. They know too well that many in the history of Christianity have departed from orthodoxy in an attempt to make the faith more palatable to those outside. These searchers have become convinced of truths outside the circle of faith and have then gone back inside the circle to adapt the faith to these supposed new truths. This pattern has often led to serious distortion of the faith of Jesus and His apostles.[1]

Does this project follow the pattern? I think not. I have not attempted to reconfigure a Christian doctrine (though of course we should always be open to seeing biblical doctrines in new ways in response to the Spirit's illumination of the biblical revelation in the light of new developments in culture). Instead I have found in the religions confirmation of familiar Christian doctrines, confirmations that enable us to see those doctrines with new vigor or application. In some cases I have identified biblical truths that never have been seen before—either because understandings given to the church centuries ago have been forgotten or neglected or because this understanding of the biblical revelation has never (as far as I know) opened up until now. For example, there is nothing precisely like the Daoist *wu-wei* in Christian thought. There are similar notions in Christian mysticism but few[2] that I know of that have quite the pungency of Lao Tzu and Chuang Tzu's admonitions to do nothing. It was through their words, however, that I came to a new depth of understanding of human inability and God's sovereignty.

My new understanding of union with Christ (derived in part from consideration of both Buddhist and Daoist themes) is not a revolu-

---

[1]See Harold O. J. Brown, *Heresies: Heresy and Orthodoxy in the History of the Church* (Peabody, Mass.: Hendrickson, 1998), for examples of this pattern.

[2]Meister Eckhart (c. 1260-1329?) and Margaret Porette (d. 1310) proposed spiritualities that contain similar elements and comparable pungency. See Winfried Corduan, "The Gospel According to Margaret," *Journal of the Evangelical Theological Society* 35 (December 1992): 515-30, and "A Hair's Breadth from Pantheism: Meister Eckhart's God-centered Spirituality," *Journal of the Evangelical Theological Society* 37 (June 1994): 263-74.

tion in the history of Christian thought. It was new to me and perhaps in some sense different from what most Christians have experienced or believed. But it does not represent a major departure from what most Christians have always taught—perhaps just an extension of it. We should not be surprised, however, if such a major change should occur after pondering other religious traditions—for example, something akin to the Christian church's revolutionary change in thinking about slavery, from tolerance to abhorrence. If Christ is infinite and His revelation infinite (both of which we believe to be true) and if God's Spirit gradually unfolds the truth of that revelation to the church over time (witness our progressive understandings of slavery, women and the gifts of the Spirit), we should imagine that as a church we have not yet understood all that is to be understood of the biblical revelation of Christ. Perhaps we still have not been shown by the Spirit half of what is there. This is not to say that our conception of basic doctrine would change, for we strive to hold fast to the "faith that was once for all entrusted to the saints" (Jude 3). But we know from church history that the church's understanding and application of revelation grow and develop over time as new historical conditions arise. We do not expect that continually fresh understanding and reappropriation of Christ to cease.

We would expect, then, for more to be illuminated of that revelation in the future. Certainly much, if not most, of that future illumination will come through disciples of Jesus meditating on the biblical revelation itself. But is that the only way it will come? If Jesus counseled His disciples to learn from pagans about faith and God, it seems arbitrary to rule out any new understanding coming from consideration of non-Christian traditions. We would be ruling out a way of learning that Jesus Himself suggested to the disciples.

Yet questions persist. I have identified five that have arisen most frequently in my discussions of these issues with other believers, particularly evangelicals. It may be helpful to spell out each objection explicitly and then to provide a response to each.

1. *Do we not know these truths already? If they are in the biblical revelation already, why go to other traditions to learn what we can learn more directly from our own faith?* We look to other faiths because Jesus did. At certain times in His teaching ministry Jesus Himself used pagans rather than Jews and their tradition to teach faith to His disciples. Jesus could have chosen, when teaching His disciples to have faith, to appeal only to Jewish exemplars such as Abraham or David or Moses, but at certain critical moments He pointed instead to pagans who knew little or nothing of the Hebrew God or His Son: the pagan widow at Zarephath in Sidon, Naaman the Syrian, the centurion and the Canaanite woman (Lk 4:14-30; 7:1-10; Mt 15:21-28). All of them, despite their relative ignorance of the true God, had the kind of faith that Jesus could commend to His disciples.

Why, at these junctures in His ministry, did Jesus choose these exemplars rather than figures who seem to have known more of the true God—such as the patriarchs or Job or the Hebrew prophets? We can never know the answer to this question with any certainty, but we can speculate that perhaps Jesus chose these pagans because they were contemporaries close at hand (the centurion and the Canaanite woman, or the Good Samaritan) whose use as object lessons would therefore be particularly vivid, or because they served to rebuke Jewish hardness of heart (the widow at Zarephath and Naaman, whose faith was greater than those who had known Jesus first-hand at Nazareth). In similar fashion, we may be rebuked and humbled by studying the faiths of others. For example, seeing the devotion of some Muslims to Allah may reveal our own poverty of commitment to Jesus.

Some of the church's greatest theologians took lessons from non-biblical traditions. Perhaps John Calvin could have learned the principle of God's accommodation from Christian theological sources, but the fact remains that God used Calvin's fascination with Renaissance humanism to teach Calvin the principle of accommodation. Thomas Aquinas developed his understanding of analogy and the goodness of creation not from Scripture alone but by interaction with Aristotelian thought. And Saint Augustine came to appreciate both God's transcendence and this world's imperfection by thinking through Scripture with the help of Neo-Platonist teachers.

Could these theologians have learned these lessons from studying the Bible alone? Once again, we do not know. The Bible contained these lessons at least in seminal form. But Aristotle had far more to say about analogy than did Moses or Isaiah, and Neo-Platonists said at least as much as Paul about the gradual return of this world to its ideal state. The extrabiblical teachers perhaps enabled these theologians to understand and develop notions that were implicit in Scripture but needed further explication to be of widespread help for the church. The Thomist principle of analogy, for example, derives in part from Aristotle and is not explicitly stated in the Bible but provides a way for us to understand better what the Bible means.

It takes a teacher to help us learn what is difficult. Although we are in principle capable of learning most things by ourselves, some matters are fraught with such inherent difficulty that it seems at times *necessary* for us to get outside help if we are to have any realistic chance of "getting it." In principle I should have been able to learn algebra on my own, by reading and listening to the teacher, but in practice it took outside tutoring to get me over the hump and begin to be able to learn on my own.

We may be able to learn at an intellectual level but fail to see why it is important or relevant. Think of history class for most children before senior high school. It often seems dry and irrelevant. But insert an enthusiastic teacher with teaching skills and a love for history, and suddenly a sleepy class is transformed into a band of curious and excited students. This is why looking at Scripture through the lens of another tradition can be helpful. It can illumine the application of a doctrine that had seemed irrelevant or reveal a concept that had been in Scripture but only, as it were, between the lines.

2. *Does this compromise the biblical canon? Does it suggest that God has more special revelation to give the church beyond what is in the Bible?* The simple answer is no. What the religions can give us is not new revelation but help to see the revelation that is already in Christ and is portrayed in Scripture. The religions can provide not new revelation that adds to the revelation in Christ but a kind of revelation (revealed type) that helps explicate the biblical revelation. Or to use familiar theological language, they can serve as tools for the Spirit's *illumination* of the (written) revelation we have been given but imperfectly understand.[3] If we think we are being given illumination when the result clearly contradicts fundamental Christian doctrine, then the illumination is not from the Holy Spirit, Who will glorify the Christ of Scripture (Jn 16:14-15). So if we think that Daoist texts have shown us that God is impersonal or that the *Upanishads* have revealed the reality of reincarnation, we are being led by something other than the Spirit of God.

The evangelical principle of a closed canon means, among other things, that we *critically* appropriate insights from the religions. For example, both Theravada Buddhism and philosophical Daoism can help us understand union with Christ. At the same time, accepting the biblical canon means that we must reject the Daoist notion of an ultimate reality that is impersonal and its corresponding (pantheist) idea that the Dao is not to be distinguished from the cosmos.

Is this method circular? It *is* in the sense that we use the biblical revelation to evaluate critically new understandings of that revelation. But this does not mean that we can never learn anything new

---

[3]As I have explained in earlier chapters, I reject Barth's identification of illumination with revelation, but I affirm illumination as one moment or aspect in revelation, which includes not only the Spirit's opening of the understanding of a person but also the written deposit in Scripture.

about that revelation. Quite the opposite is true. We continually see Christ in new ways as we look at Christ through the experiences of our lives. Yet we hold to the basic lineaments of the picture of Christ we have received through Scripture and Christian tradition. In terms of this objection, this means that we add not content but understanding to the canon.

3. *Will this not undermine the evangelical urgency for evangelism and missions? For if we say that the religions already have truth, why expend money and lives to bring them our version of the truth?* There are several answers to this objection. First, while other religions have truth, they do not have the far fuller truth revealed in and by Christ. If Muslims, for example, know about regular prayer and the signs of God in creation, they nevertheless lack assurance of salvation and the fullness of life in the Spirit. Nor do they know the fullness of the love of God that has been revealed through Christ's crucifixion and resurrection or the glory of the Trinity. Theravadin Buddhists know about the mystery of the moment, as I have called it, and can teach us some things about the ineffability of ultimate reality. They also understand, in ways that can be helpful to us, the difference between the true self and the empirical self. But they do not know the triune God! (Of course, whatever they know about reality they know about the triune God—without being aware of it—for God is not separate from reality; but they do not know that reality is because of a Person, and they know little or nothing of what that Person—or Persons—is like.) Worse, they do not know the joy of being known by God or the still greater joy of feeling loved by what they call Ultimate Reality. Without knowing the gospel they may never enjoy the bliss of eternity with Jesus. (I am not sure that they will not, but neither do I have assurance that they will. I can be sure only that those who know Christ in a saving way today will enjoy Him forever.)

But even if some non-Christians already know God in a saving way, as inclusivists have argued (Sir Norman Anderson, Clark Pinnock, C. S. Lewis, John Sanders, Millard Erickson and many others), God wants to bring them to the fullness of eternal life. Only in Christ is there fully human and fully meaningful life now. Lydia, already worshiping God, came to a fuller experience of divine grace through knowledge of Jesus Christ (Acts 16:14).

Pure Land Buddhists know something of grace from Amida (Amitabha in China) Buddha. So do Hindu *bhaktas* from the grace given by Krishna and other Hindu personal gods. But they do not know that this grace was won at infinitely painful cost to the Godhead. Knowing this will show them that grace is far more gracious than they had imagined. Thus their thanksgiving and joy will be all the deeper. Pure Land devotees and Hindu *bhaktas* may also gain greater assurance of their salvation from knowing that their Savior was a real person in real history who truly lived on planet earth—unlike the savior deities whom most Buddhists and Hindus concede to be legendary.

Second, we Christians are commanded by Scripture to share the gospel with those who do not know it. It does not matter what we think of their future prospects, nor does it matter how much truth we think they may have. We dare not neglect our duty to proclaim if we are to continue to be evangelicals who try to live our lives under Christ and His Word.[4]

Scripture also makes clear that God's primary method of bringing people to Himself is through the proclamation of the gospel. No matter how much truth non-Christians seem to have, they need more if they do not know Jesus Christ. To know Jesus in His fullness is always a good thing and never a detriment. In fact, what could be better than knowing the living God in the fullness of His revelation? How could that possibly be bad?

Third, we share the gospel in evangelism and missions out of love

---

[4]J. I. Packer, *Evangelism and the Sovereignty of God* (Downers Grove, Ill.: InterVarsity Press, 1961).

and compassion. Non-Christians can know much about God without coming into saving relationship with God. The alternative is eternal separation from the only source of love and happiness. Even if, as S. Mark Heim has suggested, the Therevadin may experience nirvana, the individual may still miss out on the greater joy of eternity with Jesus. To keep from that person the wonderful news of the gospel is therefore cruel. Jonathan Edwards said that it is the loving thing to tell a man on the second floor that the first floor of his house is on fire. To ignore the problem is an act of cruel indifference. When real war is raging, it is deceptive and heartless to cry, "Peace! Peace!" when there is no peace (Jer 8:11). So out of love for our non-Christian friends who already know something of God, we will want to share with them *more* truth, as the Spirit leads and at the proper time.

Fourth, this world is a battlefield between the forces of light and the forces of darkness. We must participate in spiritual warfare to try to roll back the forces of evil, and our best weapon is the gospel. We want to save people not only from the second death of eternal separation from the God of love but also from the first death of rebellion against God in this life (Lk 15:24). It is a familiar theme in Scripture that many know much about God without knowing God in a saving way (e.g., Mt 7:21-23). Many—and this of course includes non-Christians—can be saved from the misery of rebellion against God in this life (manifested in a myriad of ways, especially in the religions) by a Spirit-led sharing of the gospel.

4. *Why study other religions when we do not know our own?* It is a sad fact that most Christians are fairly illiterate biblically. The same can probably be said for most evangelicals. Our evangelical churches need to do a better job of teaching and preaching Scripture and of training church members to acquire the joyful habit of Scripture reading and meditation. For those who are not already well grounded in Scripture, I do not recommend that they start exploring the other religions for truth. The best thing they can do

for their own knowledge of God is to saturate themselves in the Christian Scriptures, which already reveal about God infinitely more than they presently know. Let them learn their own faith well before they begin to study others. It is good to study the religions so that we may understand better other religionists whom we befriend and with whom we perhaps eventually share the gospel. But it is a mistake to look to these religions for truth when we know Jesus is the final truth but have made very little effort to understand Him.

This book is dangerous. Unless read carefully, it could encourage novices to start chewing meat when their spiritual digestive systems are able to handle only milk (cf. Heb 5:11-14). As the author of Hebrews advised, Christians need to master the "basic teaching about Christ" or "foundation" before they go on to matters that require maturity, which comes to those "whose faculties have been trained by practice" (Heb 5:14—6:1). This is why John Calvin did not teach predestination in his catechism for children but advised it be left for those whose faith is more fully formed.[5] Like predestination, this book's subject is best left to those who have their faith firmly grounded in Scripture and at least a few years' experience. Otherwise they may worry about things they do not understand and entertain distortions that are corrected only by thorough knowledge of the Christ of Scripture.

5. *Where are you going with all this? What is the purpose of learning truth from the other religions?* This project has four goals. First, it should make evangelical evangelism more sensitive and therefore more effective. Too many evangelicals have approached Muslims and Buddhists (and other religionists) with the assumption that their religions are totally false or wholly demonic and that if they accept Christ they must discard everything they have ever known

---

[5]John T. McNeill, *The History and Character of Calvinism* (Oxford: Oxford University Press, 1954), p. 211.

about the divine. This is arrogance based on misunderstanding of the religions. These evangelicals should not be surprised if the religionists with whom they share the gospel seem never to have heard it. They probably are so offended by the evangelicals' proud dismissal of their faith as hopelessly false—even devilish—that they decide that these Christians could not possibly have religious truth. And if this is what Christianity is all about, it does not deserve a hearing. Sometimes I think it is all the more miraculous that some religionists have come to Christ despite similar attitudes held by Christians who tell them about Christ.

One object of this book is to help evangelicals share the gospel with a bit more respect and sensitivity. If non-Christian believers sense that evangelicals respect their religious traditions as systems that contain religious truth, they will generally be more open than otherwise. They will not feel that they have to deny everything they have ever believed and practiced in order to become a disciple of Jesus, or that their culture has been of no value in their religious pilgrimage. They will better be able to feel love and respect coming from the Christian evangelist. Perhaps more will see the beauty of Christ as a result.

Second, we evangelicals can become better disciples. I have always been excited by the prospect and reality of union with Christ. Soon after I came to an active faith in college, I read Watchman Nee's *Normal Christian Life*, which began to open up for me the meaning of union with Christ in an exciting way. As I look back, I now realize that Nee's insight into this mystical reality was probably shaped by his Chinese cultural experience. Because of Nee's heritage, his sense of social and psychic solidarity (mystical oneness with others) was closer to that of Paul's than that possessed by most Western interpreters of Paul. In the last decade my own reading in the Daoist and Buddhist traditions opened up for me more of the joyful mystery of this union, and my experience as a disciple has been enriched.

In the ways I have already outlined in this book, and in many more, evangelical discipleship can be enlivened and enriched by exposure to non-Christian religious experience. Our understanding of Scripture and of Christ will be deepened, and the result will be a more mature church—led by disciples who know more of Christ, both intellectually and experientially.

Third, learning from the religions can enhance ecumenical social action—or what some call missions of mercy. As the new millennium begins, evangelicals and other orthodox Christians have discovered that they often have more in common religiously and ethically with other religionists than they do with liberal Christians. For example, at the 1995 United Nations Conference on Population and Development in Cairo, Muslims and Roman Catholics worked as allies to fight an abortion-rights initiative led by a hard-edged United States delegation. Only by their united efforts was the notion of enshrining abortion on demand as an internationally recognized human right abandoned by its proponents. The chances of our winning similar battles in the future on other social and moral issues will be improved by our showing more respect for these traditions than we have in the past. In the future we may need the help of other religionists in struggles against euthanasia and infanticide, human cloning, and religious persecution.[6] We may want to work arm in arm to defend marriage and the rights of the poor. Recognizing the religious integrity and truth found in many of the religions will significantly improve the chances of success for these efforts. This is not to compromise our biblical faith but to appropriate what we share with other religionists of God's law written on every human heart (Rom 2:14-15).

Finally, there is the doxological reason for learning truth from other religions. Learning about the religions and seeing how God has revealed His truths to people of other faiths shows that God is at

---

[6]I do not mean to suggest that liberal Christians necessarily support these things. All condemn religious persecution and infanticide in principle, while debates rage over euthanasia and human cloning.

work in more ways and lands and people than many of us had imagined. The God of most evangelicals has been too small. We have conceived of His presence and Spirit as alive only among Christians, but learning from the religions will show us that God's Spirit is active far more expansively that we have ever imagined. As John said, "The true light, which enlightens *everyone,* was coming into the world" (Jn 1:9, emphasis added).

The Scriptures indicate that the purpose of the creation was the glory of God, which means the "emanation and true external expression of God's internal glory and fullness."[7] In other words, God created the world so that His attributes and Being might be known and enjoyed by all the creation. This is His glory and at the same time the creation's bliss. As the creation comes to see and rejoice in God in all the dimensions of His existence that He permits them to enjoy, He is glorified and delighted. This is both our joy and God's joy, and the reason for the creation. As we see that God's work in the world is far deeper and broader than we had imagined and that He is mysteriously revealing aspects of His reality to those outside the church—whether or not they ever come to know Jesus—our vision of God will be that much enlarged. Our praise and worship of God will be deeper and richer, and we will join the heavenly chorus that sings,

> O the depth of the riches and wisdom and knowledge of God! How unsearchable are his judgments and how inscrutable his ways!
> "For who has known the mind of the Lord?
> Or who has been his counselor?"
> "Or who has given a gift to him,
> to receive a gift in return?"
> For from him and through him and to him are all things. To him be the glory forever. Amen. (Rom 11:33-36)

---

[7]Jonathan Edwards, *Concerning the End for Which God Created the World,* ed. Paul Ramsey, The Works of Jonathan Edwards 8 (New Haven, Conn.: Yale University Press, 1989), p. 527.

Appendix

GOD & THE
⌐MASCULINE PRONOUN⌐

I MUST EXPLAIN WHY I USE THE MASCULINE PRONOUN FOR GOD WHEN some Christians argue that such use renders God sexual and diminishes the worth of females. These are important concerns and need to be taken seriously. Feminists make an important point when they argue that masculine language for God should not be used to the exclusion of all feminine imagery. The Bible itself uses feminine imagery (Num 11:12; Ps 22:9-10; 71:6; 139:13; Is 49:15; 66:9, 13; Mt 23:37); use of feminine imagery and language in prayer will surely enrich our apprehension of God's self-giving love.

But when it is suggested that the masculine pronoun for God be excised because of women's oppression by men, the cure proves worse than the disease. Avoidance of the masculine pronoun for God often forces us to use ungainly expression like "Godself," which is not only awkward but also theologically problematic because it undermines the notion that God is a person. It is particularly important to highlight God's personhood when discussing religions that deny it. Philosophical Hindus and Buddhists, for example, insist there is no personal God because there is no final distinction between God and the cosmos.

Second, avoidance of the masculine pronoun reminds me of Stanley Hauerwas's response to John Cobb's portrayal of what Cobb calls Christian progressivism: "One of the things that bothers me about John Cobb's God is that she is just too damn nice."[1] The problem with Godself is that it is too inoffensive and as a result assumes too much. It runs the risk of avoiding the scandal of particularity (the Christian God is the Father Who sent His Son to die on Pilate's cross), and it suggests that we can know the divine essence behind the biblical Father, Son and Holy Spirit. But Scripture tells us that we know the Father truly only through the Son,[2] and the creeds inform us that God is known first not as some amorphous essence but as Father.[3] In other words, we know nothing about any god but the God Who has revealed Himself as Father, Son and Holy Spirit. We do not know a supposed divine essence behind the Father and Son that can be named without the name Father and Son. All we know is that God has given us His name as Father, Son and Holy Spirit. And when God alone is invoked by Scripture, that God is the Father. Hence Father and Son are not simply metaphorical but are literal names—indeed proper names—of the deity.[4]

The problem is not only epistemological but soteriological. It is not just a question of how we know the true God but what salvation is at stake. Paul Hinlicky has pointed out recently that it is only in the story of the Father's sending of the Son and Spirit that we can fully participate in salvation from sin and death. When trinitarian

---

[1]Stanley Hauerwas, "Knowing How to Go On When You Do Not Know Where You Are," *Theology Today* 51 (January 1995): 567.

[2]Matthew 11:27; 1 John 2:23.

[3]"The Apostles' Creed does not begin with the divine essence but with the Person of the Father: 'I believe in God, the Father almighty.' The Nicene Creed does not make God first *ousia* but *hypostasis*, not essence first but person: 'I believe in one God, the Father almighty'" (Patrick Henry Reardon, "Father, Glorify Thy Name," *Pro Ecclesia* 7 [Spring 1998]: 143).

[4]Robert W. Jenson, "The Father, He . . . ," in *Speaking the Christian God: The Holy Trinity and the Challenge of Feminism*, ed. Alvin E. Kimel Jr. (Grand Rapids, Mich.: Eerdmans, 1992), pp. 95-109.

language is eliminated or obscured, a person can talk of salvation as liberation from patriarchy and other forms of oppression, but these kinds of salvation are not the salvation proclaimed by the church of the ages.[5]

If God is Trinity—a Trinity of Father, Son and Holy Spirit—there is no way to avoid the suggestion of gender, for the words Father and Son both connote the masculine. Those who keep the language of the Trinity but refuse to use the masculine pronoun cannot have it both ways. They think that in order to protect their insistence that God has no gender, they must avoid the masculine pronoun. But when they use Father and Son, they nevertheless suggest gender and must explain that this suggestion of gender is relativized by God's transcendence. Yet this argument is no different from mine: that while I use language suggesting masculinity—as we humans understand it—the revelation of the Trinity shows that its masculinity is radically different from the traditional stereotype (as Garrett Green argues below). Hence those who retain trinitarian language but avoid the masculine pronoun have the same theological problem as those who use the masculine pronoun. The problem of gender cannot be resolved linguistically without sacrificing the heart of the Christian faith. That is, only by removing all trinitarian language can all suggestion of gender be eliminated, but then one is left with a god quite different from the divine reality of Jesus Christ.

Therefore, use of the masculine pronoun for the Christian God is necessary because God cannot be truly known apart from His revelation in Christ. As Luther expressed it, to try to know God apart from the historical particularity of the Son and His cross is to construct a theology of glory.[6] Similarly, avoiding the masculine pro-

---

[5]See Paul Hinlicky, "Secular and Eschatological Conceptions of Salvation in the Controversy over the Invocation of God," in *This Is My Name Forever: The Trinity and Gender Language for God*, ed. Alvin Kimel (Downers Grove, Ill.: InterVarsity Press, forthcoming).
[6]Martin Luther, "Theses for the Heidelburg Disputation," in *Martin Luther: Selections from His Writings*, ed. John Dillenberger (Garden City, N.Y.: Anchor, 1961), pp. 502-3.

noun suggests that we can know God apart from the revelation that God is the Father of the Son. Hence they cannot be replaced. They are not human constructions in response to ineffable religious experiences, but names for God given to humans by God Himself. The very names encapsulate the entire story of the triune God. To avoid them is to suggest indirectly that God did not reveal himself as a Father to a Son, or at least that these are not divinely given names.

Does this mean that God is male? Of course not. And the best representatives of the grand tradition have always agreed. "No one in the whole conciliar and creedal tradition regarded the word 'father,' when used in reference to God, as having any sexual connotation whatsoever. The Cappadocians in particular had already gone to some length to say that paternity and sonship in God possessed no sexual reference."[7] Must we do something about the misperceptions of God and the oppression of women to which these misperceptions have contributed? Yes, but the solution is not to reject the name and thus the masculine pronoun that follows, but rather to correct the distortions of readings that assume a male gender. This involves correcting the assumption of "metaphorical theology" (that assumes that all language for God is simply metaphorical and thus can be changed without doing untoward damage to meaning) that trinitarian language simply extends the ordinary understanding of father and son to God. But the biblical authors assumed that meaning flows not from the bottom up but from the top down. Paul wrote in Ephesians that all fatherhood on earth derives its name and meaning from God's fatherhood (Eph 3:15). The same dynamic is found in divine Sonship, according to C. S. Lewis: "Divine Sonship is, so to speak, the solid of which biological sonship is merely a diagrammatic representation on the flat."[8] In other words, we are to draw a proper conception of father and son from the Trinity, as

---

[7]Reardon, "Father, Glorify Thy Name," p. 148.

[8]C. S. Lewis, *Miracles* (New York: Macmillan, 1947), p. 289.

revealed to us, rather than understanding the Trinity from our experience of human families.

Garrett Green argues that another failing of metaphorical theology is its tendency to treat metaphors atomistically—out of context. If we attend to the story from which Father and Son come, we find a God very different from the One vilified by some of those who oppose the masculine pronoun for God.

> This God does not jealously hoard his power. As husband he does not beat his unfaithful wife but cries out with the pain of a jilted lover and redoubles his efforts to win her back. As Father he does not spare his own son but gave him up for us all. As Son he did not claim the prerogatives of power and lord it over his subjects but emptied himself, taking the form of a servant—and humbled himself on a shameful cross. As Spirit he incorporates us into the mystical body of Christ, in whom there is neither slave nor free, male nor female. As king he does not isolate himself in heavenly splendor but wills to dwell with his people, to wipe away every tear from their eyes and to deliver them from all that oppresses them, even death itself.

Green concludes, "Anyone who claims that masculine metaphors . . . are 'oppressive to women' is interpreting them out of context, treating them as isolated units of meaning rather than integral elements of a living narrative."[9] According to Ellen Charry, men who abuse women have perverted notions of fatherhood and sonship, which a proper understanding of the Trinity can help correct: "If men have identified manliness with an understanding of divine fatherhood and sonship that reinforces their own proclivities to control, subjugate, or wreak violence upon others to bolster their own feelings of power, they have gerrymandered the Christian doctrine of the Trinity, the reason for the incarnation, the power of the cross, and the hope of resurrection." Hence, to eliminate trinitarian language is to deprive

---

[9]Garrett Green, "The Gender of God and the Theology of Metaphor," in *Speaking the Christian God: The Holy Trinity and the Challenge of Feminism*, ed. Alvin E. Kimel Jr. (Grand Rapids, Mich.: Eerdmans, 1992), p. 60.

the church of its "primary models" for correcting these distortions.[10]

Therefore I use the masculine pronoun for God so as not to distract readers from the biblical narrative that alone reveals the true God who is neither patriarchalist nor culturally fashionable. He is the terrifying Other who explodes our ideas about Him—whether they be that He is male or that He is culturally inoffensive. I have capitalized all masculine pronouns used for God in this book in order to highlight the infinite qualitative distinction between all human fathers and sons, on the one hand, and the divine Father and Son, on the other, and also to express the divine name with all due reverence.

[10]Ellen Charry, "Is Christianity Good for Us?" in *Reclaiming Faith: Essays on Orthodoxy in the Episcopal Church and the Baltimore Declaration,* ed. Ephraim Radner and George R. Sumner (Grand Rapids, Mich.: Eerdmans, 1993), p. 234. For another excellent essay on God-language see Katherine Greene-McCreight, "What's in a Name? On the Ecumenical Baptismal Formula," *Pro Ecclesia* 6, no. 3 (1997): 289-308.

Index of Names & Subjects

Index of Scripture References